110 TURN-OF-THE-CENTURY HOUSE DESIGNS

Robert W. Shoppell

DOVER PUBLICATIONS, INC., MINEOLA, NEW YORK

Bibliographical Note

This Dover edition, first published in 2006, is an unabridged republication of *How to Build, Furnish and Decorate,* originally published by The Co-operative Building Plan Association, Architects, New York, 1897.

International Standard Book Number: 0-486-44768-5

Manufactured in the United States of America
Dover Publications, Inc., 31 East 2nd Street, Mineola, N.Y. 11501

SHOPPELL'S MODERN HOUSES.

Cottage, Design No. 1154

PERSPECTIVE.

DESCRIPTION.

GENERAL DIMENSIONS: Width, 26 ft. 6 ins.; depth, not including veranda or porch, 28 ft. 6 ins.

HEIGHTS OF STORIES: Cellar, 6 ft. 6 ins.; first story, 9 ft.; second story, 8 ft.

EXTERIOR MATERIALS: Foundation, brick; first story, mitred clapboards; gables, panels and shingles; roof, shingles.

INTERIOR FINISH: Two coat plaster, hard white finish. Soft wood flooring and trim throughout. Staircase, yellow pine. Kitchen wainscoted. All interior wood-work grain filled, stained to suit owner and finished in hard oil varnish.

COLORS: Trim, including water-table, cornices, casings, bands, veranda posts, rail, etc., dark bottle green. Clapboards, Nile green. Shingling on gables, stained sienna. Panel work picked out with dark bottle and Nile green. Shingles on roof dipped in and brush-coated with dark red stain. Veranda floor, olive green. Veranda ceiling and outside doors, also brick-work, oiled.

ACCOMMODATIONS: Open fireplace in parlor. Fireplace opening for portable range in kitchen. China closet in dining-room. Wide portière openings connect dining-room and hall and hall and parlor. Sink, with cold water supply, in kitchen. Cellar under hall and parlor, with inside entrance and concrete floor. Ample storage space under roof in second story. No blinds.

COST: $1,470, † not including mantel, range or heater. The estimate is based on ‡ New York prices for materials and labor. In many sections of the country the cost should be less.

Price of working plans (with full details drawn to large scale), specifications and * license to build, ... $15.00
Price of †† bill of materials, ... 5.00

FEASIBLE MODIFICATIONS: General dimensions, materials and colors may be changed. Cellar may be placed under whole house with outside entrance. Open fireplace may be omitted in parlor. Two wash-tubs and hot water boiler may be placed in kitchen, and bath-room with full plumbing in second story. Veranda may be extended around hall side to angle in the dining-room.

The price of working plans, specifications, etc., for a modified design, varies according to the alterations required and will be made known upon application to the Architects.

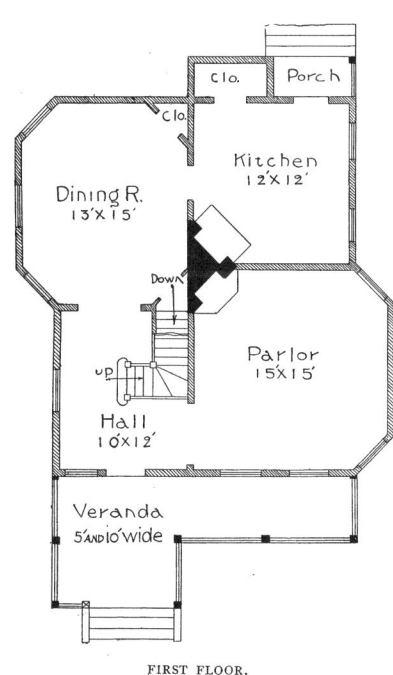

FIRST FLOOR.

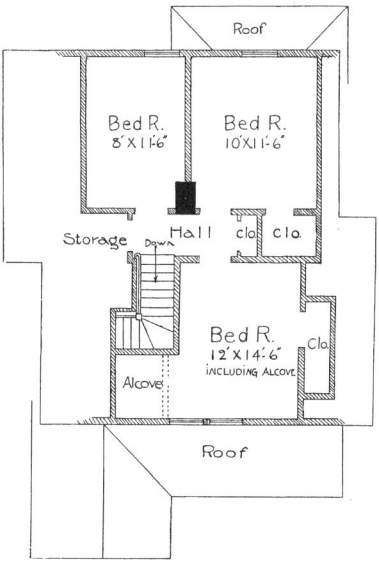

SECOND FLOOR

Cottage, Design No. 1155

PERSPECTIVE.

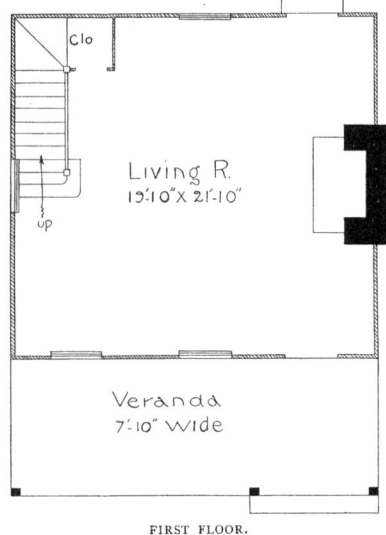

FIRST FLOOR.

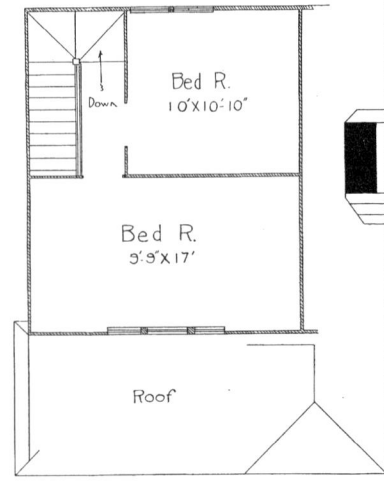

SECOND FLOOR.

DESCRIPTION.

GENERAL DIMENSIONS: Width, 22 ft.; depth, including veranda, 28 ft.

HEIGHTS OF STORIES: First story, 9 ft.; second story open to roof.

EXTERIOR MATERIALS: Foundation, posts; first story walls, 1¼ inch planking covered with clapboards; second story, gables and roofs, shingles.

INTERIOR FINISH: No plaster. All woodwork dressed to show. Staircase, flooring and trim, N. C. pine. All interior woodwork finished with one coat of hard oil varnish.

COLORS: Trim, including water-table, cornices, casings, veranda posts, white. Clapboards on side walls, buff. Shingles on side walls and roof left natural for weather stain. Sashes, dark green. Outside doors, piazza floor and rafters, etc., oiled.

ACCOMMODATIONS: The general arrangement of living-room and bedrooms, closets, etc., is shown by the floor plans. No cellar, blinds or plumbing. Large, quaint, open fireplace of rough field stone in living-room. Large French casement windows opening on to front veranda from living room. Partitions in bedrooms do not extend to ceiling, but are 8 ft. high, which is desirable in a design of this kind as it gives ample ventilation. This design is admirably adapted for a summer or mountain cottage.

COST: $375. The estimate is based on ‡ New York prices for materials and labor. In many sections of the country the cost should be less.

Price of working plans (with full details drawn to large scale), specifications and * license to build, ... $15.00

Price of †† bill of materials, . 5.00

FEASIBLE MODIFICATIONS: General dimensions, materials and colors may be changed. A brick or stone cellar may be placed under the whole or portion of house, with inside and outside entrances. Veranda may be carried around living-room at staircase side. A one or two-story kitchen extension about 12 x 12 may be placed back of living room at an additional cost of $75.00 for a one-story extension and $125.00 for a two-story extension.

The price of working plans, specifications, etc., for a modified design, varies according to the alterations required and will be made known upon application to the Architects.

Address, THE CO-OPERATIVE BUILDING PLAN ASSOCIATION, Architects, 106-108 Fulton Street, New York.

Cottage, Design No. 1156

PERSPECTIVE.

DESCRIPTION.

GENERAL DIMENSIONS: Width, 17 ft.; depth, including bay, 25 ft.

HEIGHTS OF STORIES: First story, 8 ft. 6 ins.; second story, 8 ft.

EXTERIOR MATERIALS: Foundation, posts; first story, clapboards; side walls of dormers, gables and roof, shingles.

INTERIOR FINISH: Two coat plaster, hard white finish throughout. Soft wood flooring, trim and stairs. All interior wood-work painted in colors to suit owner.

COLORS: All clapboards, light gray. Trim, white. Shingles left natural for weather stain. Veranda floor and ceiling, oiled.

ACCOMMODATIONS: The principal rooms and their sizes, closets, etc., are shown by the floor plans. No cellar. Bay-window in living-room with wide window seat. Kitchen pantry under main staircase. Second story bedroom has two large closets. The space between rear wall of the second story bedroom and the roof is floored and utilized as a storage-room.

COST: $600. The estimate is based on ‡ New York prices for materials and labor. In many sections of the country the cost should be less.

Price of working plans (with full details drawn to large scale), specifications and * license to build, ... $15.00

Price of †† bill of materials, ... 5.00

FEASIBLE MODIFICATIONS: General dimensions, materials and colors may be changed. A cellar may be added under a portion or

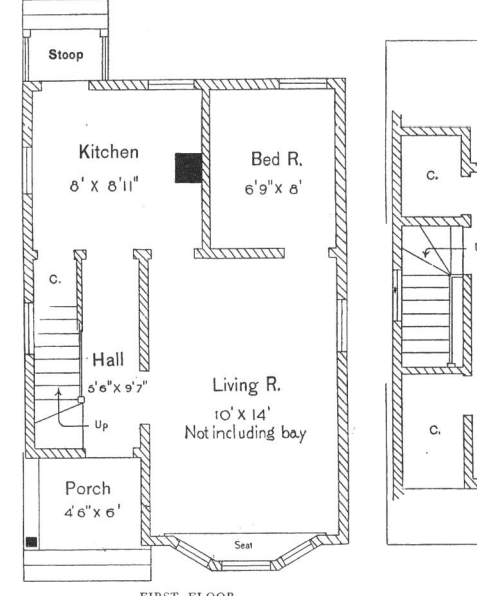

FIRST FLOOR.

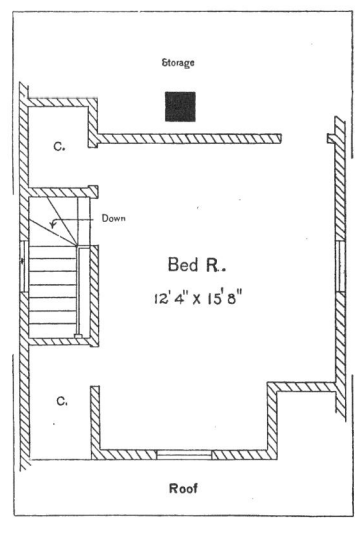

SECOND FLOOR.

the whole of the house, or a circular cellar may be used. First story bedroom may be used as a kitchen and the present kitchen as a dining-room.

The price of working plans, specifications, etc., for a modified design, varies according to the alterations required and will be made known upon application to the Architects.

Address, THE CO-OPERATIVE BUILDING PLAN ASSOCIATION, Architects, 106-108 Fulton Street, New York.

Cottage, Design No. 1166

PERSPECTIVE.

DESCRIPTION.

GENERAL DIMENSIONS: Width, 23 ft. 6 ins.; depth, including veranda, 30 ft. 6 ins.

HEIGHTS OF STORIES: First story, 8 ft. 6 ins.; second story, 8 ft.

EXTERIOR MATERIALS: Foundation, posts or piers; first story, clapboards; gables, dormers and roofs, shingles.

INTERIOR FINISH: Hard white plaster. Soft wood flooring, trim and stairs. Interior wood-work finished with hard oil.

COLORS: Body, Colonial yellow. Trim, ivory white. Shingles in gables, oiled. Roofs left natural. Sashes, dark red. Blinds, Colonial yellow. Veranda floor and ceiling, oiled.

ACCOMMODATIONS: The principal rooms and their sizes, closets, etc., are shown by the floor plans. Central chimney to serve all rooms.

COST: $700. The estimate is based on ‡ New York prices for materials and labor. In many sections of the country the cost should be less.

Price of working plans (with full details drawn to large scale), specifications and * license to build, ... $15.00

Price of †† bill of materials, ... 5.00

FEASIBLE MODIFICATIONS: Heights of stories, general dimensions, materials and colors may be changed. Cellar may be placed under part or whole of house, or a circular cellar may be built. The parlor may be enlarged by a bay-window encroaching upon the veranda. Open fireplaces and mantels may be introduced in hall, parlor and dining-room.

The price for working plans, specifications, etc., for a modified design, varies according to the alterations required and will be made known upon application to the Architects.

Address, THE CO-OPERATIVE BUILDING PLAN ASSOCIATION, Architects, 106–108 Fulton Street, New York.

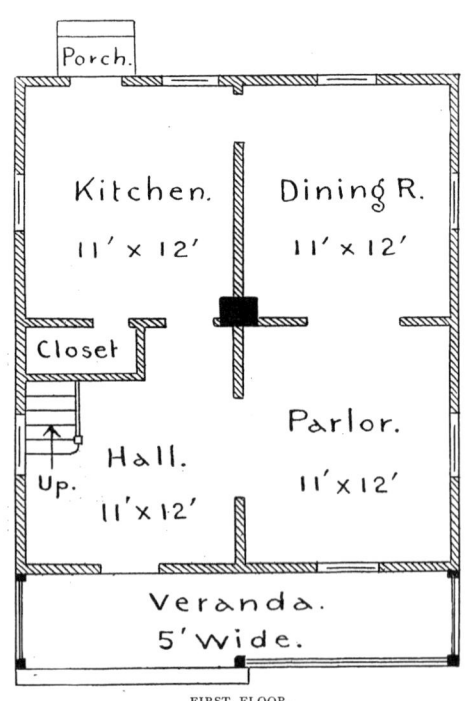

FIRST FLOOR.

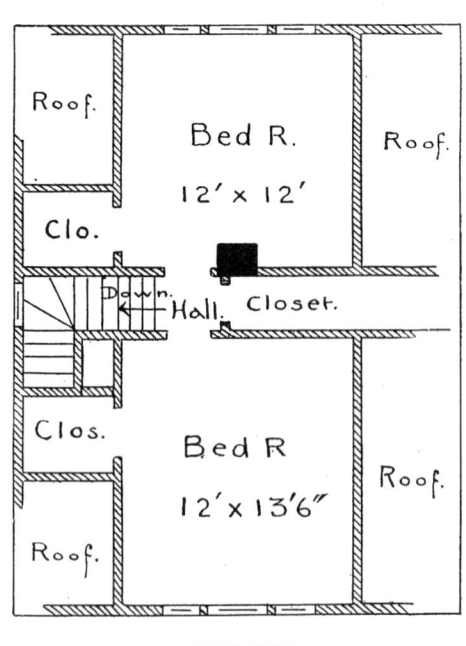

SECOND FLOOR.

Cottage, Design No. 1167

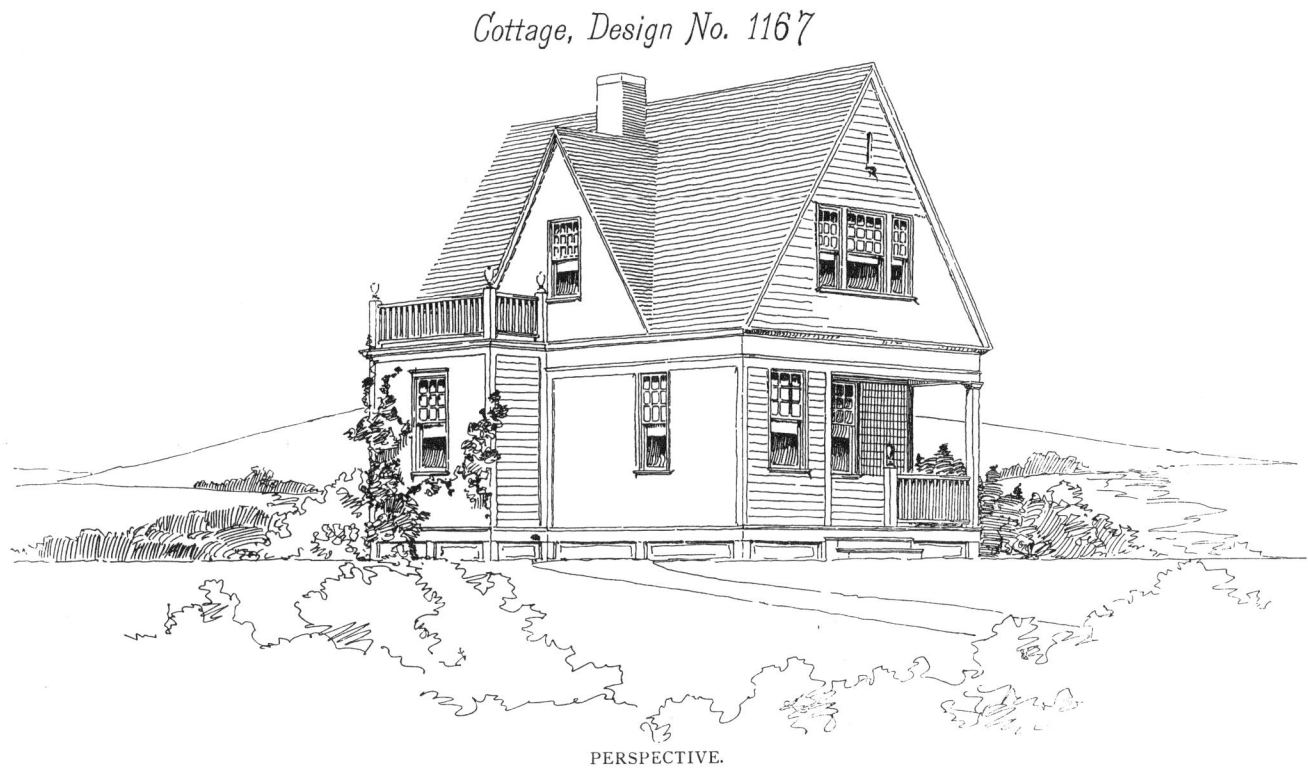

PERSPECTIVE.

DESCRIPTION.

GENERAL DIMENSIONS: Width, through kitchen and dining-room, 23 ft. 6 ins.; depth, including veranda, 29 ft. 6 ins.

HEIGHTS OF STORIES: First story, 8 ft. 6 ins.; second story, 8 ft.

EXTERIOR MATERIALS: Foundation, posts or piers; first story, clapboards; gables and roofs, shingles.

INTERIOR FINISH: Two coat plaster. Soft wood flooring, trim and staircase, painted colors to suit owner.

COLORS: All clapboards, Colonial yellow. Trim, ivory white. Shingles on gables, oiled. Roof shingles left natural. Sashes, dark red. Blinds, Colonial yellow. Veranda floor and ceiling, oiled.

ACCOMMODATIONS: The principal rooms and their sizes, closets, etc., are shown by the floor plans. A small loft is floored over second story for storage. Central chimney accessible from all first story rooms.

COST: $676. The estimate is based on ‡ New York prices for materials and labor. In many sections of the country the cost should be less.

Price of working plans (with full details drawn to large scale), specifications and * license to build, ... $15.00
Price of †† bill of materials, ... 5.00

FEASIBLE MODIFICATIONS: Heights of stories, general dimensions, materials and colors may be changed. Veranda may be widened and extended, or its present space replanned to enlarge the parlor. A vestibule may be planned in hall. Cellar may be placed under part or whole of house, or a circular cellar may be built.

The price of working plans, specifications, etc., for a modified design, varies according to the alterations required and will be made known upon application to the Architects.

Address, THE CO-OPERATIVE BUILDING PLAN ASSOCIATION, Architects, 106–108 Fulton Street, New York.

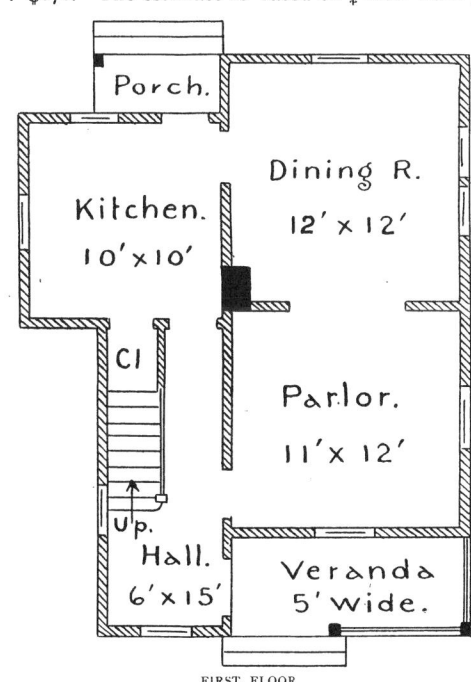

FIRST FLOOR.

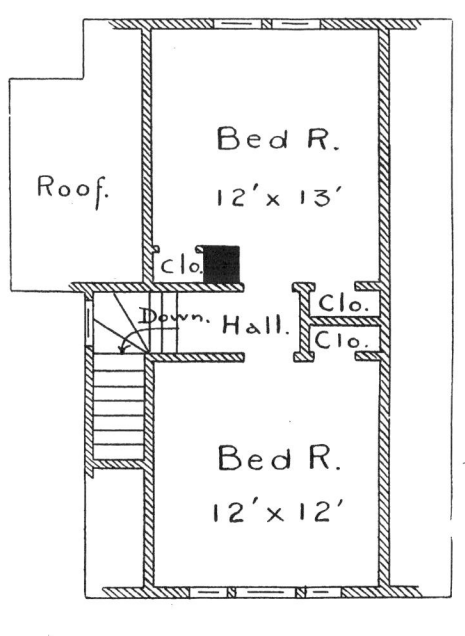

SECOND FLOOR.

Cottage, Design No. 1168

PERSPECTIVE.

DESCRIPTION.

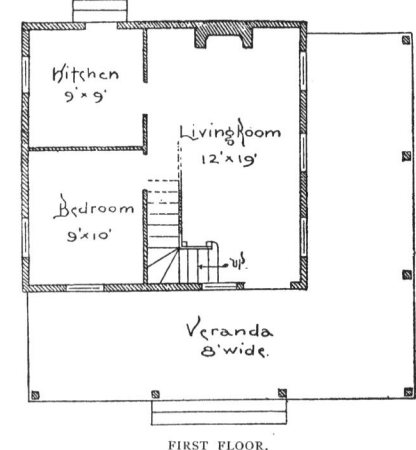

FIRST FLOOR.

GENERAL DIMENSIONS: Width, 29 ft. 8 ins.; depth, 28 ft.

HEIGHTS OF STORIES: First story, 9 ft. 3 ins.; second story, 8 ft.

EXTERIOR MATERIALS: Foundation, posts; first story, clapboards; second story and roof, shingles.

INTERIOR FINISH: Soft wood flooring, trim and stairway. Interior walls are not plastered, but finished with red building paper. Studding and all wood-work is dressed and exposed to view and finished with hard oil varnish.

COLORS: Clapboards, front door panels and veranda floor, light brown. Trim and front door framing for panels, dark brown. Roof shingles dipped in and brush coated with dark red paint. Sashes, dark red. Rafters and ceiling of veranda, varnished. Wall shingles of tower and gables, dipped in and brush coated with sienna stain.

ACCOMMODATIONS: The principal rooms and their sizes, closets, etc., are shown by the floor plans. There is no cellar. Ceiling in tower room is full height. Stairway leads up to a gallery at the side of living-room. Living room is open to roof. Fireplace with brick mantel and wood shelf of quaint design is artistic, yet simple enough to be made by an ordinary mechanic; its cost is included in the estimate. This is an appropriate design for a fishing camp, shooting lodge or summer residence.

COST: $800. The estimate is based on ‡ New York prices for materials and labor. In many sections of the country the cost should be less.

Price of working plans (with full details drawn to large scale), specifications and * license to build, ... $15.00

Price of †† bill of materials, ... 5.00

FEASIBLE MODIFICATIONS: General dimensions, materials and colors may be changed. Cellar may be put under part or whole of house. Veranda may be reduced or extended. Kitchen may be placed back of living-room and the present kitchen used as a bedroom.

The price of working plans, specifications, etc., for a modified design, varies according to the alterations required and will be made known upon application to the Architects.

Address, THE CO-OPERATIVE BUILDING PLAN ASSOCIATION, Architects, 106–108 Fulton Street, New York.

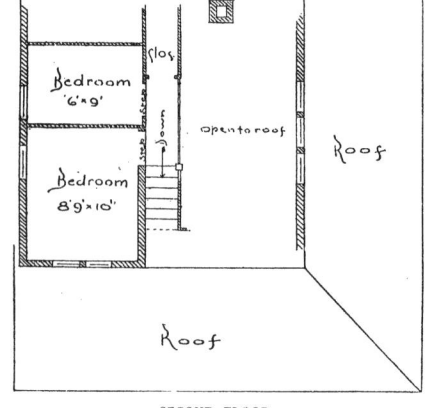

SECOND FLOOR.

Cottage, Design No. 1169

PERSPECTIVE.

DESCRIPTION.

GENERAL DIMENSIONS: Width, 20 ft. 8 ins.; depth, 24 ft.

HEIGHTS OF STORIES: Cellar, 6 ft. 6 ins.; first story, 8 ft. 8 ins.; second story, 8 ft.

EXTERIOR MATERIALS: Foundation, brick walls and piers or wood posts set in concrete; first story, clapboards; second story, gables and roofs, shingles.

INTERIOR FINISH: Two coat plaster, hard white finish. Flooring, trim and stairs, soft wood. All interior wood-work, grain filled and finished in hard oil varnish.

COLORS: Clapboards, drab. Trim, cornices and porch floor, olive green. Porch ceiling, oiled. Blinds and sashes, red. Outside doors, bronze green. All shingles dipped in and brush coated with red paint.

ACCOMMODATIONS: The principal rooms and their sizes, closets, etc., are shown by the floor plans. Cellar under living-room. Mantel in parlor is included in the estimate. By using a fireplace heater in the parlor, two upper rooms may be warmed. Large vestibule protects house from cold and dust. Sink with cold water supply in nook off living-room.

COST: $971. The estimate is based on ‡ New York prices for materials and labor. In many sections of the country the cost should be less.

Price of working plans (with full details drawn to large scale), specifications and * license to build, ... $15.00
Price of †† bill of materials, . . . 5.00

FEASIBLE MODIFICATIONS: General dimensions, materials and colors may be changed. Cellar may be extended under the whole house or may be omitted entirely. Porch may be extended indefinitely. Living-room may be made into a dining-room by placing kitchen back of same.

The price of working plans, specifications, etc., for a modified design, varies according to the alterations required and will be made known upon application to the Architects.

Address, THE CO-OPERATIVE BUILDING PLAN ASSOCIATION, Architects, 106–108 Fulton Street, New York.

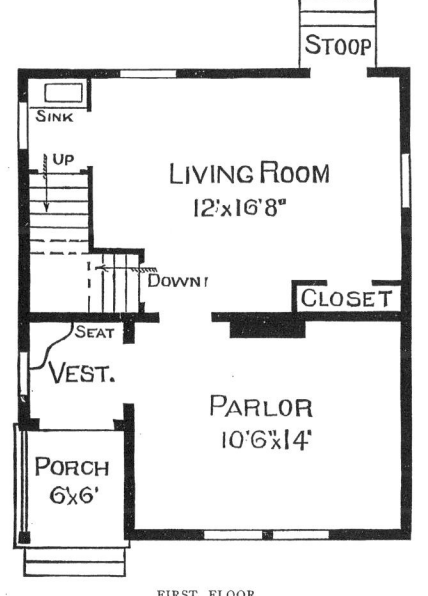

FIRST FLOOR.

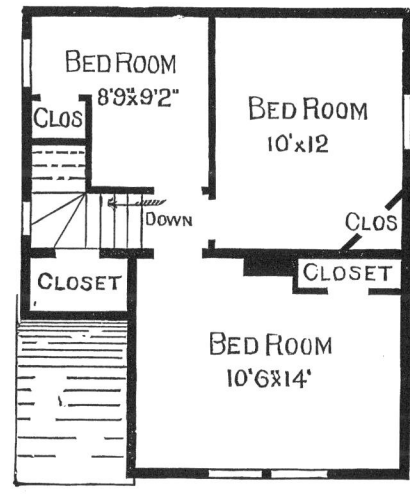

SECOND FLOOR.

Cottage, Design No. 1170

PERSPECTIVE.

DESCRIPTION.

GENERAL DIMENSIONS: Width, 24 ft.; depth, including pantry, 27 ft. 6 ins.

HEIGHTS OF STORIES: Cellar, 6 ft. 6 ins.; first story, 10 ft.; second story, 8 ft.

EXTERIOR MATERIALS: Foundation, stone; first story, clapboards; second story and roof, shingles.

INTERIOR FINISH: Hard white plaster. Soft wood flooring, trim and stairs. Interior wood-work finished with hard oil.

COLORS: All clapboards, fawn. Shingling on second story side walls, dark yellow. Trim, outside doors, veranda floor, blinds, sashes and conductors, brown.

ACCOMMODATIONS: The principal rooms and their sizes, closets, etc., are shown by the floor plans. Cellar under the whole house with inside and outside entrances. Ample veranda and numerous closets.

COST: $980, † not including heater and mantel. The estimate is based on ‡ New York prices for labor and materials. In many sections of the country the cost should be less.

Price of working plans (with full details drawn to large scale), specifications and * license to build, ... $15.00

Price of †† bill of materials, ... 5.00

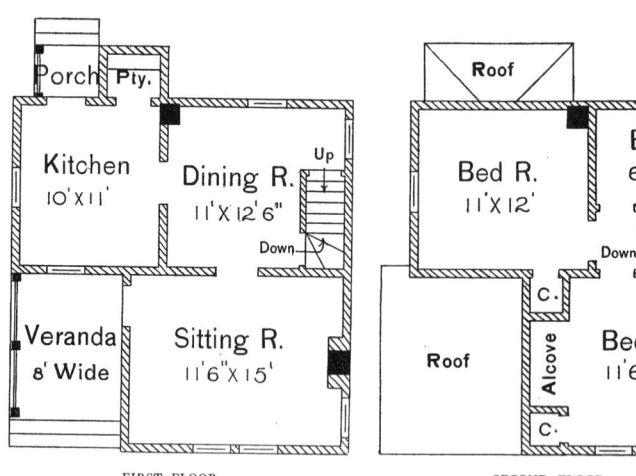

FIRST FLOOR.   SECOND FLOOR.

FEASIBLE MODIFICATIONS: Heights of stories, general dimensions, materials and colors may be changed. Cellar may be omitted and the house built on brick piers or posts. The small rear bedroom in the second story could be re-planned for a bath-room. An open fireplace could be introduced in sitting-room.

The price of working plans, specifications, etc., for a modified design, varies according to the alterations required and will be made known upon application to the Architects.

Address, THE CO-OPERATIVE BUILDING PLAN ASSOCIATION, Architects, 106-108 Fulton Street, New York.

Cottage, Design No. 1171

PERSPECTIVE

DESCRIPTION.

GENERAL DIMENSIONS: Width, including porch, 23 ft.; depth, including bay-window, 28 ft. 6 ins.

HEIGHTS OF STORIES: Cellar, 6 ft. 6 ins.; first story, 8 ft. 6 ins.; second story, 8 ft.

EXTERIOR MATERIALS: Foundation, brick; first story, main part, clapboards; lower portion of porch, bay-window, gables and roof, shingles.

INTERIOR FINISH: Two coat plaster, hard white finish throughout. Soft wood flooring, trim and stairs. All interior woodwork finished natural with hard oil.

COLORS: All clapboards, light grey. Trim, white. All shingles left natural for weather stain. Veranda floor and ceiling, oiled.

ACCOMMODATIONS: The principal rooms and their sizes, closets, etc., are shown by the floor plans. Cellar under the whole house, accessible from the kitchen. All first story rooms and front bedroom, second story, to have chimney connection. Bay-window in the parlor with wide window seat. The space between side walls and roof, in the second story, is utilized for storage purposes.

COST: $1,000. The estimate is based on ‡ New York prices for materials and labor. In many sections of the country the cost should be less.

Price of working plans (with full details drawn to large scale), specifications and * license to build, ... $15.00

Price of †† bill of materials, . . . 5.00

FEASIBLE MODIFICATIONS: General dimensions, materials and colors may be changed. Cellar may be omitted and the house built on posts or piers. The porch may be increased in size by projecting it further to the side.

The price of working plans, specifications, etc., for a modified design, varies according to the alterations required and will be made known upon application to the Architects.

Address, THE CO-OPERATIVE BUILDING PLAN ASSOCIATION, Architects, 106-108 Fulton Street, New York.

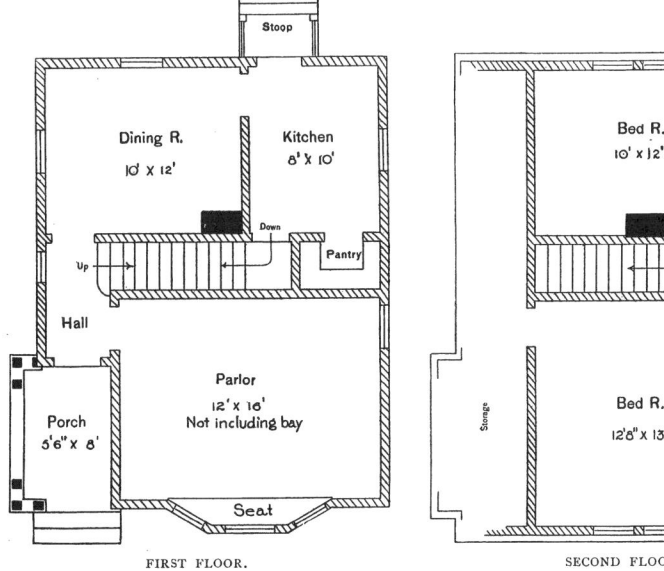

FIRST FLOOR.   SECOND FLOOR.

Cottage, Design No. 1172

PERSPECTIVE.

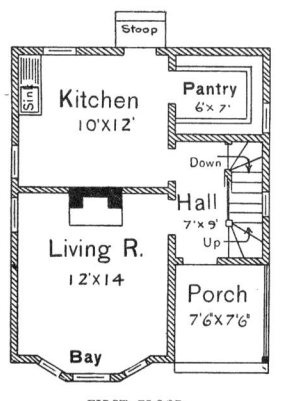

FIRST FLOOR.

DESCRIPTION.

GENERAL DIMENSIONS: Width, 20 ft. 6 ins.; depth, 25 ft. 6 ins.

HEIGHTS OF STORIES: Cellar, 6 ft. 6 ins.; first story, 8 ft.; second story, 7 ft. 6 ins.

EXTERIOR MATERIALS: Brick foundation; clapboards for first story; shingles for second story, gables and roofs.

INTERIOR FINISH: Two coat plaster, hard white finish, throughout. Floors throughout, spruce. Trim throughout, white wood. All wood-work finished with hard oil, or painted to suit owner.

COLORS: Body, all clapboards, first story, white. Trim, including water-table, corner boards, casings, cornices, bands, porch posts, rail, sashes and outside doors, Colonial yellow. Porch floor and ceiling, oiled. Shingles on side walls and roofs left natural for weather stain.

ACCOMMODATIONS: The principal rooms and their sizes, closets, etc., are shown by the floor plans. Cellar under whole house. Large pantry. Bay-window and open fireplace in living-room. Access to cellar from hall.

COST: $1,000, † not including mantel. The estimate is based on ‡ New York prices for labor and materials.

Price of working plans (with the fullest details drawn to large scale), specifications and * license to build, . . $15.00

Price of †† bill of materials, ... 5.00

FEASIBLE MODIFICATIONS: General dimensions, materials and colors may be changed. Cellar may be decreased in size or be wholly omitted. Kitchen extension may be planned at the back, the present kitchen to be used as dining-room and the present living room as parlor. The small bedroom may be re-planned as a bath-room. Air space over second story may be floored for storage use. Open fireplaces may be placed in the two large bedrooms.

The price of working plans, specifications, etc., for a modified design, varies according to the alterations required and will be made known upon application to the Architects.

Address, THE CO-OPERATIVE BUILDING PLAN ASSOCIATION, Architects, 106-108 Fulton Street, New York.

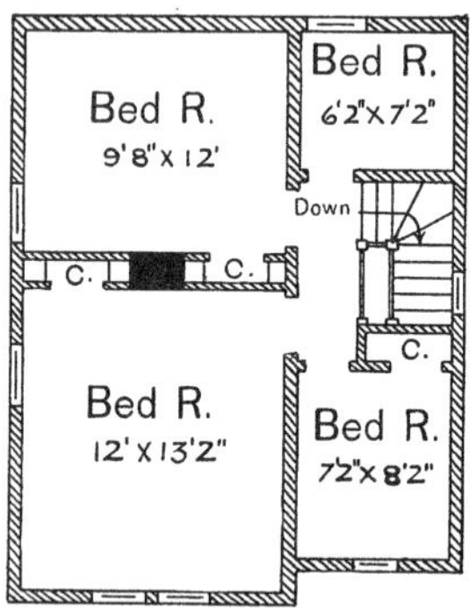

SECOND FLOOR.

Cottage, Design No. 1181

PERSPECTIVE.

DESCRIPTION.

GENERAL DIMENSIONS: Width, 24 ft. 2 ins.; depth, 30 ft. 5 ins. including verandas.

HEIGHTS OF STORIES: First story, 9 ft.; second story, 8 ft.

EXTERIOR MATERIALS: Foundation, posts; first story, clapboards; second story, gables and roofs, shingles.

INTERIOR FINISH: Two coat plaster, hard white finish. Flooring, trim and stairways, soft wood. Kitchen, wainscoted. All interior wood-work grain filled, stained to suit owner and finished in hard oil varnish.

COLORS: Clapboards, outside panels and sashes, light brown. Trim, including cornices, casings, outside door panels, veranda ceiling, rain-water conductors, dark brown. Veranda floor, oiled. Wall shingles dipped and brush coated sienna stain. Roof shingles left natural for weather stain.

ACCOMMODATIONS: The principal rooms and their sizes, closets, etc., are shown by the floor plans. No cellar. Chimney with thimble connections in kitchen, dining-room, parlor and bedrooms.

COST: $1,132. The estimate is based on ‡ New York prices for materials and labor. In many sections of the country the cost should be less.

Price of working plans (with full details drawn to large scale), specifications and * license to build, ... $15.00

Price of †† bill of materials, ... 5.00

FEASIBLE MODIFICATIONS: General dimensions, materials and colors may be changed. Cellar may be placed under portion or whole of house. Veranda may be placed around front and sides. Wide portiére opening may be made to connect dining-room and parlor, and hall and dining room. Bath-room, with full plumbing, may be introduced in second story and brick-set range, sink and boiler in kitchen. This design can be built with plank construction and interior finished with paper in place of plaster, which would make a saving in cost of about $300.

The price of working plans, specifications, etc., for a modified design, varies according to the alterations required and will be made known upon application to the Architects.

Address, THE CO-OPERATIVE BUILDING PLAN ASSOCIATION, Architects, 106-108 Fulton Street, New York.

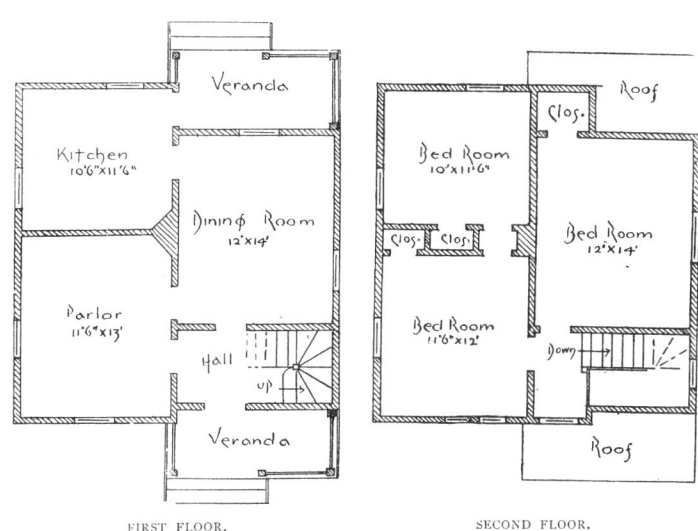

FIRST FLOOR.   SECOND FLOOR.

Cottage, Design No. 1182

PERSPECTIVE.

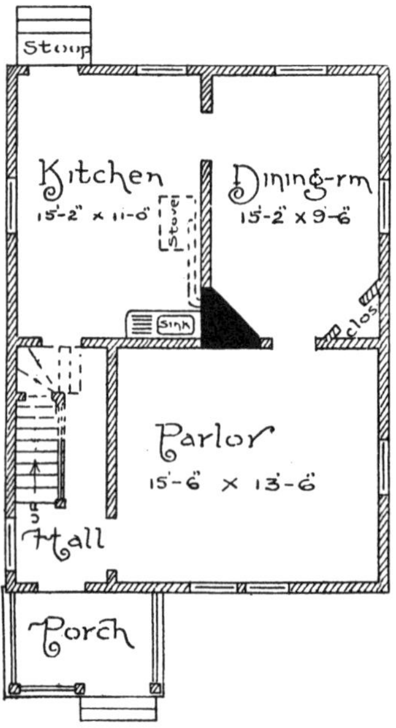

FIRST FLOOR. 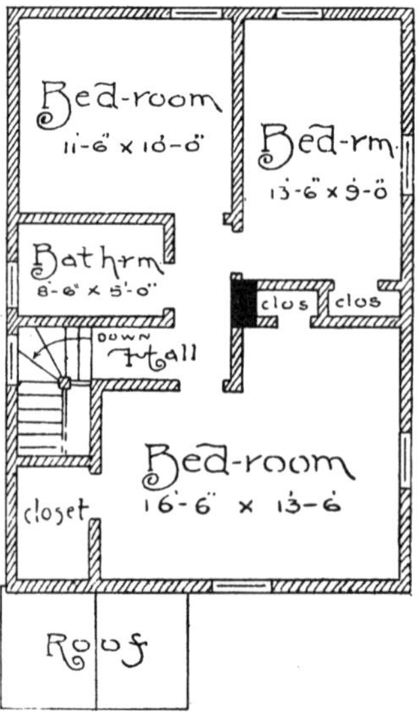   SECOND FLOOR.

DESCRIPTION.

GENERAL DIMENSIONS: Width, 22 ft.; depth, 30 ft.

HEIGHTS OF STORIES: First story, 8 ft. 6 ins.; second story, 8 ft.

EXTERIOR MATERIALS: Foundation, posts; first story, clapboards; second story, gables and roofs, shingles.

INTERIOR FINISH: Two coat plaster, hard white finish. Soft wood flooring, trim and stairs. Kitchen, wainscoted. Interior wood-work grain filled and finished in hard oil varnish.

COLORS: Clapboards, light buff. Trim, including water-table, corner boards, cornices, casings bands, porch rail, etc., white. Outside blinds, doors and conductors, maroon. Sashes, dark red. Shingles on side walls, oiled. Shingles on roof left natural for weather stain. Porch floor and ceiling, oiled.

ACCOMMODATIONS: The principal rooms and their sizes, closets, etc., are shown by the floor plans. There is no cellar. Unfinished attic accessible through scuttle in second story hall. Sink with cold water supply in kitchen. The small room for "bath-room" can be used as a bath-room, sewing room, a large closet, or as an alcove to the bedroom which it adjoins. No tub fixtures or plumbing are specified, nor are they included in the estimate. China closet in dining-room.

COST: $1,150. The estimate is based on ‡ New York prices for materials and labor. In many sections of the country the cost should be less.

Price of working plans (with full details drawn to large scale), specifications and * license to build, ... $15.00
Price of †† bill of materials, ... 5 00

FEASIBLE MODIFICATIONS: General dimensions, materials and colors may be changed. Portiére opening may be made to connect hall and parlor. Cellar may be placed under whole or part of house with inside and outside entrance and concrete floor. Porch may be extended across front.

The price of working plans, specifications, etc., for a modified design, varies according to the alterations required and will be made known upon application to the Architects.

Address, THE CO-OPERATIVE BUILDING PLAN ASSOCIATION, Architects, 106–108 Fulton Street, New York.

Cottage, Design No. 1183

PERSPECTIVE.

DESCRIPTION.

GENERAL DIMENSIONS: Width, 20 ft.; depth, 33 ft. 6 ins.
HEIGHTS OF STORIES: Cellar, 6 ft. 6 ins.; first story, 8 ft. 6 ins.; second story, 8 ft.

EXTERIOR MATERIALS: Foundation, brick; first and second story walls and porch enclosure, clapboards; gables and roofs, shingles.

INTERIOR FINISH: Two coat plaster, hard white finish. Soft wood trim. Flooring throughout, N. C. pine. Main staircase risers and treads, white pine; level rail and newel in second story, ash. Living-room, wainscoted. All interior wood-work grain filled, stained to suit owner and finished in hard oil varnish.

COLORS: Trim, including water-table, corner boards, cornices, casings, etc., dark green. Clapboards, terra-cotta. Shingles on gables left natural for weather stain. Roof shingles stained moss green. Sashes, white. Porch floor and ceiling and outside doors, oiled.

ACCOMMODATIONS: The principal rooms and their sizes, closets, etc., are shown by the floor plans. Opening for brick-set range in living-room. Sink with cold water supply in pantry. Open fireplace in parlor. Cellar under whole house with inside and outside entrances and concrete floor. Large-sized pantry. Good storage space under porch roof and over second story, accessible through a scuttle in second story hall.

COST: $1,175, † not including mantel, range or heater. The estimate is based on ‡ New York prices for materials and labor. In many sections of the country the cost should be less.

Price of working plans (with full details drawn to large scale), specifications and * license to build, ... $15.00
Price of †† bill of materials, ... 5.00

FEASIBLE MODIFICATIONS: General dimensions, materials and colors may be changed. Cellar may be reduced in size or wholly omitted Kitchen may be planned back of living-room. Porch may be extended out across the front to form veranda. Bath-room, with full plumbing, may be placed in the second story and two set-tubs in cellar.

The price of working plans, specifications, etc., for a modified design, varies according to the alterations required and will be made known upon application to the Architects.

Address, THE CO-OPERATIVE BUILDING PLAN ASSOCIATION, Architects, 106–108 Fulton Street, New York.

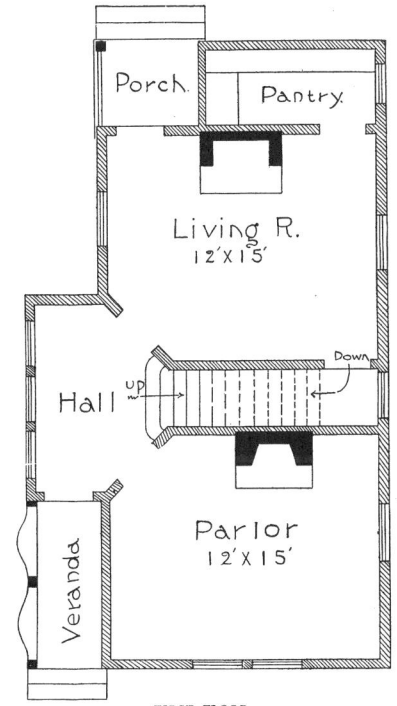

FIRST FLOOR.

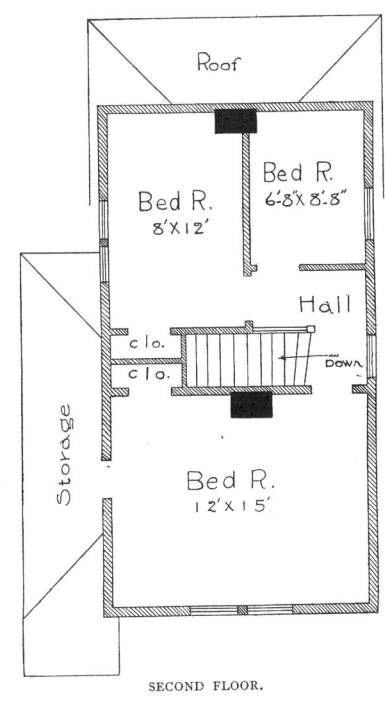

SECOND FLOOR.

Cottage, Design No. 1184

PERSPECTIVE.

DESCRIPTION.

GENERAL DIMENSIONS: Width, 49 ft., including veranda; depth, 24 ft., including veranda.

HEIGHTS OF STORIES: First story, 10 ft.; second story, 9 ft.

EXTERIOR MATERIALS: Foundation, wood posts; first story, clapboards; second story, clapboards and shingles; roof, shingles.

INTERIOR FINISH: Interior is not plastered, but is finished with heavy red paper; the wood-work is exposed to view and varnished. This pretty and inexpensive finish is very suitable for a summer cottage. Soft wood stairs, flooring and trim throughout, varnished the same as other exposed wood-work.

COLORS: Clapboards and veranda floor, light brown. All trim and front door, dark brown. Sashes, dark red. Rafters and veranda ceiling, varnished. Roof shingles dipped in and brush-coated with dark red paint. Wall shingles dipped in and brush-coated sienna stain.

ACCOMMODATIONS: The principal rooms and their sizes, closets, etc., are shown by the floor plans. No cellar. Open fireplace and mantel in hall included in estimate. Designed for a seaside or mountain cottage, suitable also for a shooting lodge or "box." Balcony in second story affords pleasant outlook.

COST: $1,194. The estimate is based on ‡ New York prices for materials and labor. In many sections of the country the cost should be less.

Price of working plans (with full details drawn to large scale), specifications and * license to build, . . . $15.00

Price of †† bill of materials, ... 5.00

FEASIBLE MODIFICATIONS: Heights of stories, colors, sizes of rooms and kinds of materials may be changed. Cellar may be placed under the whole or part of house. Veranda may be reduced or extended. Bedrooms over dining-room may be united to form one large room.

The price of working plans, specifications, etc., for a modified design, varies according to the alterations required and will be made known upon application to the Architects.

Address, THE CO-OPERATIVE BUILDING PLAN ASSOCIATION, Architects, 106-108 Fulton Street, New York.

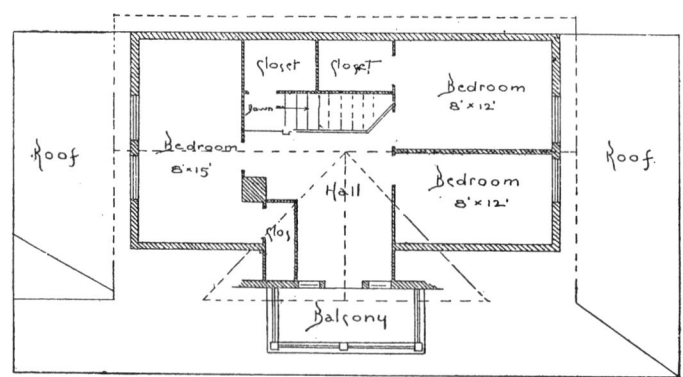

SECOND FLOOR.

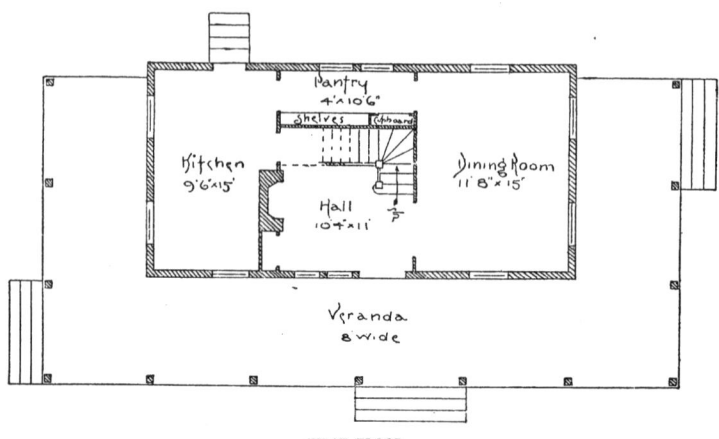

FIRST FLOOR.

Cottage, Design No. 1185

PERSPECTIVE.

DESCRIPTION.

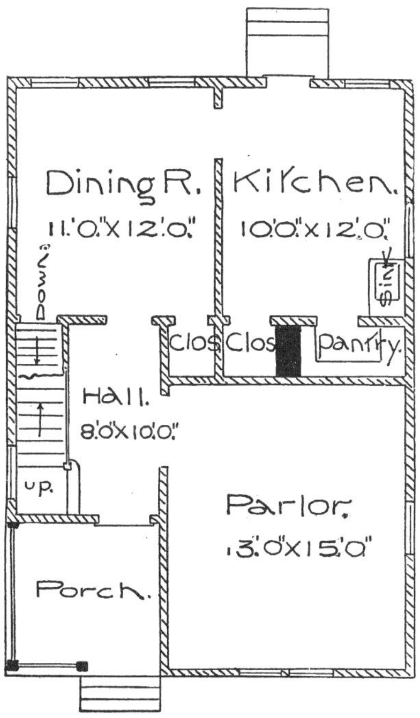

GENERAL DIMENSIONS: Width, 22 ft. 6 ins.; depth, 32 ft.

HEIGHTS OF STORIES: Cellar, 7 ft.; first story, 9 ft.; second story, 8 ft., 6 ins.

EXTERIOR MATERIALS: Foundation, stone or brick; first story, clapboards; second story, gables and roofs, shingles.

INTERIOR FINISH: Two coat plaster, hard white finish. Soft wood flooring and trim. Staircase, ash. Kitchen and bath-room, wainscoted. Chair-rail in dining-room. All interior wood-work, grain filled, stained to suit owner and finished in hard oil varnish.

COLORS: Clapboards, light brown. Trim, including cornices, casings, bands, porch posts, rail and balusters, seal brown. Wall shingles dipped and brush-coated, reddish brown stain. Roof shingles dipped and brush-coated, silver stain. Blinds, maroon.

ACCOMMODATIONS: The principal rooms and their sizes, closets, etc., are shown by the floor plans. Cellar under the whole house, with inside and outside entrances. Storage space back of bath-room and in front of second story hall, also loft over second story. Wide portière opening connects hall and parlor. Sink and boiler in kitchen, also flue for portable range. Bath-room, with full plumbing, in second story.

COST: $1,200, † not including parlor mantel, range or heater. The estimate is based on ‡ New York prices for materials and labor. In many sections of the country the cost should be less.

Price of working plans (with full details drawn to large scale), specifications and * license to build, ... $15.00

Price of †† bill of materials, ... 5.00

FEASIBLE MODIFICATIONS: General dimensions, materials and colors may be changed. Cellar may be reduced in size. Open fireplaces may be introduced in dining-room and parlor. Part or all of plumbing may be omitted. Porch may be extended around hall and dining-room side to form veranda. Wide portière opening or sliding doors may be made to connect dining-room and hall. Sliding doors may be substituted for portière openings between hall and parlor. Storage space at front of second story hall may be finished off as a hall bedroom.

The price of working plans, specifications, etc., for a modified design, varies according to the alterations required and will be made known upon application to the Architects.

Address, THE CO-OPERATIVE BUILDING PLAN ASSOCIATION, Architects, 106-108 Fulton Street, New York.

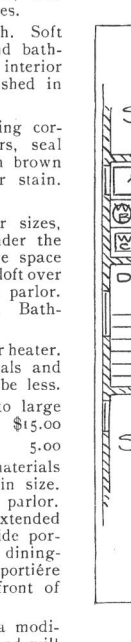

FIRST FLOOR.

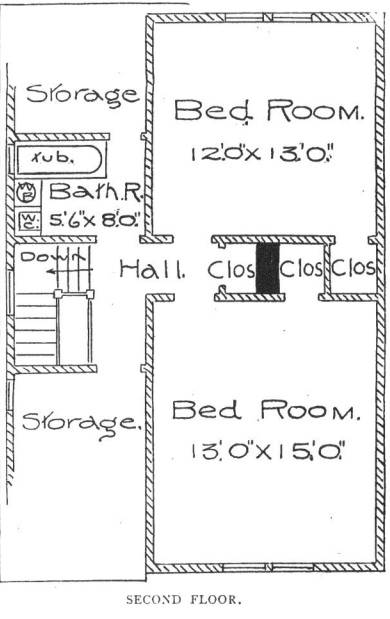

SECOND FLOOR.

Cottage, Design No. 1186

PERSPECTIVE.

DESCRIPTION.

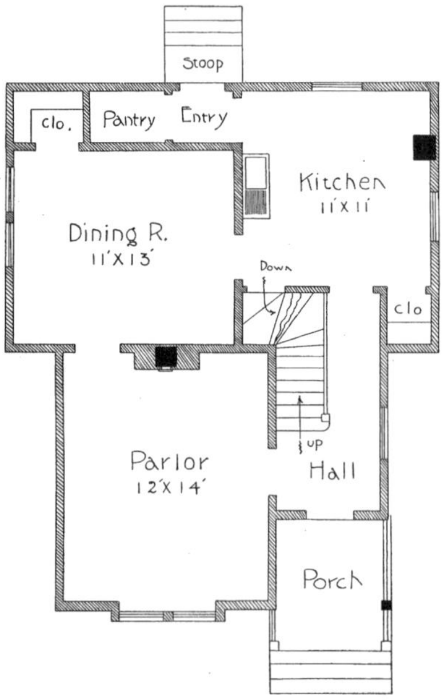

GENERAL DIMENSIONS: Extreme width, 25 ft. 6 ins.; depth, including porch, 32 ft.

HEIGHTS OF STORIES: Cellar, 6 ft. 6 ins.; first story, 8 ft. 6 ins.; second story, 8 ft.

EXTERIOR MATERIALS: Foundation, brick; first and second stories, clapboards; gables and roof, shingles.

INTERIOR FINISH: Two coat plaster, hard white finish. Soft wood for trim. Flooring throughout, N. C. pine. Main staircase newel, rails and balusters, yellow pine; risers and treads, white pine. Kitchen, wainscoted. All interior woodwork grain filled, stained to suit owner and finished in hard oil varnish.

COLORS: Trim, including cornices, casings, corner boards, bands, porch posts, rail, etc., dark green. Clapboards, white. Shingles on gables, silver gray. Roof shingles stained moss green. Sashes, dark red. Piazza floor and ceiling, oiled.

ACCOMMODATIONS: The principal rooms and their sizes, closets, etc., are shown by the floor plans. Cellar under parlor and hall, with inside entrance. Sink with cold water supply in kitchen. Chimney breast for mantel and thimble for stove pipe in parlor; also thimble connection in two bedrooms. Recessed window in parlor. China closet in dining-room. Good-sized pantry off entry large enough to admit ice-box.

COST: $1,200, † not including mantel, range or heater. The estimate is based on ‡ New York prices for materials and labor. In many sections of the country the cost should be less.

Price of working plans (with full details drawn to large scale), specifications and * license to build, . . $15.00
Price of †† bill of materials, ... 5.00

FIRST FLOOR.

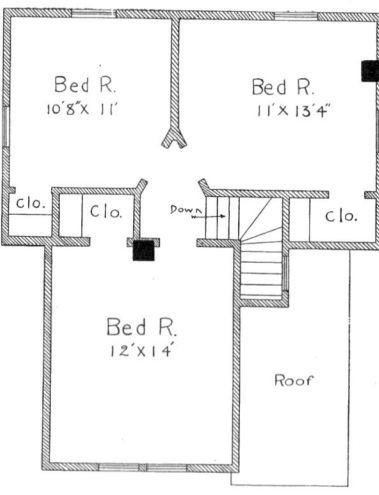

SECOND FLOOR.

FEASIBLE MODIFICATIONS: General dimensions, materials and colors may be changed. Cellar may be placed under whole house with outside entrance. Double sliding doors can be placed between dining-room and parlor by transferring chimney to side wall of parlor. Porch may be extended around hall side to kitchen closet. A 4-ft. portiere opening may be made to connect parlor and hall.

The price of working plans, specifications, etc., for a modified design, varies according to the alterations required and will be made known upon application to the Architects.

Address, THE CO-OPERATIVE BUILDING PLAN ASSOCIATION, Architects, 106-108 Fulton Street, New York.

Cottage, Design No. 1187

PERSPECTIVE.

DESCRIPTION.

GENERAL DIMENSIONS: Width, through dining-room and kitchen, including bay, 33 ft.; depth, including veranda and pantry, 43 ft.

HEIGHTS OF STORIES: First story, 9 ft.; second story, 8 ft.

EXTERIOR MATERIALS: Foundation, brick piers; first story, clapboards; second story, gables and roofs, shingles.

INTERIOR FINISH: Hard white plaster throughout. Soft wood flooring, trim and stairs. All interior wood-work finished with hard oil.

COLORS: First story, clapboards, light brown. Trim, dark brown. Outside doors, panels, light brown; stiles and rails, dark brown. Sashes, dark green. Veranda floor and ceiling, oiled. Shingles on side walls and gables stained sienna. Shingles on roof left unfinished.

ACCOMMODATIONS: The principal rooms and their sizes, closets, etc., are shown by the floor plans. No cellar, or attic. Wide veranda. Open fireplace in living-room. Bay window in dining-room.

COST: $1,200, † not including mantel. The estimate is based on ‡ New York prices for materials and labor. In many sections of the country the cost should be less.

Price of working plans (with full details drawn to large scale), specifications and * license to build, . . $15.00

Price of †† bill of materials, ... 5.00

FEASIBLE MODIFICATIONS: General dimensions, materials and colors may be changed. Stairs may be separated from living-room by a hall which will connect with dining-room and living-room. Cellar may be introduced under a portion or the whole house. Double folding doors may be used between living-room and dining-room. Bay-window could be carried up two stories. Veranda may be reduced or enlarged. The rear door of dining-room could be omitted.

The price of working plans, specifications, etc., for a modified design, varies according to the alterations required and will be made known upon application to the Architects.

Address, THE CO-OPERATIVE BUILDING PLAN ASSOCIATION, Architects, 106-108 Fulton Street, New York.

Cottage, Design No. 1188

PERSPECTIVE.

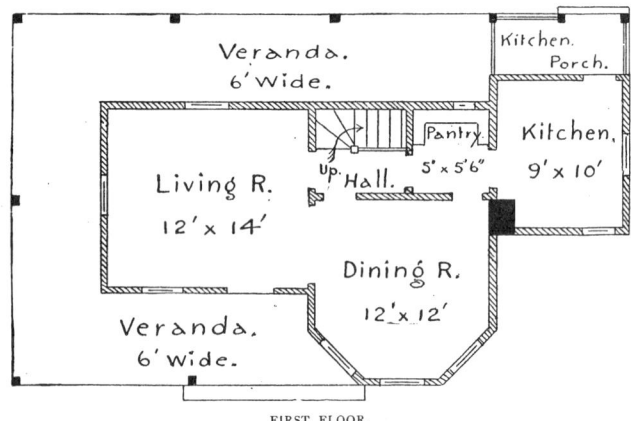

FIRST FLOOR.

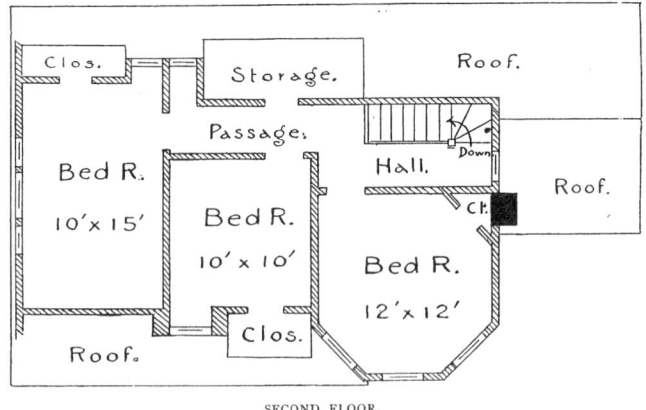

SECOND FLOOR.

DESCRIPTION.

GENERAL DIMENSIONS: Width, including veranda, 43 ft.; depth, including veranda, 25 ft.

HEIGHTS OF STORIES: First story, 8 ft. 6 ins.; second story, 8 ft.

EXTERIOR MATERIALS: Foundation, posts or piers; first and second stories, gables and dormers, shingles; roofs, shingles and metal.

INTERIOR FINISH: Two coat plaster. Soft wood flooring, trim and stairs, painted colors to suit owner.

COLORS: All shingles left natural. Trim, white. Sashes, red. Outside blinds, Colonial yellow. Veranda floor and ceiling, oiled.

ACCOMMODATIONS: The principal rooms and their sizes, closets, etc., are shown by the floor plans. No cellar. Loft floored for storage. One chimney serves for kitchen and dining-room. A stove in dining-room should comfortably warm living-room also, as the two rooms are connected by wide opening. Large pantry connects kitchen with hall and dining-room. Extensive veranda on three sides of the house. Kitchen porch enclosed by lattice work.

COST: $1,200. The estimate is based on ‡ New York prices for materials and labor. In many sections of the country the cost should be less.

Price of working plans (with full details drawn to large scale), specifications and * license to build, ... $15.00

Price of †† bill of materials, ... 10.00

FEASIBLE MODIFICATIONS: General dimensions, materials and colors may be changed. Cellar may be placed under part or whole of house. Bath-room, with partial or full plumbing, may be planned in second story. Kitchen extension may be carried up a story and enlarged to give another bedroom. Bay projection may be covered with a hipped or bell shaped roof. A part or all of the veranda at rear may be replanned to increase the size of living-room or to give extra rooms.

The price of working plans, specifications, etc., for a modified design, varies according to the alterations required and will be made known upon application to the Architects.

Address, THE CO-OPERATIVE BUILDING PLAN ASSOCIATION, Architects, 106–108 Fulton Street, New York.

Cottage, Design No. 1189

PERSPECTIVE.

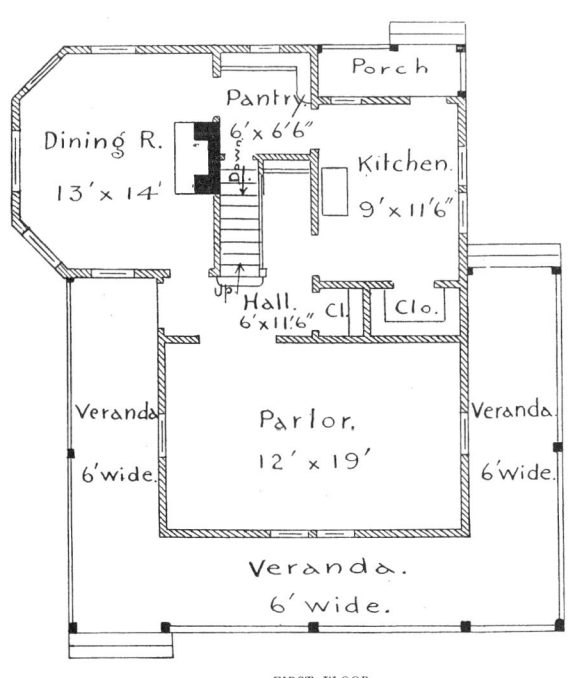

FIRST FLOOR.

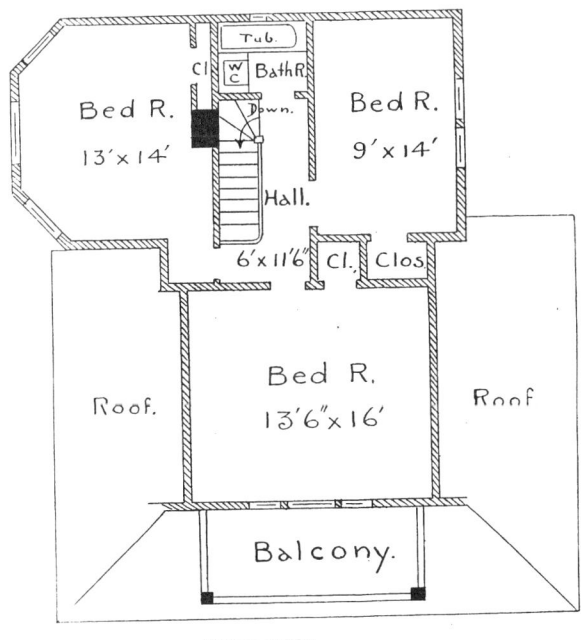

SECOND FLOOR.

DESCRIPTION.

GENERAL DIMENSIONS: Width through dining-room and kitchen, including veranda, 36 ft.; depth, including veranda, 38 ft.

HEIGHTS OF STORIES: Cellar, 6 ft. 6 ins.; first story, 8 ft. 6 ins.; second story, 8 ft.

EXTERIOR MATERIALS: Foundation, stone or brick; first story where covered by veranda, clapboards; remainder of first story and entire second story, also all gables and roofs, shingles.

INTERIOR FINISH: Two coat plaster. Soft wood flooring, trim and stairs. Interior wood-work finished with hard oil.

COLORS: Body, all clapboards under veranda, Colonial yellow. Shingles on walls and gables left natural color. Trim, white. Sashes, red. Blinds, Colonial yellow. Roof shingles dipped and brush coated red. Veranda floor and ceiling, oiled.

ACCOMMODATIONS: The principal rooms and their sizes, closets, etc., are shown by the floor plans. Cellar under rear half of the house. Attic floored for storage but otherwise unfinished. One chimney serves whole house, the kitchen stove being connected with the chimney by a tile pipe through which stove-pipe passes. Open fireplace in dining-room. Pantry connects kitchen and dining-room.

COST: $1,250, † not including mantel, range, heater or plumbing. The estimate is based on ‡ New York prices for materials and labor. In many sections of the country the cost should be less.

Price of working plans (with full details drawn to large scale), specifications and * license to build, ... $15.00

Price of †† bill of materials, ... 10.00

FEASIBLE MODIFICATIONS: General dimensions, materials and colors may be changed. Bath-room may be used as a small bedroom, and plumbing put in at any desired time. Balcony may be omitted or may be enclosed to form a part of the adjoining room, in which case two rooms may be planned where front bedroom now is. Open fireplace in dining-room may be omitted. Another chimney may be introduced between parlor and kitchen with an open fireplace in parlor, if desired. Cellar may be extended under whole house or omitted entirely.

Address, THE CO-OPERATIVE BUILDING PLAN ASSOCIATION, Architects, 106–108 Fulton Street, New York.

Cottage, Design No. 1190

PERSPECTIVE.

DESCRIPTION.

GENERAL DIMENSIONS: Width, 23 ft.; depth, 30 ft., not including rear porch.

HEIGHTS OF STORIES: Cellar, 6 ft. 6 ins.; first story, 9 ft.; second story, 8 ft.

EXTERIOR MATERIALS: Foundation, posts; first story, clapboards; second story and roof, shingles; gables, shingles and panels.

INTERIOR FINISH: Two coat plaster, hard white finish. Flooring and trim, soft wood. Kitchen wainscoted. Stairway newels, rails and balusters, ash; risers and treads, white pine. All interior woodwork grain filled and finished in hard oil varnish.

COLORS: Clapboards, outside door framing for panels and sashes, light brown. Trim, outside door panels, veranda ceiling, and rain water conductors, dark brown. Veranda floor, oiled. Wall shingles dipped in and brush coated with sienna stain. Roof shingles, unpainted.

ACCOMMODATIONS: The principal rooms and their sizes, closets, etc., are shown by the floor plans. There is a cellar 10 x 10 with plank walls, and a stairway to same from dining-room.

COST: $1,287. The estimate is based on ‡ New York prices for materials and labor. In many sections of the country the cost should be less.

Price of working plans (with full details drawn to large scale), specifications and * license to build, ... $15.00
Price of †† bill of materials, . 5.00

FEASIBLE MODIFICATIONS: General dimensions, materials and colors may be changed. Cellar may be placed under whole or portion of house, in which case brick walls would be substituted for wood posts. Porch may be extended across the front. Open fireplaces may be built in parlor and dining-room. Brick-set range, sink and boiler may be introduced in kitchen. Bath-room with full plumbing, or partial plumbing, may be put in second story. This design may be built with plank construction and built with paper interior instead of plaster for about $325 less than our estimate calls for.

The price of working plans, specifications, etc., for a modified design, varies according to the alterations required and will be made known upon application to the Architects.

Address, THE CO-OPERATIVE BUILDING PLAN ASSOCIATION, Architects, 106–108 Fulton Street, New York.

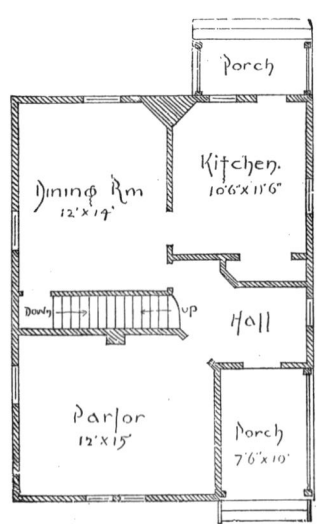

FIRST FLOOR.

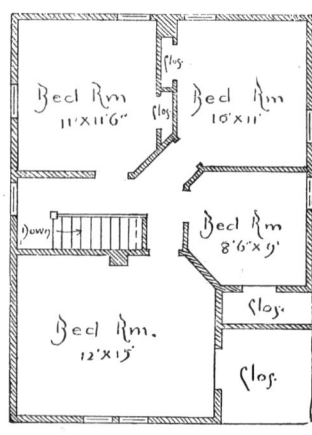

SECOND FLOOR.

Cottage, Design No. 1191

PERSPECTIVE.

DESCRIPTION.

GENERAL DIMENSIONS: Width, 20 ft.; depth, 30 ft.

HEIGHTS OF STORIES: Cellar, 6 ft. 6 ins.; first story, 9 ft.; second story, 8 ft.

EXTERIOR MATERIALS: Foundation, brick; first story, clapboards; second story and roofs, shingles; gables, panels and shingles.

INTERIOR FINISH: Two coat plaster, hard white finish. Soft wood flooring and trim. Staircase, ash. All interior wood-work grain filled and finished in hard oil varnish.

COLORS: Clapboards, porch posts, rail and balusters, light chocolate. Trim, outside doors, sashes and rain conductors, maroon. Porch floor, oiled. Wall shingles dipped and brush coated with oil. Roof shingles left natural color.

ACCOMMODATIONS: The principal rooms and their sizes, closets, etc., are shown by the floor plans. Cellar under front portion of house. Space above the second story is floored for storage, accessible through scuttle. Sink in kitchen is placed in recess to economize space. Dining-room has a bay with window-seat. This design may be built on a 25 ft. lot and still leave passage at side. Chimney is centrally located and is accessible to most of the rooms.

COST: $1,356, † not including mantels, range or heater. The estimate is based on ‡ New York prices for materials and labor. In many sections of the country the cost should be less.

Price of working plans (with full details drawn to large scale), specifications and * license to build, ... $15.00

Price of †† bill of materials, ... 5.00

FEASIBLE MODIFICATIONS: General dimensions, materials and colors may be changed. Cellar may be extended under the whole house or be omitted entirely. The porch may be extended across front to form veranda. Wide portiére opening or sliding doors may be made to connect parlor and hall. Bath-room, with full plumbing, may be introduced in second story and two wash-tubs placed in cellar.

The price of working plans, specifications, etc., for a modified design, varies according to the alterations required and will be made known upon application to the Architects.

Address, THE CO-OPERATIVE BUILDING PLAN ASSOCIATION, Architects, 106–108 Fulton Street, New York.

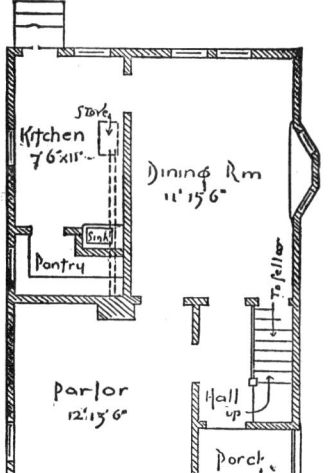

FIRST FLOOR.

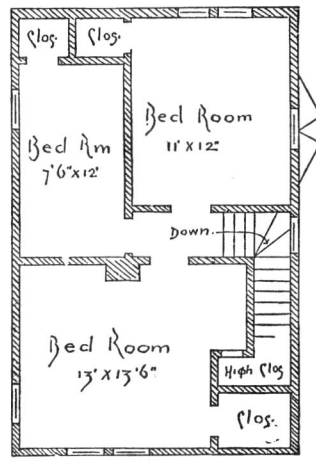

SECOND FLOOR.

21

Cottage, Design No. 1192

PERSPECTIVE.

DESCRIPTION.

GENERAL DIMENSIONS: Extreme width, 36 ft.; depth, 24 ft. 6 ins.

HEIGHTS OF STORIES: First story, 8 ft. 6 ins.; second story, 8 ft. 6 ins.; cellar, 6 ft. 6 ins.

EXTERIOR MATERIALS: Foundation, brick; first story, dormers, gables and roof, shingles.

INTERIOR FINISH: Two coat plaster, hard white finish. Soft wood flooring and trim throughout. Staircase, yellow pine. Kitchen, wainscoted. All interior wood-work grain filled and finished natural with hard oil varnish.

COLORS: Trim, including cornices, casings, veranda rail, etc., dark green. Shingles on side walls left natural for weather stain. Roof shingles dipped and brush coated dark red. Sashes, white. Veranda floor and ceiling and outside doors, oiled.

ACCOMMODATIONS: The principal rooms and their sizes, closets, etc., are shown by the floor plans. Cellar under kitchen and living-room, with outside entrance. Flue for portable range in kitchen. Thimble connecting chimney in parlor and dining-room and bedrooms over same. Ample storage space in second story under the roof. No blinds.

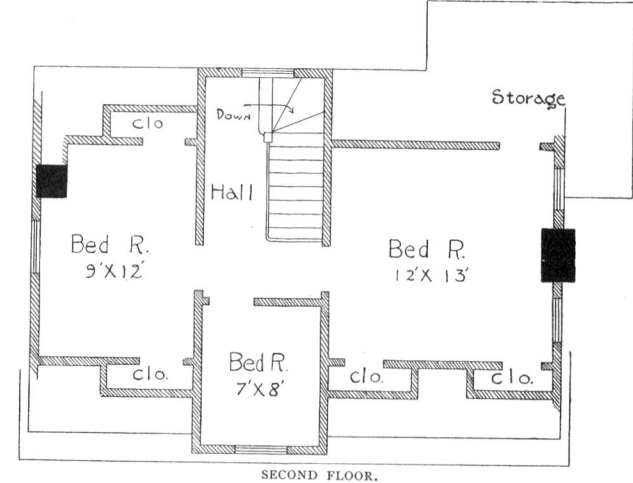

SECOND FLOOR.

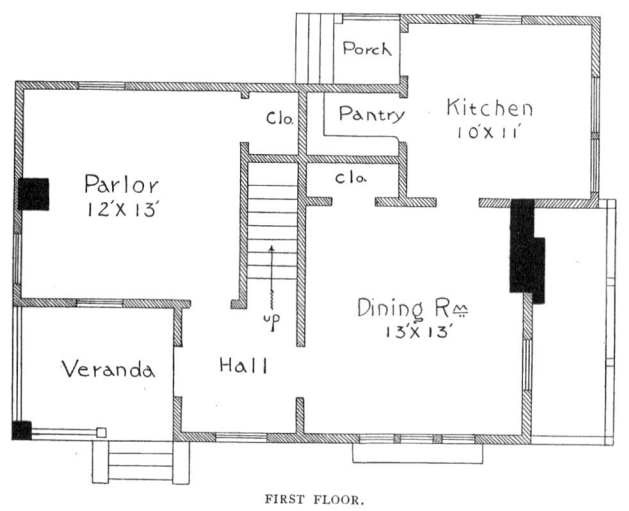

FIRST FLOOR.

COST: $1,365, † not including mantel, range or heater. The estimate is based on ‡ New York prices for materials and labor. In many sections of the country the cost should be less.

Price of working plans (with full details drawn to large scale), specifications and * license to build, ... $15.00
Price of †† bill of materials, ... 10.00

FEASIBLE MODIFICATIONS: General dimensions, materials and colors may be changed. Cellar may be placed under whole house with an inside entrance as well as outside. Fireplace may be introduced in dining-room and parlor and bedrooms over same. If cellar is placed under the whole house and furnace is used, one chimney will suffice. The uncovered veranda may be roofed over. Bath-room, with full plumbing, may be placed in second story back of bedroom, with an entrance from hall.

The price of working plans, specifications, etc., for a modified design, varies according to the alterations required and will be made known upon application to the Architects.

Address, THE CO-OPERATIVE BUILDING PLAN ASSOCIATION, Architects, 106–108 Fulton Street, New York.

Cottage, Design No. 1193

PERSPECTIVE.

DESCRIPTION.

GENERAL DIMENSIONS: Width, 18 ft.; depth, not including back veranda, 34 ft.

HEIGHTS OF STORIES: Cellar, 6 ft.; first story, 8 ft. 6 ins.; second story, 8 ft.

EXTERIOR MATERIALS: Foundation, brick; first story, clapboards; second story, gables and roofs, shingles.

INTERIOR FINISH: Two coat plaster, hard white finish. Soft wood flooring and trim. Main staircase treads and risers, white pine; newel, rail and balusters, ash. All interior wood-work grain filled and finished natural with hard oil varnish.

COLORS: Trim, including water-table, corner boards, cornices, casings, bands, veranda posts, rail, etc., bronze green. Clapboards, yellow stain. Sashes, red. Veranda floor, brown stain. Veranda ceiling, oiled. Shingling on side walls and gables stained burnt sienna. Roof shingles left natural for weather stain.

ACCOMMODATIONS: The principal rooms and their sizes, closets, etc., are shown by the floor plans. Cellar under parlor. Sink with cold water supply in living-room. Open fireplace in parlor. Wide portiére opening connects parlor and hall. Arched opening from parlor to stairs. Box-seat in hall. Large-sized veranda and kitchen pantry. Space over second story is floored for storage purposes, accessible through scuttle.

COST: $1,404, † not including mantel, range or heater. The estimate is based on ‡ New York prices for materials and labor. In many sections of the country the cost should be less.

Price of working plans (with full details drawn to large scale), specifications and * license to build, ... $15.00

Price of †† bill of materials, ... 5.00

FEASIBLE MODIFICATIONS: General dimensions, materials and colors may be changed. Cellar may be placed under whole house, with outside entrance and concrete floor. Stairway may be planned to attic to go over main stairs and one or two rooms be finished off. Veranda may be extended around one or both sides. Bath-room, with full plumbing, may be planned in rear of second story hall.

The price of working plans, specifications, etc., for a modified design, varies according to the alterations required and will be made known upon application to the Architects.

Address, THE CO-OPERATIVE BUILDING PLAN ASSOCIATION, Architects, 106–108 Fulton Street, New York.

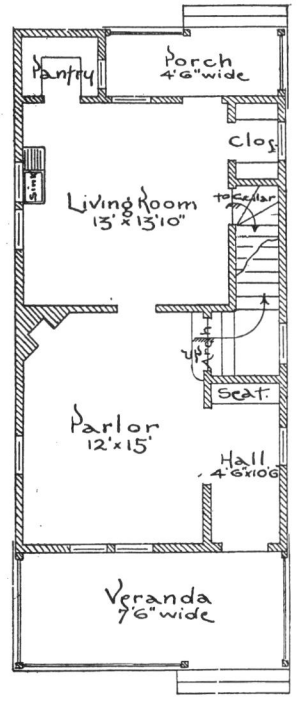

FIRST FLOOR.

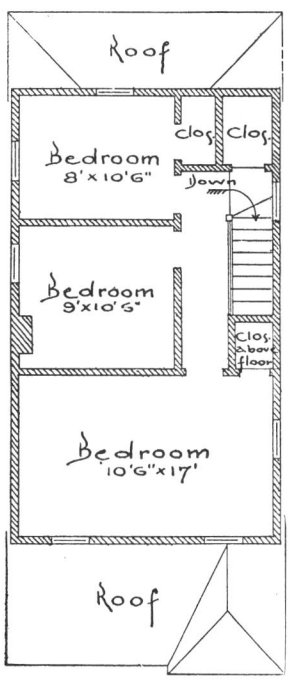

SECOND FLOOR.

Cottage, Design No. 1194

PERSPECTIVE.

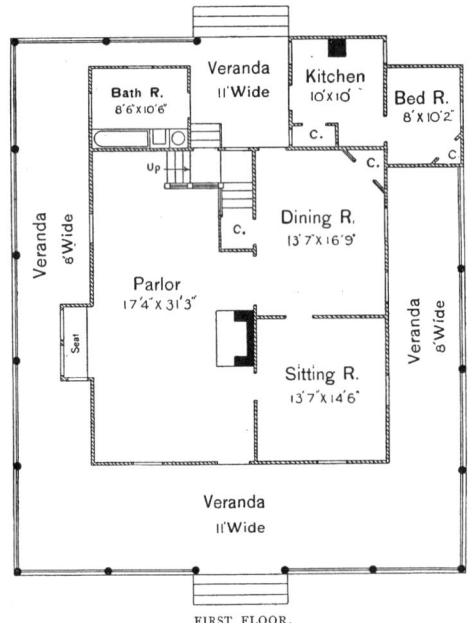

FIRST FLOOR.

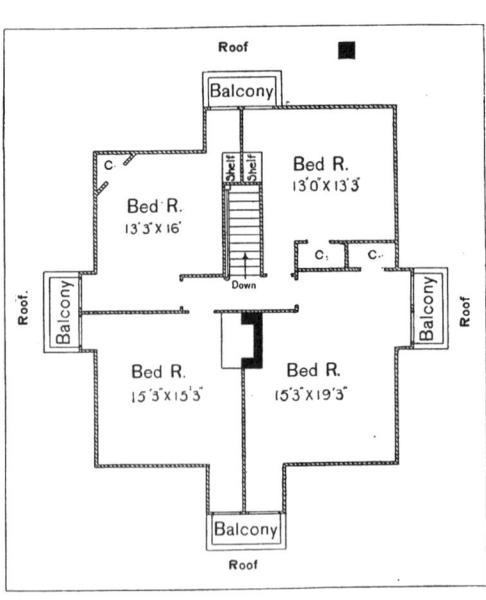

SECOND FLOOR.

DESCRIPTION.

GENERAL DIMENSIONS: Width, including veranda, 47 ft.; depth, including veranda, 53 ft. 4 ins.

HEIGHTS OF STORIES: First story, 10 ft.; second story, 9 ft.

EXTERIOR MATERIALS: Foundation, posts; first story, vertical siding; sides of dormers and all roofs, shingles.

INTERIOR FINISH: Partitions are formed of vertical boards. The second story floor joints are dressed and exposed, and the second story floor is dressed on the under side to form ceiling of first story. The second story ceilings are covered with narrow ceiling boards. All interior wood-work to be finished in hard oil.

COLORS: Body of first story, Colonial yellow. Trim, including water-table, casings, veranda rail, outside doors, etc., ivory white. Veranda floor and ceiling, oiled. All shingles left natural.

ACCOMMODATIONS: The principal rooms and their sizes, closets, etc., are shown by the floor plans. Ample veranda extending entirely around main body of house. Servants' bedroom off kitchen. Stairway accessible from parlor or veranda. Open fireplace in parlor and bedroom over parlor. Four balconies in second story.

COST: $1,480, † not including mantels and range. The estimate is based on ‡ New York prices for materials and labor. In many sections of the country the cost should be less.

Price of working plans (with full details drawn to large scale), specifications, and * license to build, . . . $15.00
Price of †† bill of materials, ... 5.00

FEASIBLE MODIFICATIONS: General dimensions, materials and colors may be changed. Cellar may be introduced under a portion or the whole of house. Bath-room may be omitted. Parlor may be divided into two rooms. Wide openings may be introduced between dining and sitting-rooms, and between parlor and sitting-room.

The price of working plans, specifications, etc., for a modified design, varies according to the alterations required and will be made known upon application to the Architects.

Address, THE CO-OPERATIVE BUILDING PLAN ASSOCIATION, Architects, 106-108 Fulton Street, New York.

Cottage, Design No. 1195

PERSPECTIVE.

DESCRIPTION.

GENERAL DIMENSIONS: Width, 35 ft.; depth, 51 ft.

HEIGHTS OF STORIES: Cellar, 7 ft; first story, 9 ft.; second story, 8 ft.

EXTERIOR MATERIALS: Foundation, brick walls and piers; first story, clapboards; second story, gables and roofs, shingles.

INTERIOR FINISH: Plaster for papering. Soft wood flooring, stairs and trim throughout. Interior wood-work varnished.

COLORS: Clapboards and veranda floor, light olive drab. Trim and rain conductors, dark olive drab. Outside doors and blinds, dark green. Sashes, brick-work and panels between piers, red. Veranda ceiling, oiled. Wall shingles, oiled. Roof shingles left natural.

ACCOMMODATIONS: The principal rooms and their sizes, closets, etc., are shown by the floor plans. Cellar under kitchen. Attic floored but otherwise unfinished. Open fireplaces in dining and sitting-room. Bath-room with tub only, in first story. Bedroom off parlor, suitable for a study, if preferred. Kitchen disconnected from main house by a covered passage.

COST: $1,470, † not including range and heater. The estimate is based on † New York prices for materials and labor. In many sections of the country the cost should be less.

Price of working plans (with full details drawn to large scale), specifications and * license to build, . . $15.00

Price of †† bill of materials, 5.00

FEASIBLE MODIFICATIONS: Heights of stories, sizes of rooms, colors and materials may be changed. Bath-room may be omitted and the space included with adjoining bedroom, or the parlor enlarged by both bedroom and bath-room. Cellar may extend under whole house. Open passage from kitchen may be enclosed to form a serving pantry. Bath room, with full or partial plumbing, may be planned in second story. Two or three small rooms may be planned in attic. Veranda may be extended or reduced.

Address, THE CO-OPERATIVE BUILDING PLAN ASSOCIATION, Architects, 106–108 Fulton Street, New York.

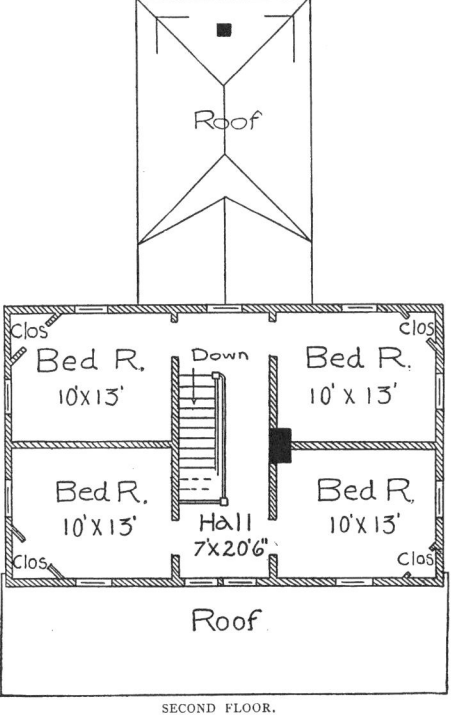

FIRST FLOOR.   SECOND FLOOR.

Cottage, Design No. 1196

PERSPECTIVE.

DESCRIPTION.

GENERAL DIMENSIONS: Width, 22 ft. 6 ins.; depth, 36 ft. 6 ins.

HEIGHTS OF STORIES: Cellar, 6 ft. 6 ins.; first story, 9 ft.; second story, 8 ft. 6 ins.

EXTERIOR MATERIALS: Foundation, brick; first story, clapboards; second story, gables and roofs, shingles.

INTERIOR FINISH: Two coat plaster, hard white finish. Trim, white wood. Flooring, N. C. pine. Main staircase, yellow pine. Kitchen, wainscoted. All interior wood-work grain filled, stained to suit owner and finished in hard oil varnish.

COLORS: Trim, including water-table, corner boards, cornices, casings, bands, veranda columns, newels, rail, etc., cream white. Clapboards, buff. Shingles on side walls dipped in and brush coated with dark sienna stain. Roof shingles dipped in and brush coated with moss green stain. Sashes, dark green. Veranda floor and ceiling, also outside doors and brick-work, oiled.

ACCOMMODATIONS: The principal rooms and their sizes, closets, etc., are shown by the floor plans. Cellar under the whole house, with inside entrance and concrete floor. Space over second story floored for storage purposes, accessible through scuttle. Flue for portable range and sink with cold water supply, in kitchen. Open fireplace in dining-room. Large pantry connecting kitchen and dining-room and hall and kitchen. Wide portière openings connect dining-room, parlor and hall. Panel slide in wall between dining-room and kitchen for passing dishes. No blinds.

COST: $1,495, † not including mantels, range or heater. The estimate is based on ‡ New York prices for materials and labor. In many sections of the country the cost should be less.

Price of working plans (with full details drawn to large scale), specifications and * license to build, . $15.00

Price of †† bill of materials, ... 5.00

FEASIBLE MODIFICATIONS: General dimensions, materials and colors may be changed. Cellar may be reduced in size or wholly omitted. Bath-room, with full plumbing, may be planned in second story. Double sliding doors may be placed between dining-room and parlor. Veranda may be extended around hall side. A dresser may be placed in pantry.

The price of working plans, specifications, etc., for a modified design, varies according to the alterations required and will be made known upon application to the Architects.

Address, THE CO-OPERATIVE BUILDING PLAN ASSOCIATION Architects, 106–108 Fulton Street, New York.

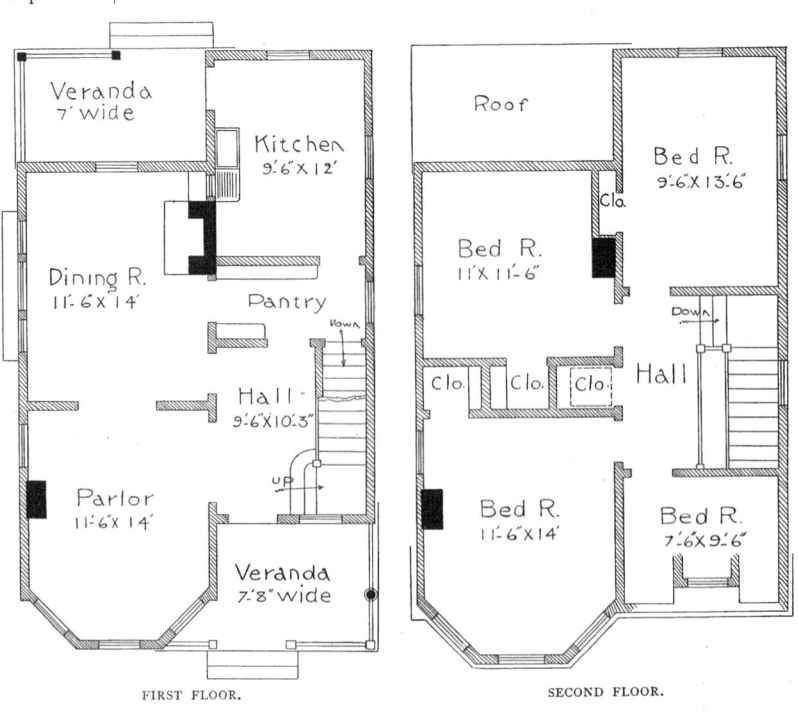

FIRST FLOOR.   SECOND FLOOR.

26

Cottage, Design No. 1197

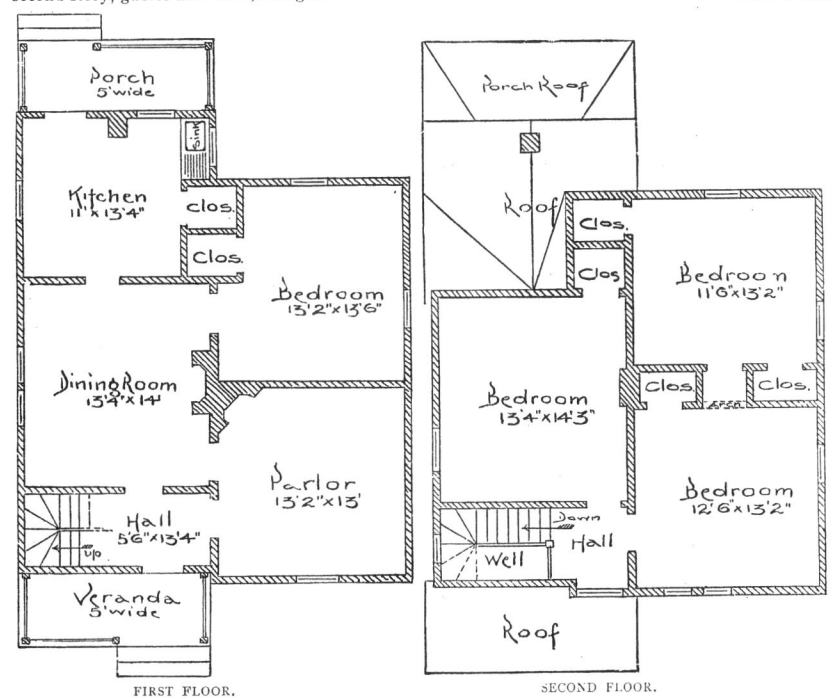

PERSPECTIVE.

DESCRIPTION.

General Dimensions: Width, 28 ft.; depth, not including veranda, 32 ft. 8 ins.

Heights of Stories: First story, 9 ft.; second story, 8 ft.

Exterior Materials: Foundation, wood posts; first story, clapboards; second story, gables and roofs, shingles.

Interior Finish: Two coat plaster, hard white finish. Soft wood flooring, trim and stairs. All interior wood-work to be grain filled and finished with three coats of hard oil varnish.

Colors: Trim, including water table, corner boards, casings, cornices, bands, veranda posts, rail, etc, dark brown. Clapboards, light brown. Sashes, red. Veranda floor and ceiling, oiled. Shingles on side walls dipped in and brush coated with light sienna stain. Roof shingles left natural for weather stain.

Accommodations: The principal rooms and their sizes, closets, etc., are shown by the floor plans. Open fireplace in dining-room and parlor. Sink with cold water supply and flue for portable range or stove, in kitchen. No cellar. Thimbles connecting with chimney for stove-pipe in all bedrooms. Ample porch and veranda room.

Cost: $1,495, † not including mantels, range or heater. The estimate is based on ‡ New York prices for materials and labor. In many sections of the country the cost should be less.

Price of working plans (with full details drawn to large scale), specifications and * license to build, ... $15.00
Price of †† bill of materials, ... 5.00

Feasible Modifications: General dimensions, materials and colors may be changed. Cellar may be placed under the whole house, with inside and outside entrance and concrete floor, at an additional cost of about $175. Veranda may be extended around dining-room side. Bath-room, with full plumbing, may be planned over kitchen, and passage way leading to same may be made by taking off part of the bedroom over dining-room. Boiler and two wash-tubs may be introduced in kitchen.

The price of working plans, specifications, etc., for a modified design, varies according to the alterations required and will be made known upon application to the Architects.

Address, The Co-operative Building Plan Association, Architects, 106–108 Fulton Street, New York.

Cottage, Design No. 1198

PERSPECTIVE.

DESCRIPTION.

GENERAL DIMENSIONS: Width, 20 ft.; depth, 44 ft.

HEIGHTS OF STORIES: Cellar, 6 ft. 6 ins.; first story, 8 ft. 6 ins.; second story, 8 ft.

EXTERIOR MATERIALS: Foundation, stone and brick; first and second stories, porch enclosure, gables and roofs, shingles.

INTERIOR FINISH: Two coat plaster, hard white finish, for ceilings; side walls plastered for papering. Flooring, trim and stairs, soft wood stained in colors to suit owner and finished in hard oil varnish.

COLORS: Cornices, mouldings, window frames, sashes, rails, panels for front door, light brown. Door panels and panels between all windows, dark brown. Wall shingles dipped in and brush coated silver stain. Roof shingles left natural color. Porch floor and steps, dark brown. Porch ceilings, varnished.

ACCOMMODATIONS: The principal rooms and their sizes, closets, etc., are shown by the floor plans. Cellar under the dining-room. Storage space over second story and over kitchen. The size and shape of this design makes it suitable for a 25 ft. lot.

COST: $1,497, † not including mantels, range or heater. The estimate is based on ‡ New York prices for materials and labor. In many sections of the country the cost should be less.

Price of working plans (with full details drawn to large scale), specifications and * license to build, . . $15.00
Price of †† bill of materials, ... 5.00

FEASIBLE MODIFICATIONS: General dimensions, materials and colors may be changed. Cellar may be extended under the whole house or may be omitted entirely. Clapboards with mitered corners may be used instead of shingles. Porch may be carried across the front. Kitchen extension may be two stories high. Roof could be raised somewhat and this would make the space available for one or two rooms. If heater is used, one chimney will suffice.

The price of working plans, specifications, etc., for a modified design, varies according to the alterations required and will be made known upon application to the Architects.

Address, THE CO-OPERATIVE BUILDING PLAN ASSOCIATION, Architects, 106–108 Fulton Street, New York.

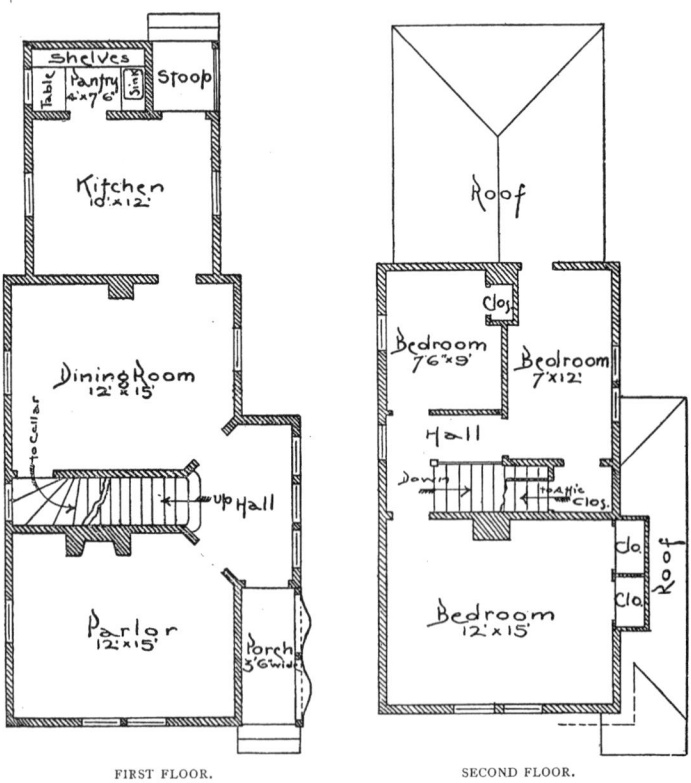

FIRST FLOOR.   SECOND FLOOR.

Cottage, Design No. 1199

PERSPECTIVE.

DESCRIPTION.

GENERAL DIMENSIONS: Width, 25 ft. 2 ins.; depth, including veranda and pantry, 35 ft. 6 ins.

HEIGHTS OF STORIES: Cellar, 6 ft. 6 ins.; first story, 8 ft. 8 ins.; second story, 8 ft.

EXTERIOR MATERIALS: Foundation, wood posts; first story and sides and rear of second story, clapboards; staircase annex, second story front and roof, shingles; gables, panels.

INTERIOR FINISH: Two coat plaster, hard white finish. Soft wood flooring and trim. Yellow pine stairs. Kitchen, wainscoted. Interior wood-work grain filled, stained to suit owner and finished in hard oil varnish.

COLORS: Trim, including water-table, corner boards, casings, cornices, etc., light brown. Clapboards, outside doors, sashes, porch floor and ceiling, brown. Outside blinds, rain conductors, light brown. Brick-work, red. Wall shingles dipped in and brush coated with umbre stain. Gable panels, light brown with light drab framing. Roof shingles dipped in and brush coated, slate color.

ACCOMMODATIONS: The principal rooms and their sizes, closets, etc., are shown by the floor plans. Attic floored but unfinished. Open fireplace in hall, parlor and dining-room. Plank cellar under dining-room with outside entrance. Pantry connection between dining-room and kitchen. Sink in pantry. Central chimney accessible in five rooms and hall. Wide portiére opening connects hall and parlor.

COST: $1,498,† not including mantels, range or heater. The estimate is based on ‡ New York prices for materials and labor. In many sections of the country the cost should be less.

Price of working plans (with full details drawn to large scale), specifications and * license to build, ... $15.00

Price of †† bill of materials, ... 5.00

FEASIBLE MODIFICATIONS: General dimensions, materials and colors may be changed. Cellar may be placed under whole or part of house with inside and outside entrance and concrete floor. Bath-room with part or all of plumbing may be introduced in second story, or water-closet may be planned in second story and bath-room, with tub only, in attic thus avoiding the sacrifice of one bedroom in second story. Vestibule on front porch may be omitted. Porch may be extended or reduced. Kitchen may be sitting-room with a door leading to the parlor and a new kitchen planned at the rear of pantry. One or two bedrooms may be finished off in attic, still leaving ample storage room.

The price of working plans, specifications, etc., for a modified design, varies according to the alterations required and will be made known upon application to the Architects.

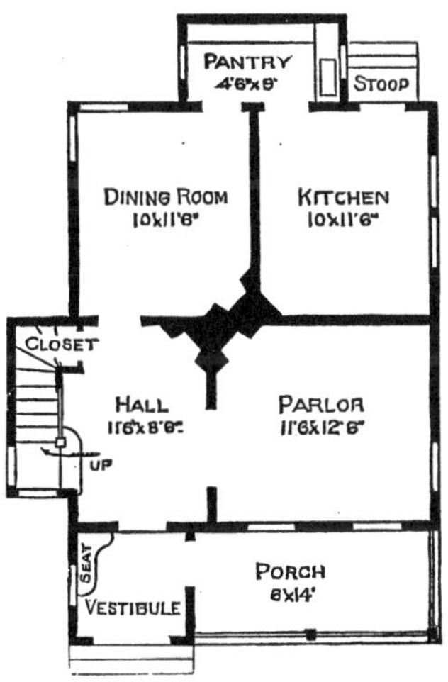

FIRST FLOOR.

SECOND FLOOR.

Residence, Design No. 1200

PERSPECTIVE

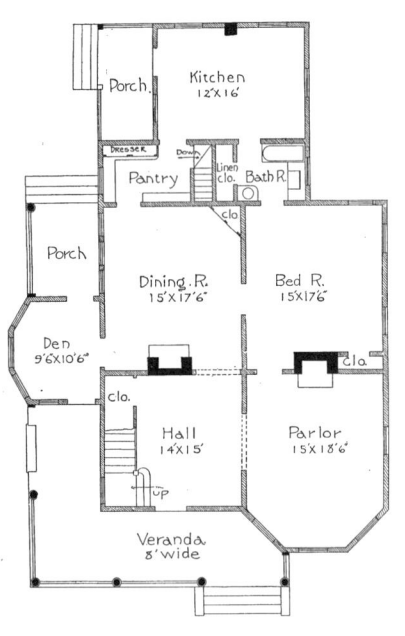

FIRST FLOOR.

DESCRIPTION.

GENERAL DIMENSIONS: Width, 41 ft. 6 ins.; depth, not including veranda, 56 ft. 6 ins.

HEIGHTS OF STORIES: Cellar, 7 ft.; first story, 10 ft.; second story, 8 ft. 6 ins.

EXTERIOR MATERIALS: Foundation, stone; first story, clapboards; second story, gables, roofs and bay-window walls of den, shingles.

INTERIOR FINISH: Two coat plaster, sand finish. Flooring and trim throughout, N. C. pine. Staircase, yellow pine. Kitchen and bath-room, wainscoted. All interior wood-work grain filled and finished natural with hard oil varnish.

COLORS: Trim, including water-table, corner-boards, casings, veranda columns, etc., dark bottle green. Clapboards, white. Shingles on side walls and roof left natural for weather stain. Sashes, dark red. Veranda floor, dark gray. Veranda ceiling and outside doors, varnished.

ACCOMMODATIONS: The principal rooms and their sizes, closets, etc., are shown by the floor plans. Cellar under dining-room and bedroom, with inside and outside entrances and concrete floor. Portable range, sink and boiler in kitchen. Bath-room, with full plumbing, accessible from kitchen and bedroom. Large butler's pantry containing shelving and dresser, connects dining-room and kitchen. China closet in dining-room. Large linen closet in bath-room. Open fireplace in dining-room and parlor. Horse block at side veranda. Wide portière openings connect hall and parlor and dining-room and hall. Two rooms as shown on floor plan finished off in second story attic; remainder of space floored for storage purposes.

COST: $2,500, † not including mantels, plumbing, range or heater. The estimate is based on ‡ New York prices for materials and labor. In many sections of the country the cost should be less.

Price of working plans (with full details drawn to large scale), specifications and * license to build, ... $25.00

Price of †† bill of materials, ... 10.00

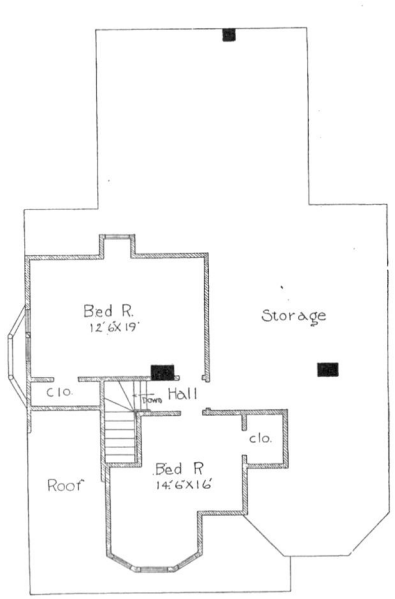

SECOND FLOOR.

FEASIBLE MODIFICATIONS: General dimensions, materials and colors may be changed. Cellar may be extended under the whole house or wholly omitted and house set upon brick or stone piers. Any or all fireplaces and part or all of plumbing may be omitted. Steps may be substituted for horse block at side veranda. One or two additional bedrooms may be finished off in second story, still leaving ample room for storage space.

The price of working plans, specifications, etc., for a modified design, varies according to the alterations required and will be made known upon application to the Architects.

Address, THE CO-OPERATIVE BUILDING PLAN ASSOCIATION, Architects, 106-108 Fulton Street, New York.

Cottage, Design No. 1209

PERSPECTIVE.

DESCRIPTION.

GENERAL DIMENSIONS: Width, 20 ft. 6 ins.; depth, not including porch and vestibule, 44 feet.

HEIGHTS OF STORIES: Cellar, 7 ft.; first story, 9 ft.; second story, 8 ft.

EXTERIOR MATERIALS: Foundation and first story, local rubble stone; gables and roof, shingles; porch roof, tin.

INTERIOR FINISH: Two coat plaster, sand finish. Trim, white wood. Staircase, ash. Flooring, N. C. pine. Chair-rail in dining-room. Kitchen, wainscoted. All interior wood-work grain filled, stained to suit owner, and finished in hard oil varnish.

COLORS, if blue or gray stone is used: Trim, including cornices, casings, leaders, etc., white. Shingles on side walls stained silver gray. Roof shingles stained moss green. Sashes, dark bottle green. Porch floor, light gray. Porch ceiling and outside doors finished in hard oil varnish.

ACCOMMODATIONS: The principal rooms and their sizes, closets, etc., are shown by the floor plans. Cellar under dining-room, bedroom and kitchen, with inside entrance, and concrete floor. Sink, with cold water supply and flue for portable range or stove, in kitchen. Closet for china in dining-room. Hat and coat closet under main stairs. Wide portiére opening connects dining-room and living room. Storage space over kitchen, accessible from second story rear bedroom.

COST: $1,640, † not including mantels, range or heater. The estimate is based on ‡ New York prices for materials and labor. In many sections of the country the cost should be less.

Price of working plans (with full details drawn to large scale), specifications and * license to build, ... $15.00

Price of †† bill of materials, ... 5.00

FEASIBLE MODIFICATIONS: General dimensions, materials and colors may be changed. Cellar may be placed under whole house. Kitchen extension may be omitted and first story bedroom made into a kitchen. Open fireplaces may be introduced in living-room and dining-room. Brick-set range, boiler for hot water supply and bath-room, with full plumbing, may be introduced. Three stationary wash-tubs may be placed in cellar. Double sliding doors may be made to connect bedroom and dining-room.

The price of working plans, specifications, etc., for a modified design, varies according to the alterations required and will be made known upon application to the Architects.

Address, THE CO-OPERATIVE BUILDING PLAN ASSOCIATION, Architects, 106–108 Fulton Street, New York.

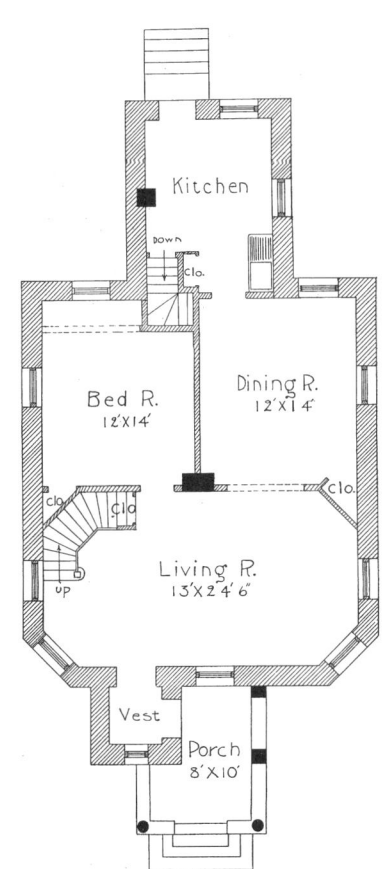

FIRST FLOOR.

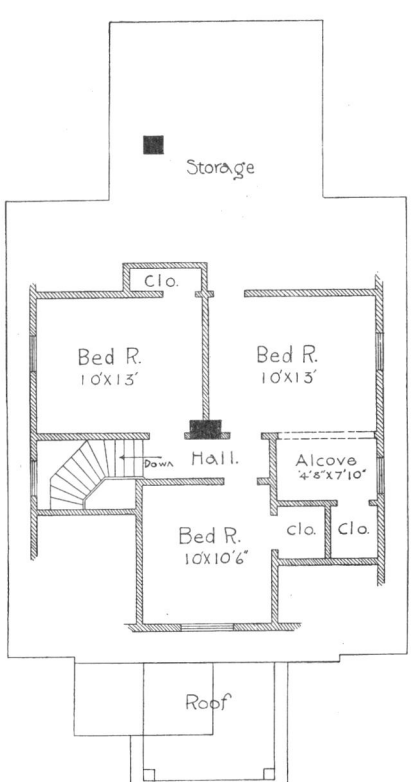

SECOND FLOOR.

Cottage, Design No. 1210

PERSPECTIVE.

DESCRIPTION.

GENERAL DIMENSIONS: Width, not including stoop, 27 ft 6 ins.; depth, not including rear stoop, 38 ft. 6 ins.

HEIGHTS OF STORIES: Cellar, 6 ft. 6 ins.; first story, 9 ft.; second story, 8 ft.

EXTERIOR MATERIALS: Foundation, stone; first story, gables and roof, shingles.

INTERIOR FINISH: Two coat plaster, hard white finish. Staircase, ash. Trim in parlor, white wood; elsewhere, N. C. pine. Flooring throughout, N. C. pine. Kitchen and bath-room, wainscoted. Trim in parlor grain filled, stained mahogany and finished in hard oil varnish; elsewhere grain filled and finished in hard oil varnish.

COLORS: Trim, including cornices, casings, columns, etc., dark green. Shingles on side walls dipped in and brush coated with dark sienna stain. Roof shingles dipped in and brush coated with red stain. Sashes, dark bottle green. Porch floor, dark yellow. Porch ceiling and outside doors, grain filled and finished natural in hard oil varnish.

ACCOMMODATIONS: The principal rooms and their sizes, closets, etc., are shown by the floor plans. Cellar under the whole house, with inside and outside entrances and concrete floor. Open fireplace in parlor. Flue for portable range, also sink and boiler, in kitchen. Bath-room between kitchen and bedroom, containing tub. Double sliding doors connect dining-room and parlor. Dish-pass in kitchen closet, connecting with dining-room. Large linen closet in second story hall.

COST: $1,700, † not including mantels, plumbing, range or heater. The estimate is based on ‡ New York prices for materials and labor. In many sections of the country the cost should be less.

Price of working plans (with full details drawn to large scale), specifications and * license to build, ... $20.00

Price of †† bill of materials, . . 10.00

FEASIBLE MODIFICATIONS: General dimensions, materials and colors may be changed. Porch may be extended across front of house. Three stationary tubs may be placed in laundry in cellar. Three feet may be taken off dining-room and form an addition to stairs to give a good sized hall. Full plumbing may be introduced in bath-room.

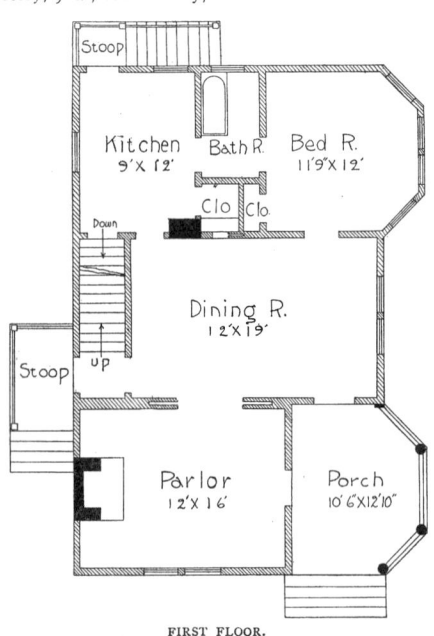

FIRST FLOOR.

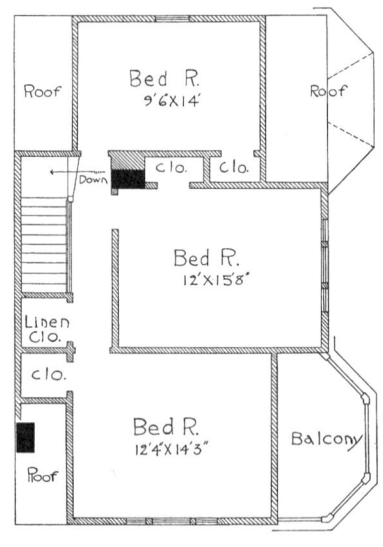

SECOND FLOOR.

The price of working plans, specifications, etc., for a modified design, varies according to the alterations required and will be made known upon application to the Architects.

Address, THE CO-OPERATIVE BUILDING PLAN ASSOCIATION, Architects, 106–108 Fulton Street, New York.

Cottage, Design No. 1211

PERSPECTIVE.

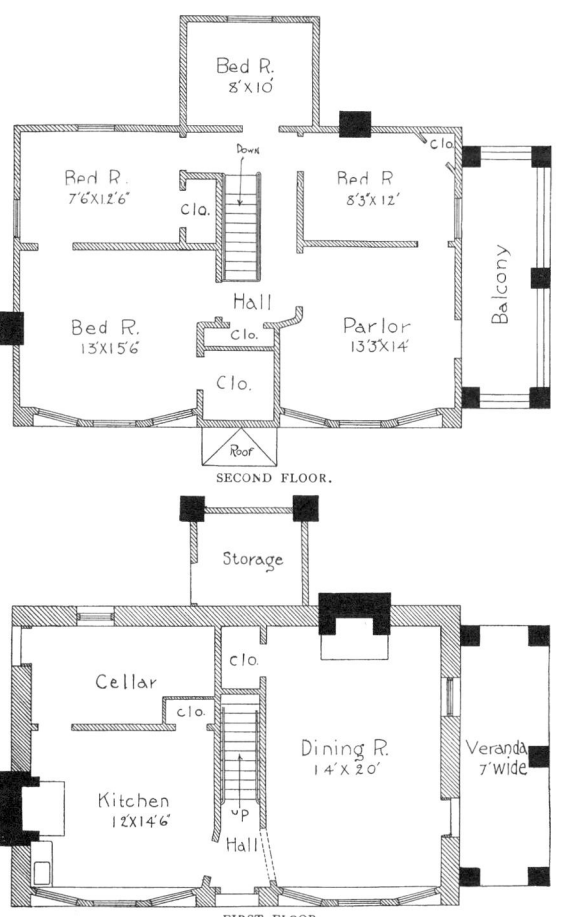

SECOND FLOOR.

FIRST FLOOR.

DESCRIPTION.

GENERAL DIMENSIONS: Width, including veranda, 42 ft. 6 ins.; depth, 31 ft. 6 ins.

HEIGHTS OF STORIES: First story, 9 ft.; second story, 9 ft.

EXTERIOR MATERIALS: Foundation and first story, rubble stone; second story bays and hood roof, shingles; flat tin roof.

INTERIOR FINISH: Two coat plaster, hard white finish. First story floor, double with paper between. Flooring and trim, soft wood. Kitchen, wainscoted. Chair-rail in dining-room. All interior wood-work grain filled, stained antique oak in hall, elsewhere to suit owner and all finished in hard oil varnish, rubbed to a dull gloss.

COLORS: Trim, including cornices, casings, rail, etc., dark green. Shingles on side walls left natural for weather stain. Roof shingles dipped and brush coated dark red. Sashes, white. Veranda floor and ceiling and outside doors, oiled.

ACCOMMODATIONS: The principal rooms and their sizes, closets, etc., are shown by the floor plans. Cellar back of kitchen with inside and outside entrance and concrete floor. Hall door of first story, glazed. Open fireplace in dining-room. Brick-set range, sink and boiler in kitchen. Portiére opening connects hall and parlor. Large-sized veranda with balcony above. Closet for china in dining-room.

COST: $1,765, † not including mantels, range or heater. The estimate is based on ‡ New York prices for materials and labor. In many sections of the country the cost should be less.

Price of working plans (with full details drawn to large scale), specifications and * license to build, ... $20.00

Price of †† bill of materials, ... 10.00

FEASIBLE MODIFICATIONS: General dimensions, materials and colors may be changed. The porch may be extended across front to form veranda. Portiére opening may be omitted. Bath-room, with full plumbing, may be introduced in second story and two wash-tubs placed in kitchen.

The price of working plans, specifications, etc., for a modified design, varies according to the alterations required and will be made known upon application to the Architects.

Address, THE CO-OPERATIVE BUILDING PLAN ASSOCIATION, Architects, 106–108 Fulton Street, New York.

Cottage, Design No. 1212

PERSPECTIVE.

DESCRIPTION.

GENERAL DIMENSIONS: Width through pantry, kitchen and living-room, 38 ft.; depth, through bedroom and kitchen, 23 ft.

HEIGHTS OF STORIES: First story, 9 ft.; second story, 8 ft. 6 ins.

EXTERIOR MATERIALS: Foundation, veranda enclosure and columns, stone; first story, clapboards; gables and roofs, shingles.

INTERIOR FINISH: Two coat plaster, hard white finish. Soft wood flooring and trim. Staircase, ash. All interior wood-work grain filled, stained to suit owner and finished in hard oil varnish.

COLORS: Trim, including cornices, casings, bands, corner boards, etc., white. Clapboards, gray. Shingles and gables, oiled. Roof shingles stained dark brown. Sashes, dark green. Veranda floor, Colonial yellow. Outside doors and veranda ceiling, finished in hard oil varnish.

ACCOMMODATIONS: Open fireplace of field stone in living-room. Ice-box off porch. Sink, with cold water supply, in kitchen. Large-sized kitchen pantry. No cellar. Covered and open veranda. Covered balcony or lookout over veranda, accessible from front bedroom. This design is suitable for a seaside or summer cottage.

COST: $1,800, † not including mantels, range or heater. The estimate is based on ‡ New York prices for materials and labor. In many sections of the country the cost should be less.

Price of working plans (with full details drawn to large scale), specifications and * license to build, ... $20.00

Price of †† bill of materials, ... 10.00

FEASIBLE MODIFICATIONS: General dimensions, materials and colors may be changed. Cellar may be introduced under whole or portion of house, with inside and outside entrance and concrete floor. Bath-room, with full or partial plumbing, may be introduced in second story. Tin-covered portion of veranda may be omitted without detracting from the general appearance of the design.

The price of working plans, specifications, etc., for a modified design, varies according to the alterations required and will be made known upon application to the Architects.

Address, THE CO-OPERATIVE BUILDING PLAN ASSOCIATION, Architects, 106-108 Fulton Street, New York.

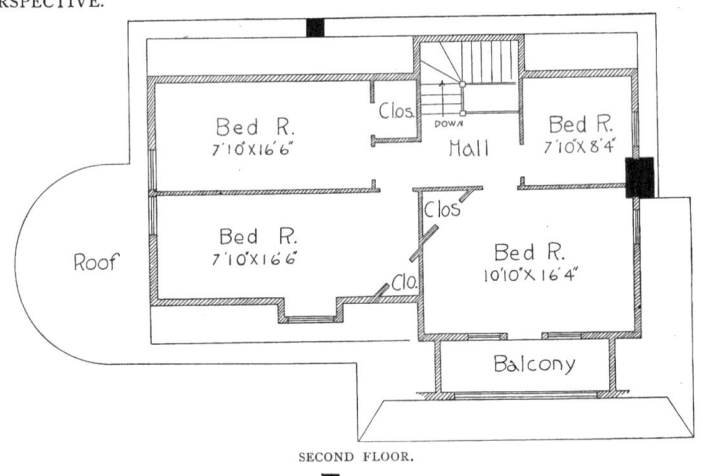

SECOND FLOOR.

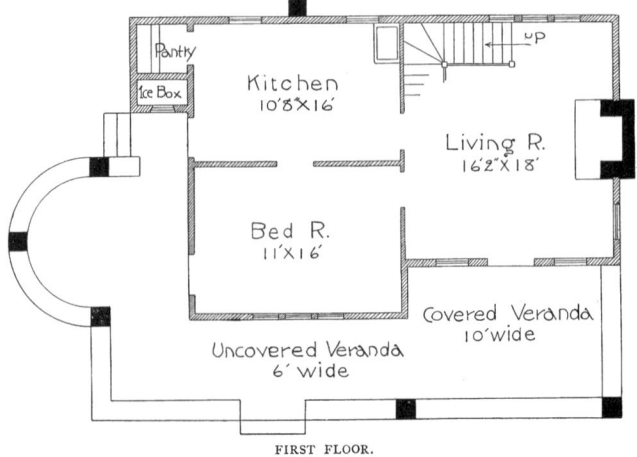

FIRST FLOOR.

Residence, Design No. 1213.

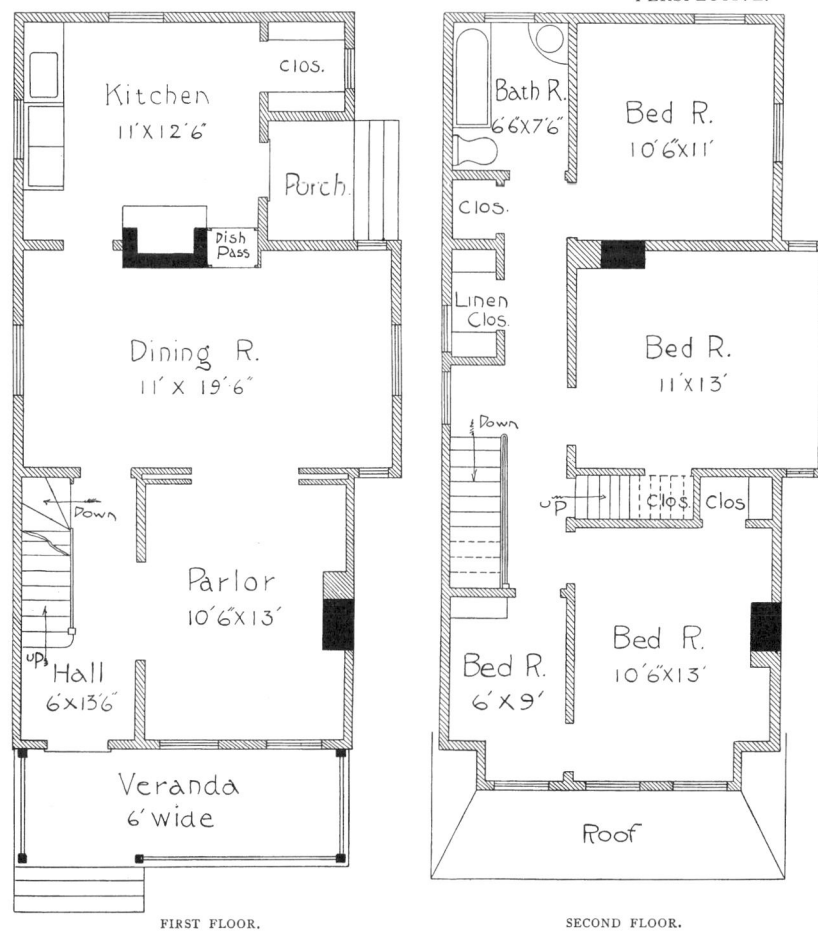

PERSPECTIVE.

FIRST FLOOR.

SECOND FLOOR.

DESCRIPTION.

GENERAL DIMENSIONS: Width, 20 ft. 6 ins.; depth, not including veranda, 37 ft. 6 ins.

HEIGHTS OF STORIES: Cellar, 6 ft. 6 ins.; first story, 9 ft.; second story, 8 ft.

EXTERIOR MATERIALS: Foundation, brick; first story, clapboards; second story, gables and roof, shingles.

INTERIOR FINISH: Two coat plaster, hard white finish. White wood trim. Flooring throughout, N. C. pine. Main staircase, ash. Kitchen and bath-room, wainscoted. Chair-rail in dining-room. All interior wood-work grain filled, stained to suit owner and finished in hard oil varnish.

COLORS: Trim, including water-table, corner boards, cornices, casings, veranda posts, rail, etc., white. Clapboards, cream. Shingles on side walls, stained light sienna. Roof shingles left natural for weather stain. Sashes, dark green. Veranda floor, light brown. Veranda ceiling and outside doors grain filled and finished in hard oil varnish.

ACCOMMODATIONS: The principal rooms and their sizes, closets, etc., are shown by the floor plans. Cellar under the whole house, with inside and outside entrances and concrete floor. Wide portière opening connects parlor and hall, and double sliding doors connect dining-room and parlor. Brick-set range, sink, boiler and wash-tubs in kitchen. Dish-pass, with drawers underneath and shelves above, between kitchen and dining-room. Large-sized kitchen pantry. Chimney breast for mantel in parlor. Bath-room, with full plumbing, in second story. Attic unfinished, but floored for storage purposes. Large linen closet, as well as closet for rear bedroom, in second story hall.

COST: $1,825,† not including mantels, range or heater. The estimate is based on ‡ New York prices for materials and labor. In many sections of the country the cost should be less.

Price of working plans (with full details drawn to large scale), specifications and * license to build, . . . $20.00

Price of †† bill of materials, ... 10.00

FEASIBLE MODIFICATIONS: General dimensions, materials and colors may be changed. Cellar may be reduced in size or wholly omitted. Open fireplace may be introduced in parlor and bedroom over same. Veranda may be extended on one or both sides. One or two bedrooms may be finished off in attic. Double sliding doors may be placed between parlor and hall. Position of pantry and porch may be transposed.

The price of working plans, specifications, etc., for a modified design, varies according to the alterations required and will be made known upon application to the Architects. Address, THE CO-OPERATIVE BUILDING PLAN ASSOCIATION, Architects, 106–108 Fulton Street, New York.

Cottage, Design No. 1214

PERSPECTIVE.

DESCRIPTION.

GENERAL DIMENSIONS: Width, 28 ft. 6 ins.; depth, including veranda, 50 ft. 10 ins.

HEIGHTS OF STORIES: First story, 9 ft.; second story, 8 ft.

EXTERIOR MATERIALS: Foundation, brick piers; first story, clapboards; second story and roof, shingles.

INTERIOR FINISH: Two coat plaster, hard white finish. Floor, trim and stairs, soft white wood. All wood-work finished in hard oil.

COLORS: Clapboards, lattice-work on front gable, sashes and veranda floor, light brown. Siding below window-sills in first story, all trim and doors, dark brown. Brick-work, dark red. Wall shingles dipped in and brush coated with buff stain. Roof shingles left natural.

ACCOMMODATIONS: The principal rooms and their sizes, closets, etc., are shown by the floor plans. No cellar. Bath-room over kitchen. Alcove off library, with neat arch. Pantry, with a tier of wide shelves, connects kitchen and dining-room; also, there is a large pantry in kitchen.

COST: $1,888, † not including mantels in parlor and library. The estimate is based on ‡ New York prices for materials and labor. In many sections of the country the cost should be less.

Price of working plans (with full details drawn to large scale), specifications and * license to build, $20.00

Price of †† bill of materials, . . . 5 00

FEASIBLE MODIFICATIONS: General dimensions, materials and colors may be changed. Cellar may be placed under whole or part of house. Veranda may be reduced in size. A portion or all of plumbing may be omitted. If heating apparatus is used, one chimney will suffice.

The price of working plans, specifications, etc., for a modified design, varies according to the alterations required and will be made known upon application to the Architects.

Address, THE CO-OPERATIVE BUILDING PLAN ASSOCIATION, Architects, 106-108 Fulton Street, New York.

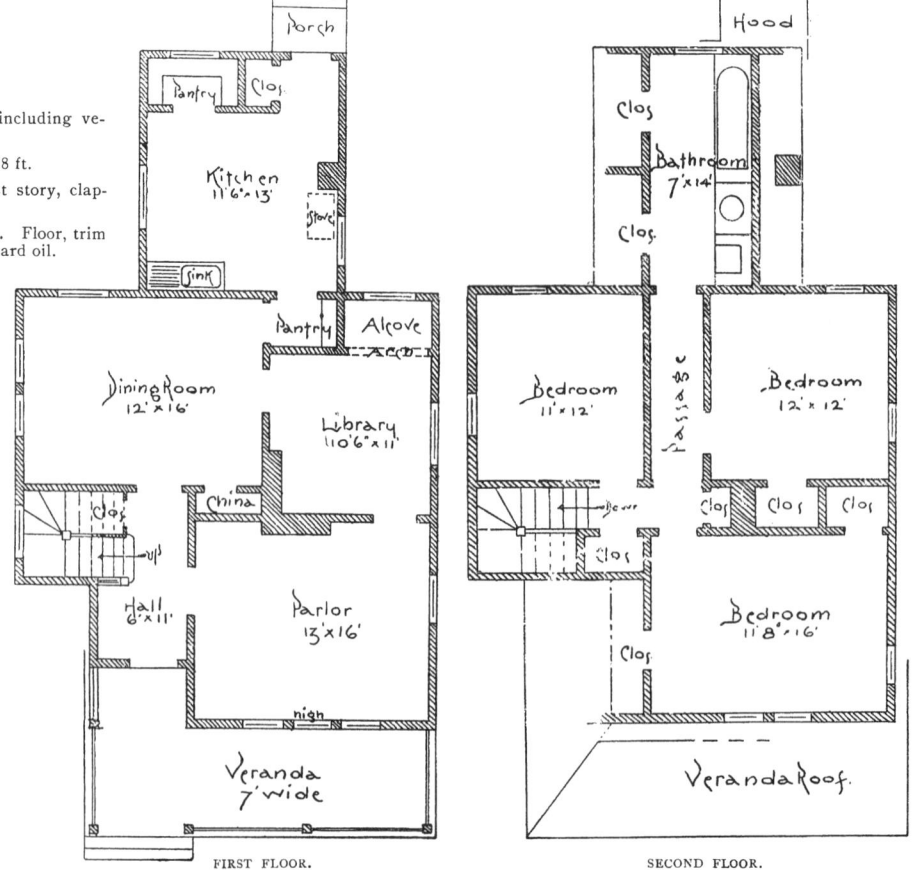

FIRST FLOOR.   SECOND FLOOR.

Cottage, Design No. 1215

PERSPECTIVE.

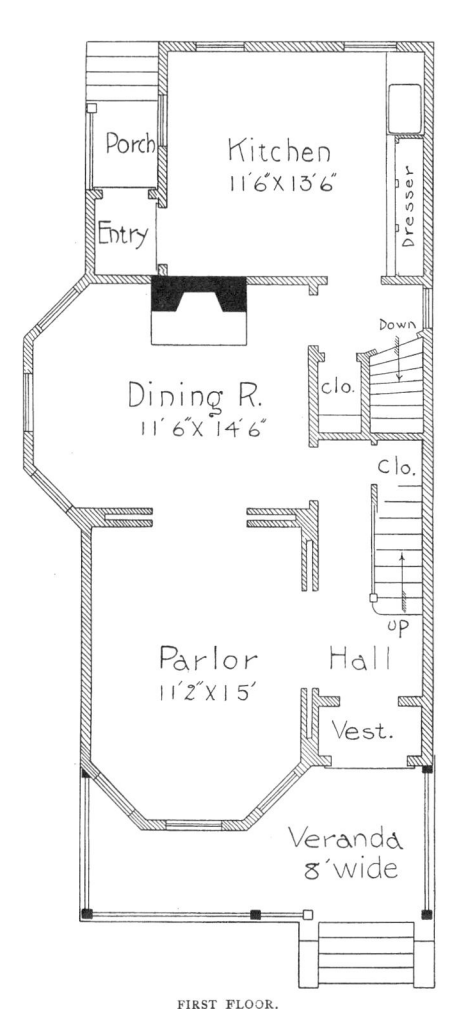

DESCRIPTION.

GENERAL DIMENSIONS: Extreme width, 21 ft. 6 ins.; depth, including piazza, 45 ft.

HEIGHTS OF STORIES: Cellar, 7 ft.; first story, 9 ft. 6 ins.; second story, 8 ft. 10 ins.

EXTERIOR MATERIALS: Foundation, brick; first and second stories, clapboards; second story clapboards mitered; gables, roofs and band between first and second story windows, shingles.

INTERIOR FINISH: Two coat plaster, hard white finish. White wood trim. Flooring N. C. pine. Main staircase, ash. Kitchen and bath-room, wainscoted. Chair-rail in dining-room. All interior wood-work grain filled, stained to suit owner and finished in hard oil varnish.

COLORS: Clapboards in first story, fawn brown. Clapboards on second story, cream. Trim, including water-table, corner boards, casings, cornices, bands, veranda posts, rail, etc., white. All shingles left natural for weather stain. Sashes, dark green. Outside blinds, maroon.

ACCOMMODATIONS: The principal rooms and their sizes, closets, etc, are shown by the floor plans. Cellar under the whole house, with inside and outside entrances and concrete floor. Double sliding doors connect dining-room, parlor and hall. Open fireplaces in dining-room. Thimble connecting flue for portable range in kitchen. Bath-room, with full plumbing, in second story. Sink and dresser in kitchen. Double front entrance doors and large single vestibule door. Two rooms and hall finished off in attic.

COST: $1,930, † not including mantels, range or heater. The estimate is based on ‡ New York prices for materials and labor. In many sections of the country the cost should be less.

Price of working plans (with full details drawn to large scale), specifications and * license to build, . . $20.00

Price of †† bill of materials, ... 10.00

FEASIBLE MODIFICATIONS: General dimensions, materials and colors may be changed. Cellar may be reduced in size or wholly omitted. Open fireplace may be introduced in parlor and bedroom over same. Veranda may be extended on one or both sides. Kitchen extension may be carried up another story which would give an additional bedroom. Sliding doors may be omitted, and openings used for portières. Attic may be left unfinished but floored for storage purposes.

The price of working plans, specifications, etc., for a modified design, varies according to the alterations required and will be made known upon application to the Architects.

Address THE CO-OPERATIVE BUILDING PLAN ASSOCIATION, Architects, 106-108 Fulton Street, New York.

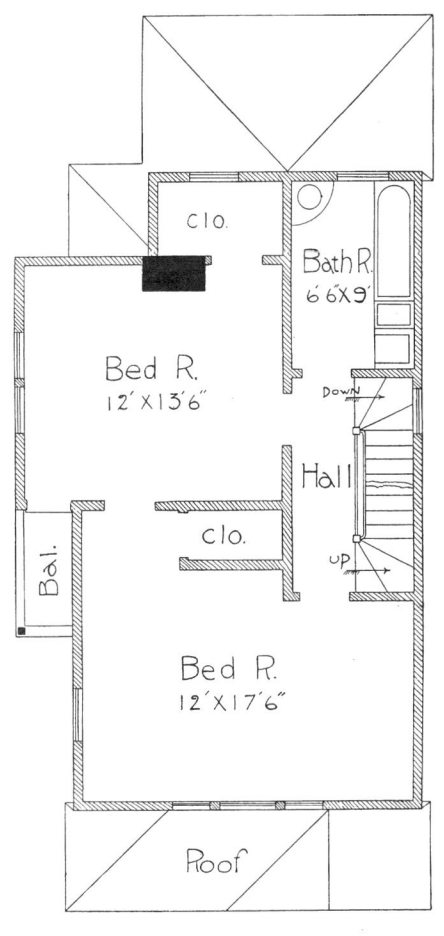

FIRST FLOOR.

SECOND FLOOR.

Cottage, Design No. 1216

PERSPECTIVE.

DESCRIPTION.

GENERAL DIMENSIONS: Width, not including veranda, 26 ft.; depth, 39 ft. 6 ins.

HEIGHTS OF STORIES: Cellar, 7 ft.; first story, 9 ft.; second story, 8 ft.

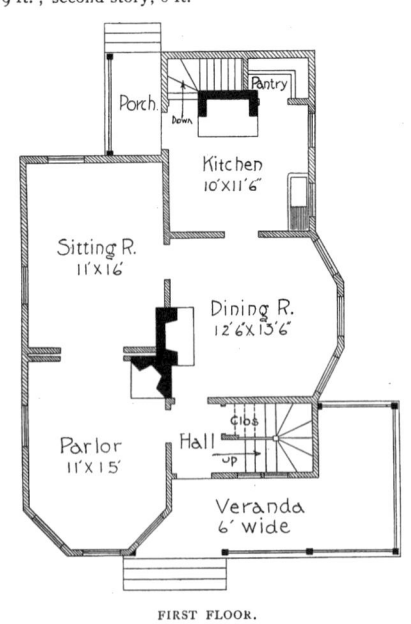

EXTERIOR MATERIALS: Foundation, stone; first story, clapboards; second story, gables and roofs, shingles.

INTERIOR FINISH: Two coat plaster, hard white finish. Flooring and trim, N. C. pine. Chair-rail in dining-room. Kitchen wainscoted. All interior wood-work grain filled and finished in hard oil varnish.

COLORS: Trim, including water-table, cornices, casings, bands, veranda posts, rail, etc., dark green. Clapboards, terra-cotta. Shingles on side walls, red. Roof shingles, oiled. Veranda floor, dark gray. Veranda ceiling and outside doors, varnished. Sashes, white.

ACCOMMODATIONS: The principal rooms and their sizes, closets, etc., are shown by the floor plans. Cellar under kitchen, dining-room and hall, with inside entrances and concrete floor. Brick-set range, sink and boiler in kitchen. Double sliding doors between parlor and sitting-room. Hat and coat closet under main stairs. Open fireplaces in parlor and dining-room. Space over second story, floored over for storage purposes and accessible through scuttle. Linen closet in second story hall.

COST: $1,950, † not including mantels, range or heater. The estimate is based on ‡ New York prices for materials and labor. In many sections of the country the cost should be less.

Price of working plans (with full details drawn to large scale), specifications and * license to build, ... $20.00

Price of †† bill of materials, . . . 10.00

FEASIBLE MODIFICATIONS: General dimensions, materials and colors may be changed. Cellar may be extended under the whole house or wholly omitted and house set upon brick or stone piers, or wood posts. Bath-room, with full plumbing, may be placed in second story in space marked storage, with door leading from hall. Two stationary wash-tubs may be placed in cellar under kitchen. Any or all fireplaces and part or all of plumbing may be omitted.

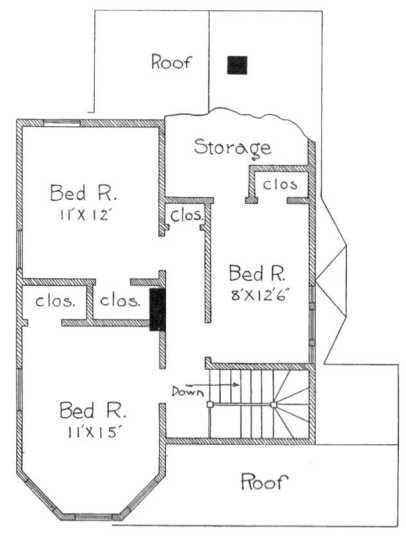

Price of working plans, specifications, etc., for a modified design, varies according to the alterations required and will be made known upon application to the Architects.

Address, THE CO-OPERATIVE BUILDING PLAN ASSOCIATION, Architects, 106–108 Fulton Street, New York.

FIRST FLOOR.

SECOND FLOOR.

Residence, Design No. 1217

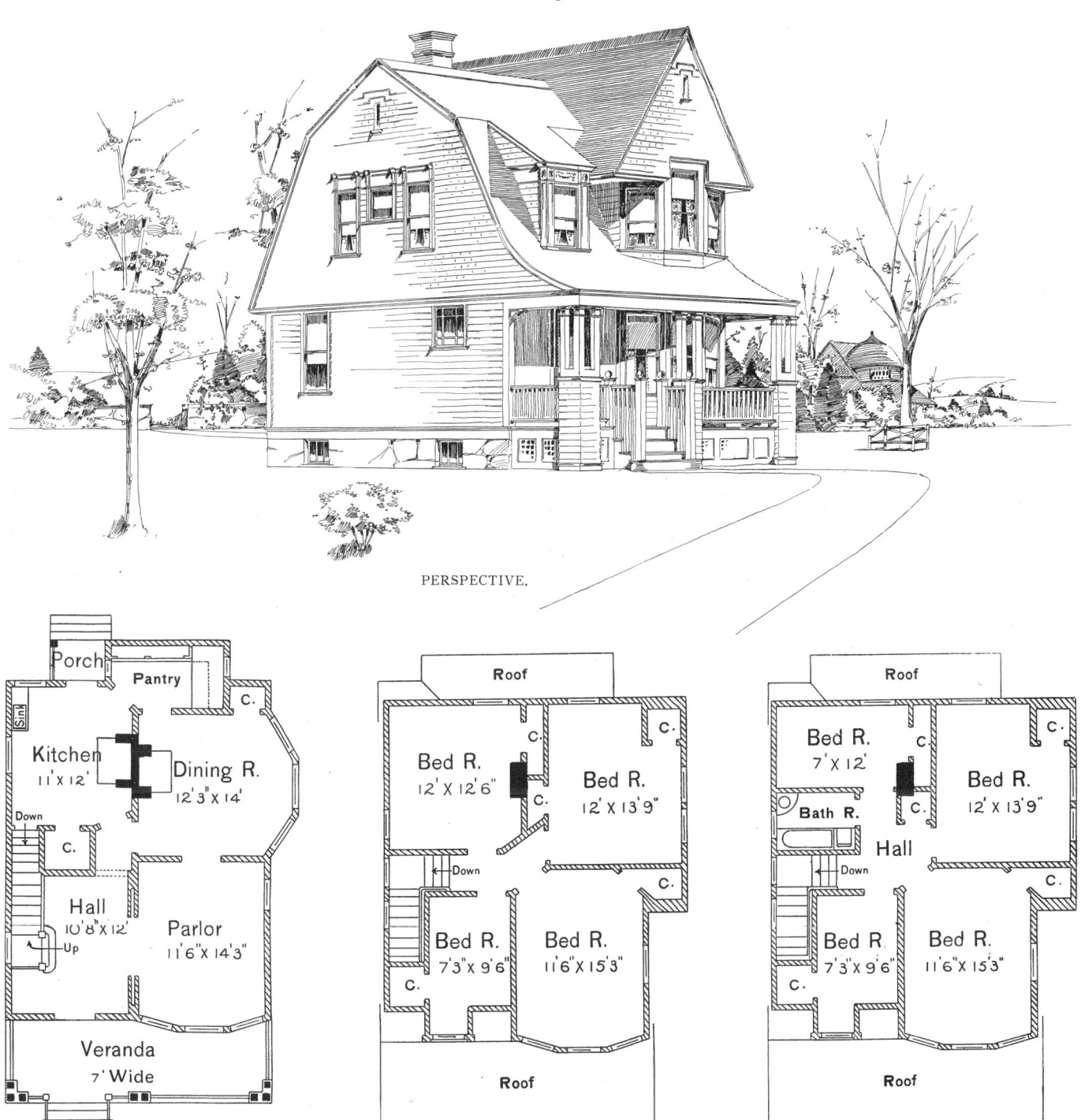

PERSPECTIVE.

FIRST FLOOR.   SECOND FLOOR.   SECOND FLOOR, PLAN "A".

DESCRIPTION.

GENERAL DIMENSIONS: Width, through dining-room and kitchen, 26 ft. 6 ins.; depth, including veranda, 40 ft.

HEIGHTS OF STORIES: Cellar, 6 ft. 6 ins.; first story, 9 ft.; second story, 8 ft. 6 ins.

EXTERIOR MATERIALS: Foundation, stone; first story, clapboards; second story, gables, roofs and piers of veranda, shingles.

INTERIOR FINISH: Two coat plaster, hard white finish. Soft wood flooring and trim. Ash stairs. Interior trim finished with hard oil.

COLORS: Clapboards, Colonial yellow. Trim, white Outside doors finished natural with hard oil. Blinds, Colonial yellow. Sashes, white. Shingles on side walls, gables and roofs left unfinished for weather stain.

ACCOMMODATIONS: The principal rooms and their sizes, closets, etc., are shown by the floor plans. Cellar under the whole house, with inside and outside entrances. Attic floored for storage and accessible through a scuttle in second story hall. Fireplace in dining-room. Double sliding doors between hall and parlor. Wide veranda extends across the entire front of the house. Brick-set range in kitchen. Numerous and large closets.

COST: $2,000, † not including mantels, range and heater. The estimate is based on ‡ New York prices for materials and labor. In many sections of the country the cost should be less.

Price of working plans (with full details drawn to large scale), specifications and * license to build, ... $20.00
Price of †† bill of materials, ... 10.00

FEASIBLE MODIFICATIONS: General dimensions, materials and colors may be changed. A bath room could be introduced in second story as shown on second floor, plan "A." Cellar may be omitted or reduced in size. A portable range could be used instead of the brick-set one. Double sliding doors could be introduced between dining-room and parlor. An additional chimney could be introduced, which would give open fireplaces in parlor and bedroom above, if desired.

The price of working plans, specifications, etc., for a modified design, varies according to the alterations required and will be made known upon application to the Architects.

Cottage, Design No. 1218

PERSPECTIVE.

DESCRIPTION.

GENERAL DIMENSIONS: Width, 22 ft.; depth, 48 ft. 6 ins.

HEIGHTS OF STORIES: Cellar, 7 ft.; first story, 9 ft.; second story, 8 ft. 6 ins.

EXTERIOR MATERIALS: Foundation, stone; first story, clapboards; second story, gables and roofs, shingles.

INTERIOR FINISH: Two coat plaster, hard white finish. Trim, white wood. Flooring throughout, N. C. pine. Chair-rail in dining-room. Kitchen, wainscoted. All interior wood-work grain filled and stained mahogany down stairs; finished natural upstairs.

COLORS: Trim, including water-table, corner boards, cornices, casings, bands, etc., very dark red. Clapboards, fawn brown. Shingles on side walls stained umber. Roof shingles stained two shades of dark green to produce a mottled effect. Sashes, white. Porch floor, dark yellow. Outside doors finished natural with hard oil varnish.

ACCOMMODATIONS: The principal rooms and their sizes, closets, etc., are shown by the floor plans. Cellar under main part of house, with inside entrance and concrete floor. Open fireplace in dining-room. Wide portière opening connects hall and parlor. Portable range, sink and boiler in kitchen. Bath-room, containing full plumbing, in second story. Good-sized pantry connecting kitchen and dining-room contains drawers and shelves. China closet in dining-room. Hat and coat closet under main stairs. Ample porch room. Space over second story is floored for storage purposes and is accessible through a scuttle.

COST: $2,000,† not including mantels, range or heater. The estimate is based on ‡ New York prices for materials and labor. In many sections of the country the cost should be less.

Price of working plans (with full details drawn to large scale), specifications and * license to build, ... $20.00

Price of †† bill of materials, ... 10.00

FEASIBLE MODIFICATIONS: General dimensions, materials and colors may be changed. Cellar may be placed under whole house. Open fireplace may be introduced in parlor and bedroom over same. Stationary wash-tubs may be placed in cellar. Brickset range may be placed in kitchen. Part or all of plumbing may be omitted. Porch may be carried around hall and bedroom side. Bay-window in dining-room may be made to take in the full length of the room.

The price of working plans, specifications, etc., for a modified design, varies according to the alterations required and will be made known upon application to the Architects.

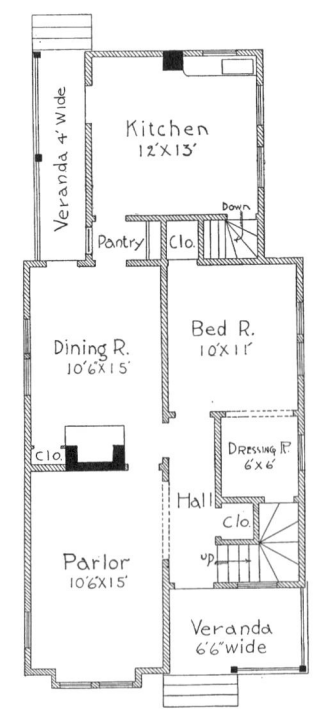

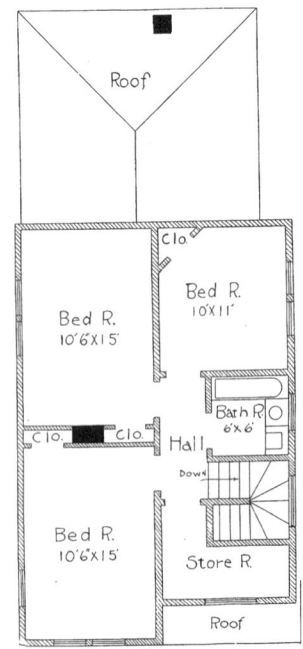

Address, THE CO-OPERATIVE BUILDING PLAN ASSOCIATION, Architects, 106–108 Fulton Street, New York.

FIRST FLOOR.   SECOND FLOOR.

Residence, Design No. 1227

PERSPECTIVE.

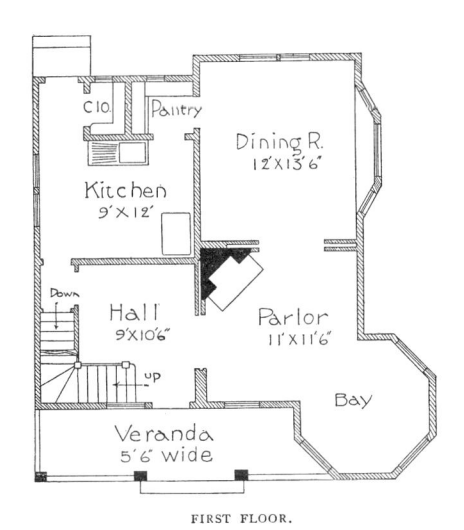

FIRST FLOOR.

SECOND FLOOR.

DESCRIPTION.

GENERAL DIMENSIONS: Width through kitchen and dining-room, 25 ft. 6 ins.; extreme width, 31 ft.; depth, including veranda, 32 ft.

HEIGHTS OF STORIES: Cellar, 6 ft. 6 ins.; first story, 9 ft.; second story, 9 ft.

EXTERIOR MATERIALS: Foundation, stone; first and second stories, roofs, and veranda enclosure, shingles.

INTERIOR FINISH: Two coat plaster, hard white finish. Staircase, ash. Trim in kitchen and dining-room, N. C. pine; elsewhere white wood. Flooring throughout, N. C. pine. Chair-rail in dining-room. Kitchen and bath-room wainscoted. Trim in kitchen and dining-room finished natural with hard oil varnish; elsewhere grain filled, stained to suit owner and finished in hard oil varnish.

COLORS: Trim, including cornices, casings, mouldings, etc., white. Shingles on side walls stained a dark shade of moss green. Sashes, dark bottle green. Veranda ceiling and outside doors, finished natural with hard oil varnish. Veranda floors, olive green.

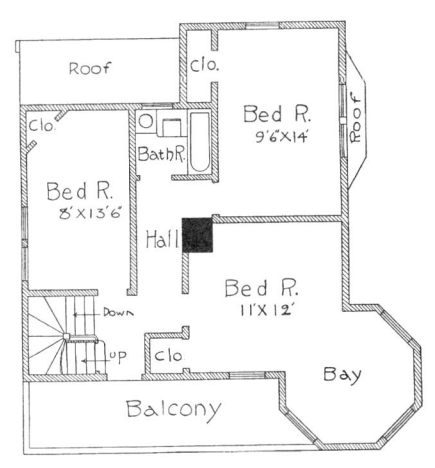

ACCOMMODATIONS: The principal rooms and their sizes, closets, etc., are shown by the floor plans. Cellar under the whole house, with inside and outside entrances and concrete floor. Open fireplace in parlor. Attic left unfinished but floored for storage purposes. Flue for portable range or stove, also sink and boiler in kitchen. Bath-room containing full plumbing, in second story. Double sliding doors connect dining-room and parlor, and single sliding door, dining-room and hall. Pantry connecting kitchen and dining-room contains dresser and corner-shelf.

COST: $2,100, † not including mantel, range or heater. The estimate is based on ‡ New York prices for materials and labor. In many sections of the country the cost should be less.

Price of working plans (with full details drawn to large scale), specifications and * license to build, ... $20.00

Price of †† bill of materials, ... 10.00

FEASIBLE MODIFICATIONS: General dimensions, materials and colors may be changed. Open fireplace may be introduced in dining-room and brick-set range in kitchen. Part or all of plumbing may be omitted. Stationary wash-tubs may be placed in cellar. A bedroom may be finished off in attic still leaving ample storage space.

The price of working plans, specifications, etc., for a modified design, varies according to the alterations required and will be made known upon application to the Architects.

Address, THE CO-OPERATIVE BUILDING PLAN ASSOCIATION, Architects, 106–108 Fulton Street, New York.

Residence, Design No. 1228

PERSPECTIVE.

DESCRIPTION.

GENERAL DIMENSIONS: Width, including veranda, 36 ft. 6 ins.; depth, including veranda, 50 ft. 3 ins.

HEIGHTS OF STORIES: First story, 8 ft. 6 ins.; second story, 8 ft.

EXTERIOR MATERIALS: Foundation, wood posts; main chimney, stone; first story, clapboards; second story, gables and roof, shingles.

INTERIOR FINISH: Two coat plaster, hard white finish. Soft wood flooring and trim. Yellow pine stairs. Kitchen wainscoted. Interior wood-work grain filled, stained to suit owner and finished in hard oil varnish.

COLORS: Trim, including water-table, corner boards, casings, cornices, etc., light brown. Clapboards, outside doors, sashes, porch floor and ceiling, brown. Rain conductors, light brown. Wall shingles dipped in and brush coated with umbre stain. Roof shingles dipped in and brush coated, slate color.

ACCOMMODATIONS: The principal rooms and their sizes, closets, etc., are shown by the floor plans. Attic floored but unfinished. Open fireplace in parlor and flue for dining-room and kitchen stoves. Plank cellar under kitchen with outside entrance. Sink in pantry. Wide portiére opening connects parlor and dining-room. Closet for china in dining-room. Large-sized kitchen pantry. Seat in nook.

COST: $2,200, † not including mantels. The estimate is based on ‡ New York prices for materials and labor. In many sections of the country the cost should be less.

Price of working plans, (with full details drawn to large scale), specifications and * license to build, ... $20.00

Price of †† bill of materials, ... 10.00

FEASIBLE MODIFICATIONS: General dimensions, materials and colors may be changed. Cellar may be placed under main or whole part of house, with inside and outside entrance and concrete floor. Bath-room, with part or all of plumbing, may be introduced in second story. Veranda may be extended. Open fireplace may be built in dining-room, and brick-set range in kitchen.

The price of working plans, specifications, etc., for a modified design, varies according to the alterations required and will be made known upon application to the Architects.

Address, THE CO-OPERATIVE BUILDING PLAN ASSOCIATION, Architects, 106–108 Fulton Street, New York.

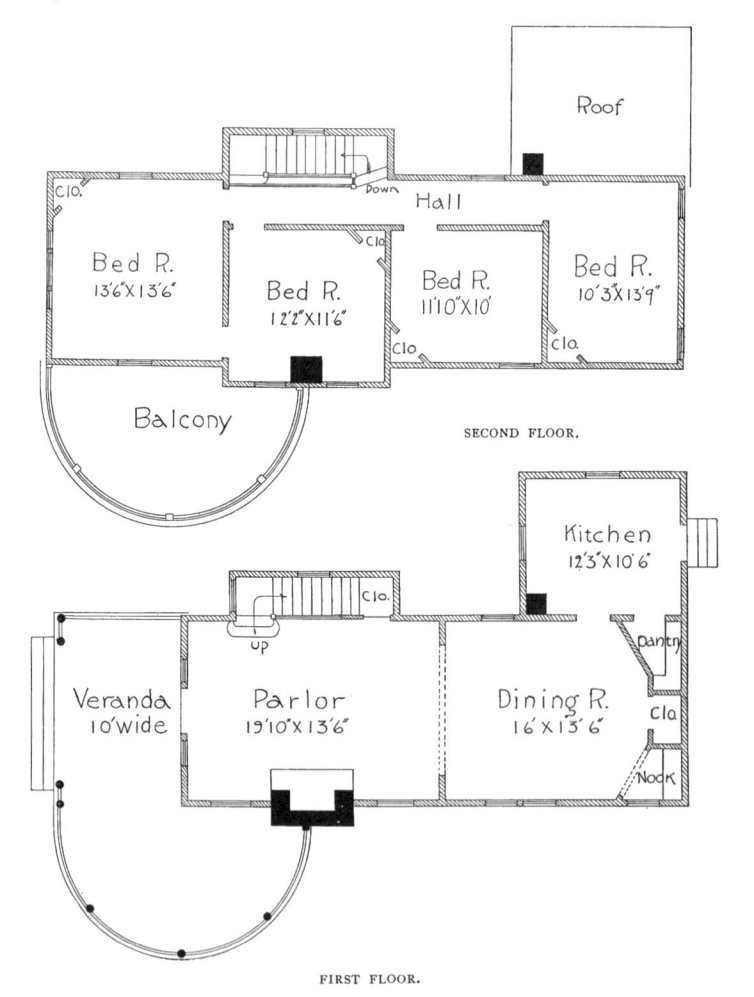

SECOND FLOOR.

FIRST FLOOR.

Residence, Design No. 1231

PERSPECTIVE.

DESCRIPTION.

GENERAL DIMENSIONS: Width, 32 ft.; depth over all, 44 ft.
HEIGHTS OF STORIES: Cellar, 7 ft.; first story, 9 ft.; second story, 8 ft.
EXTERIOR MATERIALS: Foundation, stone; first story, clapboards and shingles; second story, gables and roofs, shingles.
INTERIOR FINISH: Hard white plaster. Soft wood trim and stairway; all finished in hard oil, stained to suit owner.

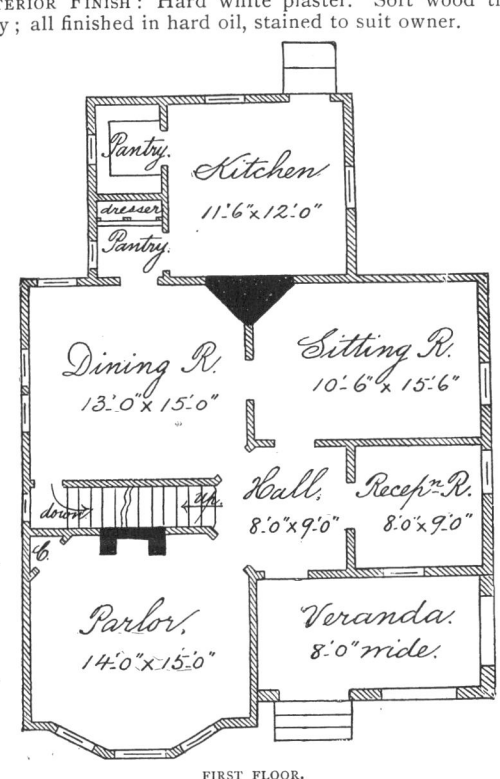

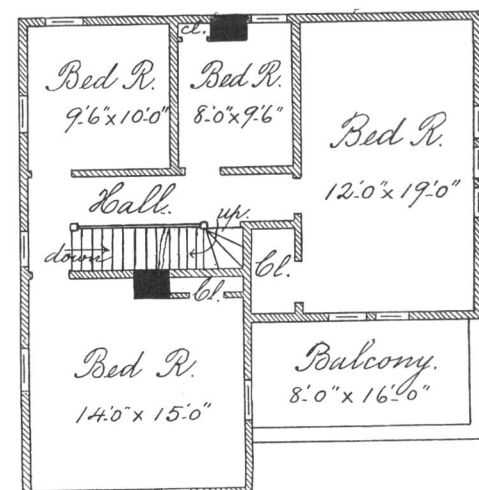

FIRST FLOOR.

SECOND FLOOR

COLORS: Entire body and gables painted Colonial (medium shade of) yellow. All trim, all mouldings, brackets, window and door frames, white. Outside doors treated with wood filler and finished with oil, showing natural colors. Roof shingles oiled. Veranda ceiling and floor oiled and finished natural.

ACCOMMODATIONS: The principal rooms and their sizes, closets, etc., are shown by the floor plans. Cellar under main house, with inside and outside entrances. Garret floored for storage. Balcony tinned and top floored. Parlor mantel included in estimate. The exterior is a combination of the Colonial and Romanesque, unusual and striking in appearance.

COST: $2,200, † not including range and heater. The estimate is based on ‡ New York prices for materials and labor. In many sections of the country the cost should be less.

Price of working plans, specifications and * license to build, ... $20.00
Price of †† bill of materials, ... 10.00

FEASIBLE MODIFICATIONS: Heights of stories, sizes of rooms, colors and materials may be changed. Cellar may be enlarged or reduced in size. The hall may be enlarged by including the reception-room. The sitting-room may be used as a bedroom, the reception-room serving as a dressing-room. The small bedroom in second story may be converted into a bath-room.

Address, THE CO-OPERATIVE BUILDING PLAN ASSOCIATION, Architects, 106–108 Fulton Street, New York.

Residence, Design No. 1232

PERSPECTIVE.

DESCRIPTION.

GENERAL DIMENSIONS: Width, 30 ft.; depth, not including veranda, 37 ft. 6 ins.

HEIGHTS OF STORIES: Cellar, 6 ft. 6 ins.; first story, 8 ft. 6 ins.; second story, 8 ft.

EXTERIOR MATERIALS; Foundation, stone; first story, clapboards; second story, gables and roofs, shingles.

INTERIOR FINISH: Two coat plaster, hard white finish. Trim, white wood. Flooring, N. C. pine. Main staircase, yellow pine. Kitchen, wainscoted. All interior wood-work grain filled, stained to suit owner and finished in hard oil varnish.

COLORS: Trim, including water-table, corner boards, cornices, casings, bands, veranda columns, rail, etc., cream white. Clapboards, buff. Shingles on side walls dipped in and brush coated with dark sienna stain. Roof shingles dipped in and brush coated with moss green stain. Sashes, dark green. Veranda floor and ceiling, also outside doors and brick-work, oiled.

ACCOMMODATIONS: The principal rooms and their sizes, closets, etc., are shown by the floor plans. Cellar under kitchen and hall, with inside entrance and concrete floor. Space over second story floored for storage purposes. Brick-set range, boiler and sink in kitchen. Open fireplace in parlor. Large pantry and china closet. Wide portière openings connect dining-room, parlor and hall. Panel slide in wall between dining-room and kitchen pantries for passing dishes. Bath-room, with full plumbing, in second story.

COST: $2,250, † not including mantels, range or heater. The estimate is based on ‡ New York prices for materials and labor. In many sections of the country the cost should be less.

Price of working plans (with full details drawn to large scale), specifications and * license to build, $25.00

Price of †† bill of materials, . . . 10.00

FEASIBLE MODIFICATIONS: General dimensions, materials and colors may be changed. Cellar may be put under whole house or wholly omitted. Bath-room plumbing may be omitted. Double sliding doors may be placed between the dining-room and parlor. Veranda may be extended around hall side. A dresser may be placed in pantry.

The price of working plans, specifications, etc., for a modified design, varies according to the alterations required and will be made known upon application to the Architects.

Address, THE CO-OPERATIVE BUILDING PLAN ASSOCIATION, Architects, 106-108 Fulton Street, New York.

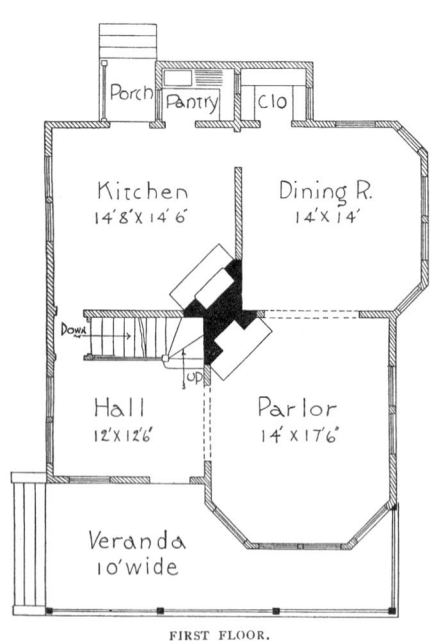

FIRST FLOOR.

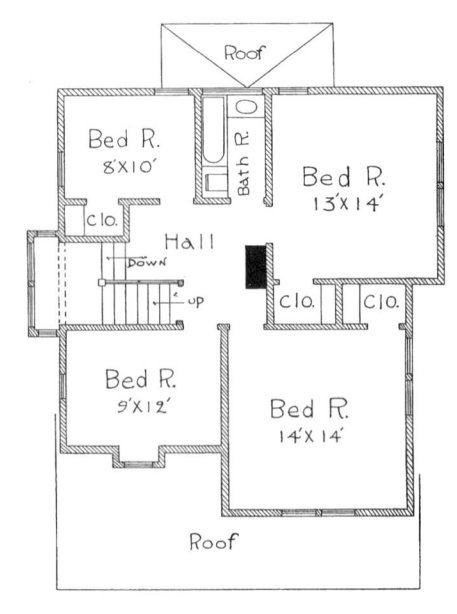

SECOND FLOOR.

44

Residence, Design No. 1233

PERSPECTIVE.

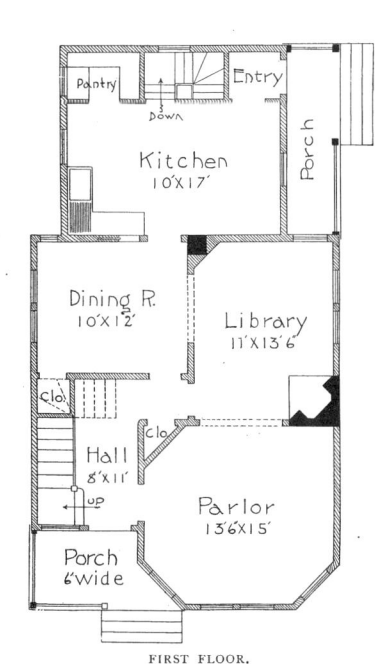

DESCRIPTION.

GENERAL DIMENSIONS: Width, 24 ft. 6 ins.; depth, 43 ft.

HEIGHTS OF STORIES: Cellar, 7 ft.; first story, 9 ft.; second story, 8 ft. 6 ins.

EXTERIOR MATERIALS: Foundation, stone and brick; first story and veranda enclosure, clapboards; second story, gables and roofs, shingles.

INTERIOR FINISH: Two coat plaster, hard white finish. Plaster cornices and centres in parlor and library. Flooring and trim throughout, white wood. Chair-rail in dining-room. All interior wood-work grain filled and finished in hard oil varnish.

COLORS: All clapboards, apple green. All trim, including water-table, corner boards, cornices, casings, bands, lattice work on veranda, posts, etc., dark bronzed green. Shingles on second story and gables dipped in and brush coated with light bronzed green stain. Roof shingles, dark terra-cotta stain. Piazza floor and ceiling oiled. Outside doors grain filled and finished with hard oil varnish.

ACCOMMODATIONS: The principal rooms and their sizes, closets, etc., are shown by the floor plans. Cellar under the whole house, with inside and outside entrances and concrete floor. Two set-tubs in cellar. Sink and convenient dresser in kitchen. Fireplace in library with wood mantel. Bath-room, with complete plumbing, in second story. One room finished off in attic. Portiére openings connect parlor with library and library with dining-room. Hat and coat closet in first story hall.

COST: $2,300, † not including mantels, range or heater. The estimate is based on ‡ New York prices for materials and labor. In many sections of the country the cost should be less.

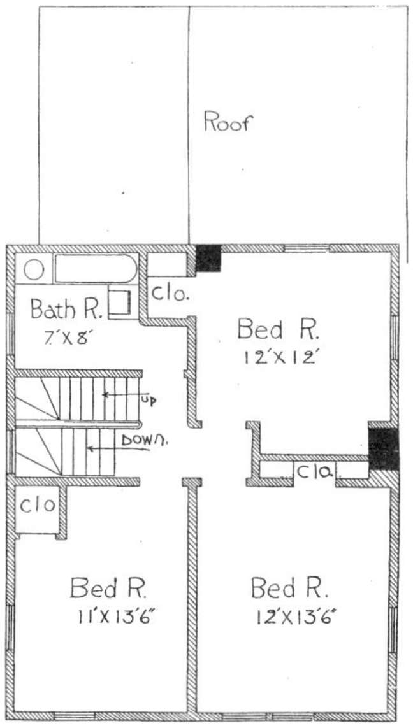

FIRST FLOOR.

SECOND FLOOR.

Price of working plans (with full details drawn to large scale), specifications and * license to build, ... $25.00

Price of †† bill of materials, ... 10.00

FEASIBLE MODIFICATIONS: General dimensions, materials and colors may be changed. Bay-window may be placed in library. Tubs may be transferred to kitchen. Open fireplace may be introduced in parlor. Veranda may be enlarged and carried around hall side to the rear of dining-room. Kitchen extension may be carried up another story, thus making an additional bedroom.

The price of working plans, specifications, etc., for a modified design, varies according to the alterations required and will be made known upon application to the Architects.

Address, THE CO-OPERATIVE BUILDING PLAN ASSOCIATION, Architects, 106-108 Fulton Street, New York.

Residence, Design No. 1234

PERSPECTIVE.

FIRST FLOOR.

SECOND FLOOR.

DESCRIPTION.

GENERAL DIMENSIONS: Width, including stoop, 31 ft. 3 ins.; depth, including veranda, 31 ft. 6 ins.

HEIGHTS OF STORIES: Cellar, 6 ft. 6 ins.; first story, 9 ft.; second story, 8 ft.

EXTERIOR MATERIALS: Foundation, brick; first story, clapboards; second story, shingles; roof, shingles.

INTERIOR FINISH: Two coat plaster, hard white finish. Soft wood flooring and trim. Picture moulding in principal rooms and hall, first story. Bath-room and kitchen, wainscoted. Main stairs, yellow pine. All wood-work to be grain filled and finished with two coats hard oil varnish.

COLORS: Clapboards, yellow stone. Trim, including water-table, corner boards, casings, cornices, bands, veranda floor, veranda posts, rail, etc, light brown. Sashes, bronze green. Rain conductors and brick-work, Pompeian red. Outside doors, bronze green. Shingling on walls and gables, oiled. Roof shingles left natural. Veranda ceiling, oiled.

ACCOMMODATIONS: The principal rooms and their sizes, closets, etc., are shown by the floor plans. Hall, one room and closet, finished in attic. Remainder of attic floored for storage purposes. Stairs from kitchen connecting with main staircase. Cellar under the whole house, with inside and outside entrances and concrete floor. Inside folding blinds to all windows. Open fireplace in hall. Wide openings between parlor and dining-room and parlor and hall. Bath-room with complete plumbing. Sink, portable range and boiler in kitchen. Bay-window in parlor, with plaster arch over same. Large open stairway. China closet in dining-room. Dresser in kitchen. Ample veranda.

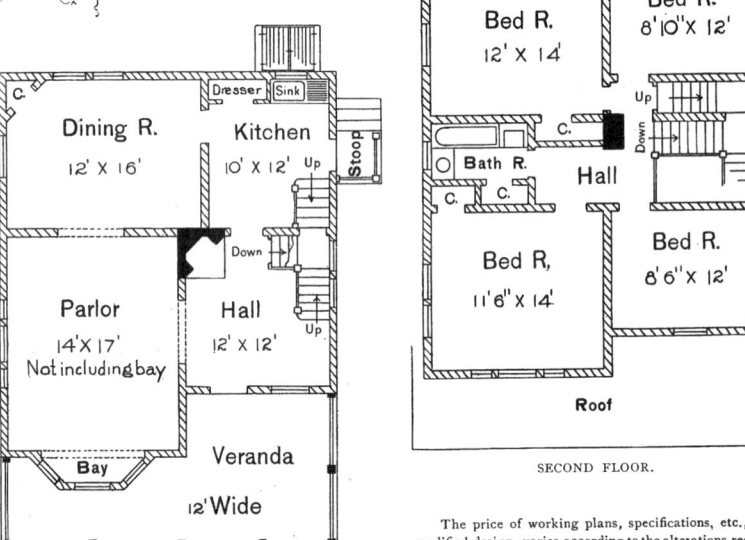

The price of working plans, specifications, etc., for a modified design, varies according to the alterations required and will be made known upon application to the Architects. Address, THE CO-OPERATIVE BUILDING PLAN ASSOCIATION, Architects, 106–108 Fulton Street, New York.

COST: $2,300, † not including mantels, range and heater. The estimate is based on ‡ New York prices for materials and labor. In many sections of the country the cost should be less.

Price of working plans (with full details drawn to large scale), specifications and * license to build, ... $25.00

Price of †† bill of materials, ... 10.00

FEASIBLE MODIFICATIONS: General dimensions, materials and colors may be changed. Stationary tubs may be introduced in kitchen or in cellar. Cellar may be reduced in size or wholly omitted. Fireplace in hall may be omitted or transferred to parlor. Veranda can be extended around sides.

Residence, Design No. 1235

PERSPECTIVE.

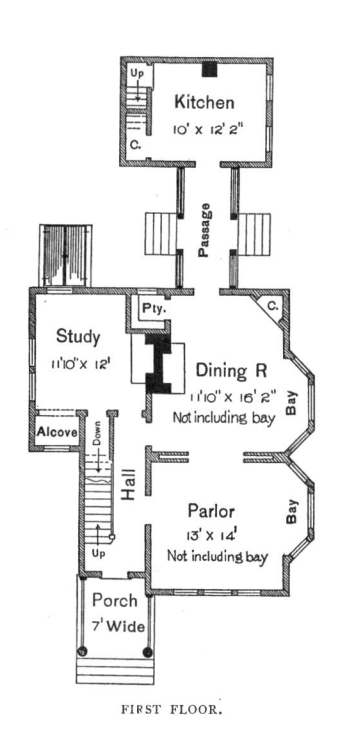

DESCRIPTION.

GENERAL DIMENSIONS: Width over all, 31 ft.; depth, including kitchen and front porch, 60 ft. 10 ins.

HEIGHTS OF STORIES: Cellar, 7 ft.; first story, 9 ft. 6 ins.: second story, 8 ft. 6 ins.

EXTERIOR MATERIALS: Foundation, stone and brick; first story, clapboards; gables and roofs, shingles.

INTERIOR FINISH: Two coat plaster, hard white finish. Main staircase, flooring and trim, yellow pine. Picture moulding in principal rooms and hall of first story. All wood-work to be grain filled and finished with hard oil varnish.

COLORS: All clapboards, buff. Trim, including water-table, corner boards, cornices, casings, bands, veranda posts, etc., cream white. Outside doors, oiled. Sashes, Tuscan yellow. Porch floor and ceiling, oiled. Conductors, Pompeian red. Shingles on gables, Pompeian red. Shingled roofs left natural for weather stain.

ACCOMMODATIONS: The principal rooms and their sizes, closets, etc., are shown on the floor plans. Cellar under study, hall and parlor, with inside and outside entrances and concrete floor. Open fireplaces in dining-room and study. Sliding doors between dining-room and parlor. Kitchen separated from main part of house by a breeze-way. No plumbing. China closet in dining room. Large and numerous closets.

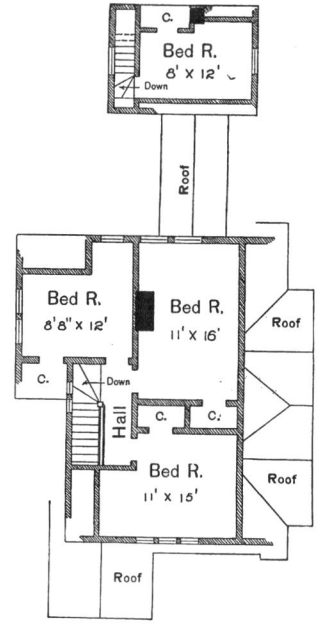

FIRST FLOOR.

SECOND FLOOR.

COST: $2,300, † not including mantels, range or heater. The estimate is based on ‡ New York prices for materials and labor. In many sections of the country the cost should be less.

Price of working plans (with full details drawn to large scale), specifications and * license to build, ... $25.00

Price of †† bill of materials, ... 10.00

FEASIBLE MODIFICATIONS: General dimensions, materials and colors may be changed. Cellar may be placed under the whole house. Kitchen may be omitted and study made into a kitchen. Present kitchen could be placed immediately back of dining-room by doing away with breeze-way. Partial or full plumbing may be introduced. Veranda may be extended at side of house and across front.

The price of working plans, specifications, etc., for a modified design, varies according to the alterations required and will be made known upon application to the Architects.

Address, THE CO-OPERATIVE BUILDING PLAN ASSOCIATION, Architects, 106–108 Fulton Street, New York.

Residence, Design No. 1236

PERSPECTIVE.

DESCRIPTION.

GENERAL DIMENSIONS: Width, 28 ft.; depth, including veranda and pantry, 35 ft. 6 ins.

HEIGHTS OF STORIES: Cellar, 6 ft. 6 ins.; first story, 8 ft. 6 ins.; second story, 8 ft.

EXTERIOR MATERIALS: Foundation, stone; first and second stories, clapboards; gables and roof, shingles.

INTERIOR FINISH: Two coat plaster, hard white finish. Soft wood flooring and trim. Yellow pine stairs. Kitchen and bath-room, wainscoted. Interior wood-work grain filled, stained to suit owner and finished in hard oil varnish.

COLORS: Trim, including water-table, corner boards, cornices, casings, veranda posts, rail, etc., very dark green. Clapboards, Nile green. Roof shingles dipped and brush-coated Indian red stain. Shingles on gables stained burnt sienna. Veranda floors, buff. Veranda ceiling, also brick-work, oiled. Outside doors grain filled and finished natural with hard oil varnish rubbed to a dull gloss.

ACCOMMODATIONS: The principal rooms and their sizes, closets, etc., are shown by the floor plans. Cellar under the whole house, with inside and outside entrances and concrete floor. Open fireplaces in dining-room and parlor. One room and hall finished off in attic, remainder of space floored for storage purposes. Brick-set range, sink and boiler in kitchen. Linen closet in second story hall. Bath-room, with full plumbing, in second story. Wide portière opening connects dining-room and parlor. Bay-window in dining-room.

COST: $2,330, † not including mantels, range or heater. The estimate is based on ‡ New York prices for materials and labor. In many sections of the country the cost should be less.

Price of working plans (with full details drawn to large scale), specifications and * license to build, . . $25.00

Price of †† bill of materials, ... 10.00

FEASIBLE MODIFICATIONS: General dimensions, materials and colors may be changed. Tubs may be introduced in kitchen or placed in cellar. Double sliding doors may be placed between parlor and dining-room. Open fireplaces may be omitted. An additional bedroom may be finished off in attic, still leaving ample storage space, or attic may be left unfinished. Cellar may be reduced in size. A part or all of plumbing may be omitted.

The price of working plans, specifications, etc., for a modified design, varies according to the alterations required and will be made known upon application to the Architects.

Address, THE CO-OPERATIVE BUILDING PLAN ASSOCIATION, Architects, 106-108 Fulton Street, New York.

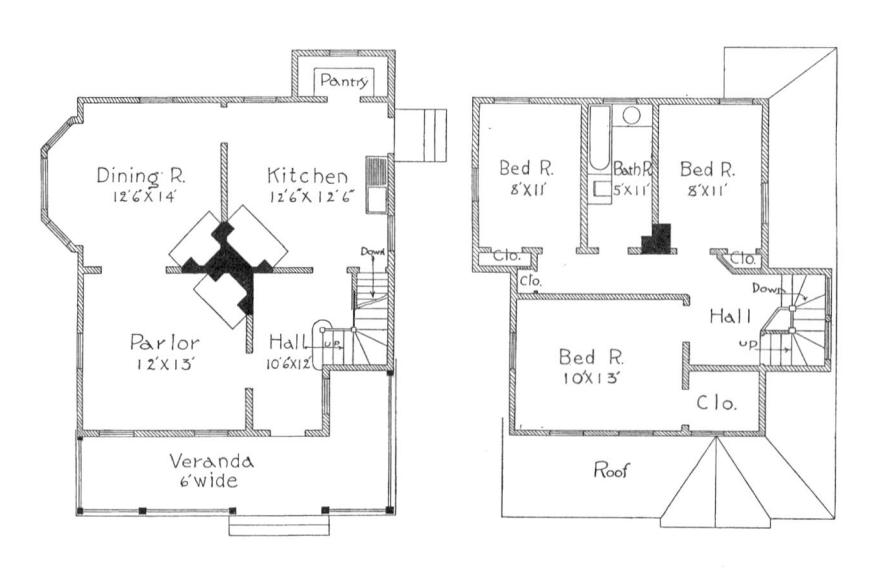

FIRST FLOOR. SECOND FLOOR.

48

Residence, Design No. 1237.

PERSPECTIVE.

DESCRIPTION.

GENERAL DIMENSIONS: Extreme width, 36 ft. 6 ins.; depth, 44 ft.

HEIGHTS OF STORIES: First story, 9 ft.; second story, 8 ft. 6 ins.; cellar, 7 ft.

EXTERIOR MATERIALS: Foundation, stone; first story, dormers, gables, etc., and roof, shingles.

INTERIOR FINISH: Two coat plaster, hard white finish. Soft wood flooring and trim throughout. Staircase, yellow pine. Kitchen and bath-room, wainscoted. All interior woodwork grain filled and finished natural with hard oil varnish.

COLORS: Trim, including cornices, casings, veranda rail, etc., dark green. Shingles on side walls left natural for weather stain. Roof shingles dipped and brush coated dark green. Sashes, white. Veranda ceiling and outside doors, varnished. Veranda floor, dark gray.

ACCOMMODATIONS: The principal rooms and their sizes, closets, etc., are shown by the floor plans. Cellar under the whole house, with inside and outside entrances and concrete floor. Portable range, sink and boiler in kitchen. Bath room, with full plumbing, in second story. Pantry connects dining-room and kitchen containing shelving, etc. Entrance to kitchen from rear is through lobby, which is large enough to admit ice box. An attractive bay-window in dining-room. Wide portière opening between dining-room and parlor. Large piano alcove off parlor. Open fireplace in parlor.

COST: $2,429, † not including mantel, range or heater. The estimate is based on ‡ New York prices for materials and labor. In many sections of the country the cost should be less.

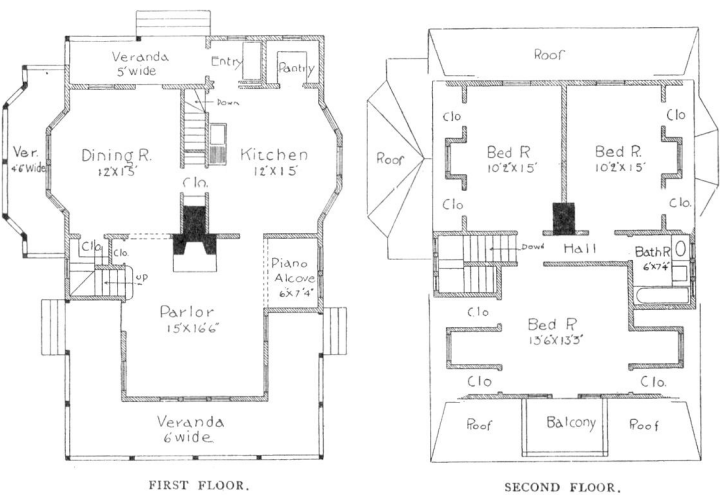

FIRST FLOOR.   SECOND FLOOR.

Price of working plans (with full details drawn to large scale), specifications and * license to build, ... $25.00

Price of †† bill of materials, ... 10.00

FEASIBLE MODIFICATIONS: General dimensions, materials and colors may be changed. Brick-set range may be built in kitchen and open fireplace introduced in dining-room. Cellar may be reduced in size. Dining-room veranda may be turned into a conservatory. Servants' water-closet may be introduced in cellar. A part or all of plumbing may be omitted.

The price of working plans, specifications, etc., for a modified design, varies according to the alterations required and will be made known upon application to the Architects.

Residence, Design No. 1238

PERSPECTIVE.

DESCRIPTION.

GENERAL DIMENSIONS: Extreme width, 32 ft.; depth, including veranda, 36 ft. 6 ins.

HEIGHTS OF STORIES: Cellar, 6 ft. 6 ins.; first story, 9 ft.; second story, 8 ft. 3 ins.

EXTERIOR MATERIALS: Foundations, stone and brick; first story, clapboards; second story and roof, shingles; gables, panels and shingles. Outside blinds to all windows, except those of the cellar and attic.

INTERIOR FINISH: Hard white plaster. Plaster cornices and centers in hall, parlor and dining-room. Soft wood flooring and trim. Ash stairs. Bath-room and kitchen, wainscoted. All interior wood-work finished in hard oil.

COLORS: Clapboards, seal brown. Trim, outside doors, blinds and veranda floor, maroon. Sashes and rain conductors, dark green. Brick-work, Indian red. Wall shingles dipped and brush coated light sienna stain. Roof shingles dipped and brush coated Indian red stain.

ACCOMMODATIONS: The principal rooms and their sizes, closets, etc., are shown by the floor plans. Cellar under hall and parlor. Attic floored but unfinished; space for two good rooms. Bath-room, with complete plumbing. Fireplaces, with hard wood mantels, in parlor and dining-room.

COST: $2,430.54, † not including mantels, range, heater, or plumbing. The estimate is based on ‡ New York prices for materials and labor. In many sections of the country the cost should be less.

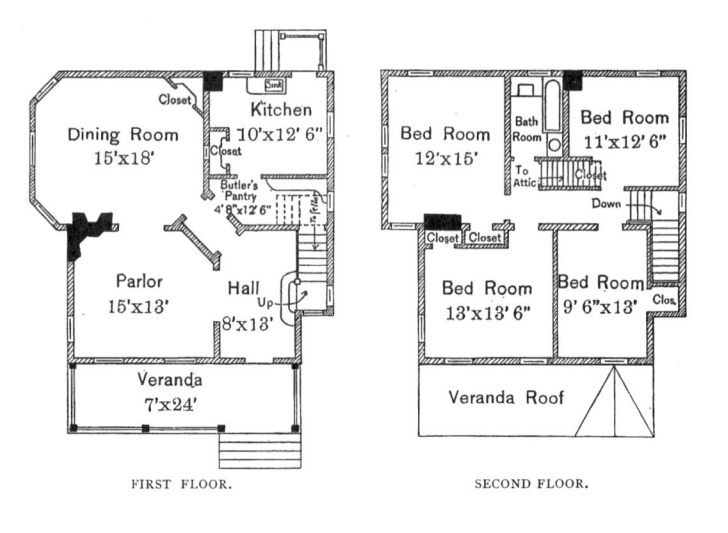

FIRST FLOOR.   SECOND FLOOR.

Price of working plans (with full details drawn to large scale), specifications and * license to build, ... $25.00

Price of †† bill of materials, ... 10.00

FEASIBLE MODIFICATIONS: General dimensions, materials and colors may be changed. Cellar may be extended under the whole house or omitted entirely. A part or all of plumbing may be omitted. If heating apparatus be used in cellar one chimney will suffice.

The price of working plans, specifications, etc., for a modified design, varies according to the alterations required and will be made known upon application to the Architects.

Address, THE CO-OPERATIVE BUILDING PLAN ASSOCIATION, Architects, 106-108 Fulton Street, New York.

Residence, Design No. 1239

PERSPECTIVE

DESCRIPTION.

GENERAL DIMENSIONS: Width, including dining-room bay and overhanging balcony, 34 ft. 6 ins.; depth, including veranda and butler's pantry projection, 42 ft.

HEIGHTS OF STORIES: Cellar, 7 ft.; first story, 9 ft.; second story, 8 ft.

EXTERIOR MATERIALS: Foundation, brick; first story, clapboards; second story, gables and roofs, shingles.

INTERIOR FINISH: Two coat plaster, hard white finish. Flooring and trim throughout, N. C. pine. Main staircase, yellow pine. Kitchen and bath-room wainscoted. Chair-rail in dining-room. All interior wood-work grain filled and finished natural with hard oil varnish.

COLORS: Trim, including water-table, corner boards, cornices, casings, veranda columns, rail, etc., dark bottle green. Clapboards, yellow brown. Shingles on side walls dipped in and brush coated with dark sienna stain. Roof shingles left natural for weather stain. Sashes and outside blinds, maroon. Veranda floor, dark gray. Veranda ceiling and outside doors, varnished.

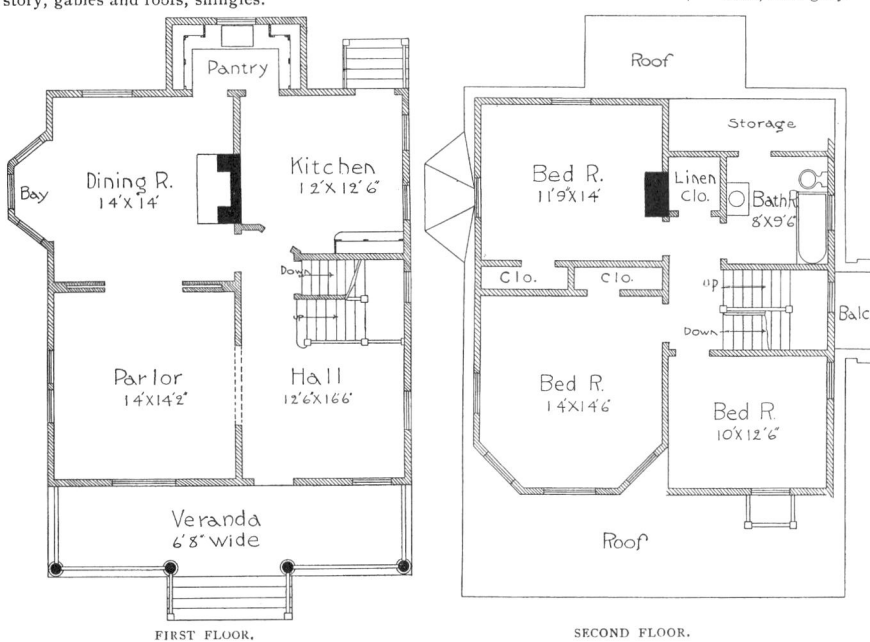

ACCOMMODATIONS: The principal rooms and their sizes, closets, etc., are shown by the floor plans. Cellar under the whole house, with inside and outside entrances and concrete floor. Portable range, sink and boiler, also dresser in kitchen. Bath-room, with full plumbing, in second story. Large butler's pantry connecting kitchen and dining-room, contains counter-shelf and two dressers. Bay-window and open fireplace in dining-room. Double sliding doors connect dining-room and parlor, and wide portière opening connects parlor and hall. Attractive platform staircase. Large-sized glazed front entrance door. Open balcony, accessible from platform of staircase. Attic unfinished, but floored for storage purposes.

COST: $2,490, † not including mantel, range or heater. The estimate is based on ‡ New York prices for materials and labor. In many sections of the country the cost should be less.

Price of working plans (with full details drawn to large scale), specifications and * license to build, . $25.00

Price of †† bill of materials, ... 10.00

FEASIBLE MODIFICATIONS: General dimensions, materials and colors may be changed. Cellar may be reduced in size or wholly omitted. Open fireplace may be introduced in parlor and bedroom over same. Bedroom may be finished off in attic. Butler's sink may be introduced in butler's pantry. Servants' water-closet may be introduced in cellar. Veranda may be extended around either side.

The price of working plans, specifications, etc., for a modified design, varies according to the alterations required and will be made known upon application to the Architects.

FIRST FLOOR.

SECOND FLOOR.

51

Residence, Design No. 1240

PERSPECTIVE.

DESCRIPTION.

GENERAL DIMENSIONS: Width, 21 ft.; depth, including veranda, 44 ft. 6 ins.

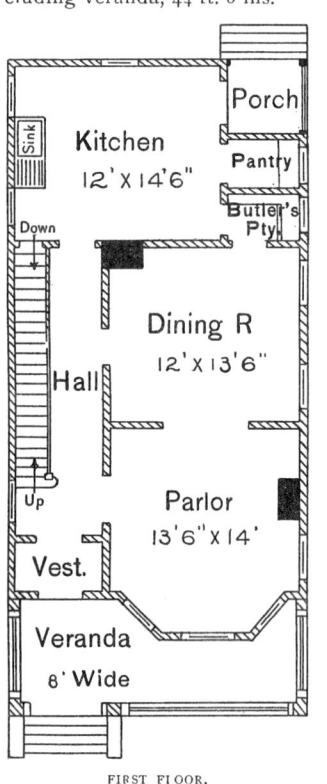

HEIGHTS OF STORIES: Cellar, 6 ft. 6 ins.; first story, 9 ft.; second story, 8 ft.

EXTERIOR MATERIALS: Foundation, stone; first story, clapboards; second story, gables and roofs, shingles.

INTERIOR FINISH: Hard white plaster throughout. Hard wood flooring and trim. Main staircase, ash. Interior woodwork grain filled and finished with hard oil varnish.

COLORS: Clapboards, maroon. Trim, outside doors and blinds, bronze green. Sashes, red. Veranda and porch floors, gray. Veranda and porch ceilings, oiled. Shingles on side walls dipped and brush coated light yellow stain. Shingles on gables dipped and brush coated sienna stain. Roof shingles oiled.

ACCOMMODATIONS; The principal rooms and their sizes, closets, etc., are shown by the floor plans. Cellar under the entire house, with inside and outside entrances and concrete floor. Attic unfinished. Bay-window in parlor and bedroom over. Double folding doors between the parlor and dining-room. Bath room with complete plumbing in second story.

COST: $2,500, † not including range and heater. The estimate is based on ‡ New York prices for materials and labor. In many sections of the country the cost should be less.

Price of working plans (with full details drawn to large scale), specifications and * license to build, . . . $25.00

Price of †† bill of materials, ... 10.00

FEASIBLE MODIFICATIONS: General dimensions, materials and colors may be changed. The cellar may be reduced in size or wholly omitted. By continuing the main stairs to the attic, two additional rooms may be obtained. Open fireplaces may be introduced in dining-room, parlor and two bedrooms over these rooms. Second story balcony may be omitted and the dressing-room enlarged.

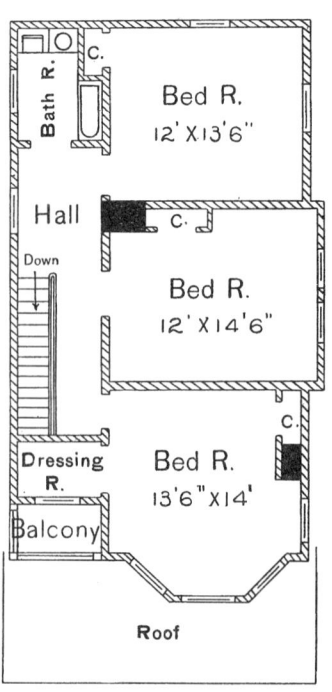

FIRST FLOOR.

SECOND FLOOR.

The price of working plans, specifications, etc., for a modified design, varies according to the alterations required and will be made known upon application to the Architects.

Address, THE CO-OPERATIVE BUILDING PLAN ASSOCIATION, Architects, 106-108 Fulton Street, New York.

Residence, Design No. 1241

PERSPECTIVE.

DESCRIPTION.

GENERAL DIMENSIONS: Width, including veranda, 34 ft.; depth, including veranda, 40 ft. 6 ins.

HEIGHTS OF STORIES: Cellar, 7 ft.; first story, 9 ft.; second story, 8 ft. 6 ins.

EXTERIOR MATERIALS: Foundation, brick; first story, clapboards; second story, gables, roofs and lower portion of veranda and porch railing, shingles.

INTERIOR FINISH: Two coat plaster, hard white finish. Soft wood flooring and trim throughout. Staircase, ash. All interior wood-work, grain filled and finished with hard oil.

COLORS: All clapboards and veranda and porch floors, fawn. First story trim, including watertable, corner boards, casings and outside doors, brown. Second story and attic trim, including casings, cornices, etc., ecru. All sashes, ecru. Blinds, olive green. Veranda and porch ceilings, oiled. Shingling on side walls, and shingles on veranda and porch roofs, stained dark red. Shingling on main roofs, stained dark brown.

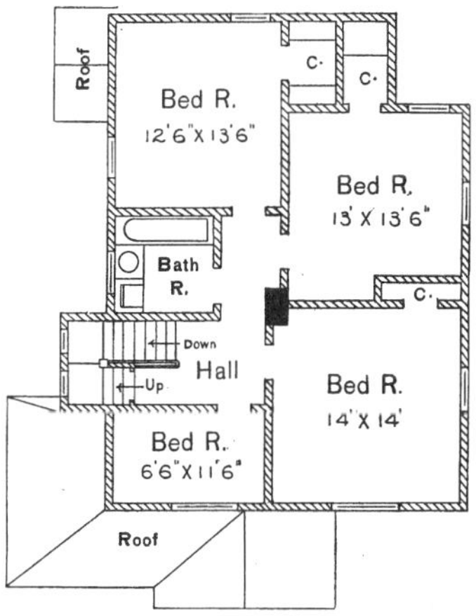

ACCOMMODATIONS: Cellar under whole house, with inside and outside entrances. The attic is floored for storage only. Bath-room with complete plumbing in second story. Open fireplace in parlor. Double sliding doors between parlor and hall, and double folding doors between dining-room and parlor.

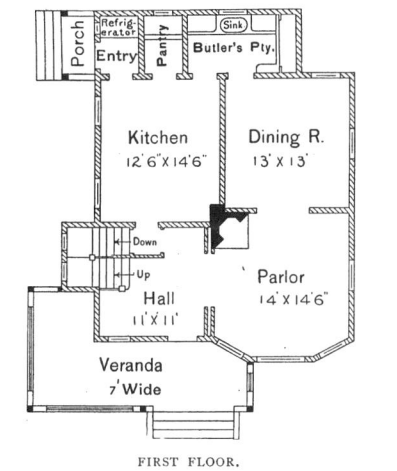

COST: $2,500,† not including mantel, range and heater. The estimate is based on ‡ New York prices for materials and labor. In many sections of the country the cost should be less.

Price of working plans (with full details drawn to large scale), specifications, and
* license to build, ... $25.00

Price of †† bill of materials, ... 10.00

FEASIBLE MODIFICATIONS: General dimensions, materials and colors may be changed. Cellar may be reduced in size or wholly omitted. A servants' water-closet and laundry could be planned in cellar, or stationary wash trays could be placed in kitchen. There is space in the attic to finish off two rooms and still have ample room for storage. Fireplace may be introduced in dining-room. A portion or all of the plumbing may be omitted.

The price of working plans, specifications, etc., for a modified design, varies according to the alterations required and will be made known upon application to the Architects.

Address, THE CO-OPERATIVE BUILDING PLAN ASSOCIATION, Architects, 106-108 Fulton Street, New York.

SECOND FLOOR.

FIRST FLOOR.

Residence, Design No. 1242.

PERSPECTIVE.

DESCRIPTION.

GENERAL DIMENSIONS: Width through dining-room and library, 26 ft. 6 ins.; depth, including veranda, 45 ft. 10 ins.

HEIGHTS OF STORIES: Cellar, 7 ft.; first story, 9 ft. 6 ins.; second story, 9 ft.

EXTERIOR MATERIALS: Foundation, stone to grade and brick above grade; first story, clapboards; second story and roofs, shingles; gables, panels and shingles. Floors of balconies covered with heavy canvas.

INTERIOR FINISH: Three coat plaster, hard white finish. Soft wood flooring and trim. Main staircase, ash. Picture moulding in principal rooms and hall, first story. Kitchen and bath-room, wainscoted. All interior wood-work grain filled and finished with hard oil varnish.

COLORS: All clapboards and spindle work of balconies, fawn. Trim, including water-table, corner boards, casings, cornices, bands, veranda posts, rail, etc., Tuscan yellow. Outside doors, blinds, sashes and stiles and rails of panels, dark green. Brick-work, painted dark red. Shingling on side walls and gables stained sienna. Roof shingles stained dark brown.

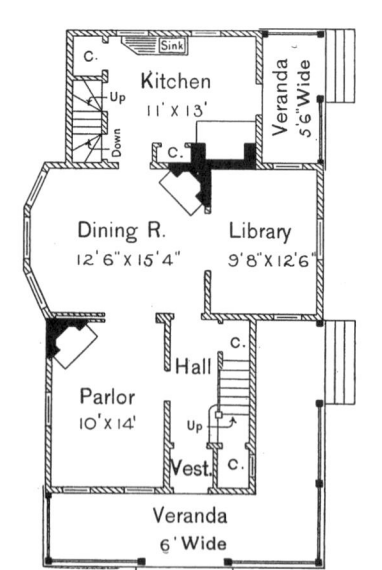

ACCOMMODATIONS: The principal rooms and their sizes, closets, etc., are shown by the floor plans. Cellar under whole house, with inside and outside entrances and concrete floor. The attic floored for storage purposes. Open fireplaces in parlor and dining-room. Brick-set range in kitchen. Double folding doors between dining-room and library, and wide, single sliding door between parlor and dining-room. Bath-room with complete plumbing. Ample veranda and closet room.

COST: $2,500,† not including mantels, range and heater. The estimate is based on ‡ New York prices for materials and labor. In many sections of the country the cost should be less.

Price of working plans (with full details drawn to large scale), specifications and * license to build, ... $30.00

Price of †† bill of materials, ... 10.00

FEASIBLE MODIFICATIONS: General dimensions, materials and colors may be changed. Cellar may be reduced in size or wholly omitted. Stationary wash-tubs could be introduced in kitchen, or a separate laundry planned in cellar. Sliding doors may be used between library and dining-room. Double doors may be introduced connecting parlor and hall. A servant's room may be finished in the attic. Open fireplace could be planned in library. Veranda space may be increased or diminished.

The price of working plans, specifications, etc., for a modified design, varies according to the alterations required and will be made known upon application to the Architects.

The CO-OPERATIVE BUILDING PLAN ASSOCIATION, Architects, 106–108 Fulton Street, New York.

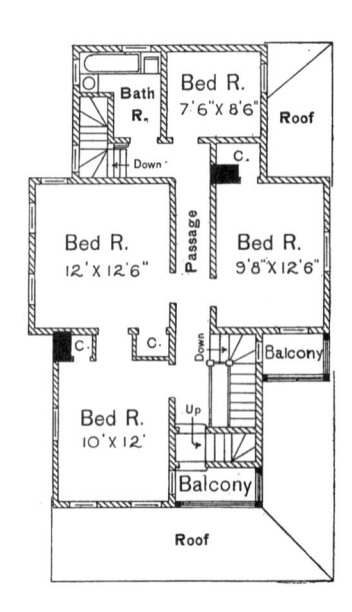

FIRST FLOOR.

SECOND FLOOR.

Residence, Design No. 1243

PERSPECTIVE.

DESCRIPTION.

GENERAL DIMENSIONS: Width, 28 ft. 6 ins.; depth, not including veranda, 37 ft.

HEIGHTS OF STORIES: Cellar, 6 ft. 6 ins.; first story, 9 ft.; second story, 8 ft. 6 ins.

EXTERIOR MATERIALS: Foundation, stone; first story, clapboards; second story, gables and roof, shingles.

INTERIOR FINISH: Two coat plaster, hard white finish. First story floor double with paper between. Soft wood flooring and trim, except in hall of first story, where the trim, flooring and staircase is of yellow pine. Chair-rail in dining-room. Kitchen and bath-room wainscoted. All interior wood-work grain filled and finished natural with hard oil varnish.

COLORS: Trim, including cornices, casings, columns, posts, rail, etc., dark green. Clapboards, light terra-cotta. Wall shingles stained dark red. Outside blinds and sashes, also veranda floor and ceiling and outside doors, oiled. Rain-water conductors, dark green. Roof shingles left natural.

ACCOMMODATIONS: The principal rooms and their sizes, closets, etc., are shown by the floor plans. Cellar under the whole house, with inside and outside entrances and concrete floor. Laundry with three wash-tubs in cellar. Portable range, sink and boiler in kitchen. Bath-room, with full plumbing, in second story. Open fireplaces in dining-room and parlor. Double sliding doors connect parlor, hall and dining-room. Large-sized butler's pantry connects kitchen and dining-room, and contains dresser. Good-sized kitchen pantry and porch. Ample storage space in attic. Linen-closet in second story hall.

COST: $2,500, † not including mantels, range or heater. The estimate is based on ‡ New York prices for materials and labor. In many sections of the country the cost should be less.

Price of working plans (with full details drawn to large scale), specifications and * license to build, ... $25.00

Price of †† bill of materials, ... 10 00

FEASIBLE MODIFICATIONS: General dimensions, materials and colors may be changed. Cellar may be reduced in size. Open fireplaces may be omitted in dining-room and parlor. Double sliding doors may be omitted and openings used for portières. Uncovered veranda may be extended around side to dining-room. Part or all of plumbing may be omitted. Wash-tubs may be transferred to kitchen. Brick-set range may be introduced in kitchen.

The price of working plans, specifications, etc., for a modified design, varies according to the alterations required and will be made known upon application to the Architects.

Address, THE CO-OPERATIVE BUILDING PLAN ASSOCIATION, Architects, 106–108 Fulton Street, New York.

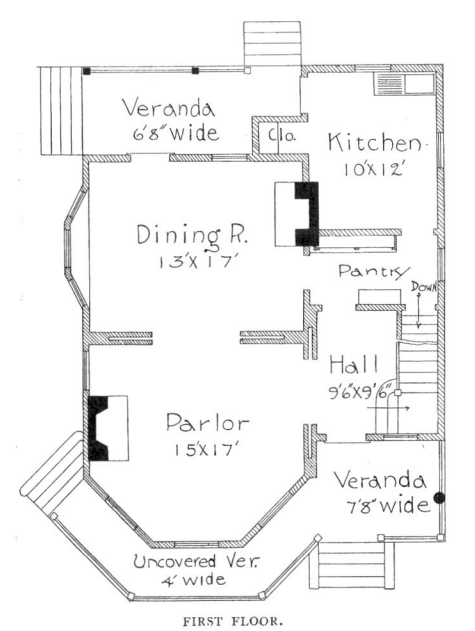

FIRST FLOOR.

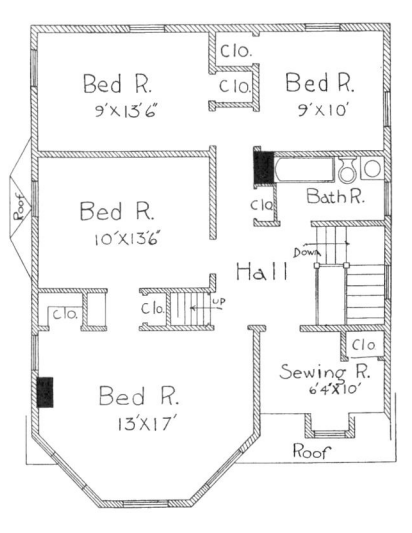

SECOND FLOOR.

Residence, Design No. 1244

PERSPECTIVE.

DESCRIPTION.

GENERAL DIMENSIONS: Width, including dining-room bay and tower projection, 44 ft. 4 ins.; depth, including veranda, 35 ft. 2 ins.

HEIGHTS OF STORIES: Cellar, 6 ft. 6 ins.; first story, 9 ft.; second story, 8 ft. 6 ins.; attic, 8 ft.

EXTERIOR MATERIALS: Foundation, stone; first and second story walls, gables and roofs, shingles.

INTERIOR FINISH: Three coat plaster, hard white finish. Plaster centres in hall and principal rooms of first story. Soft wood flooring and trim throughout. Ash staircase. Panel backs under windows in hall and principal rooms, first story. Kitchen and bath-room, wainscoted. Chair-rail in dining-room. All interior wood-work grain filled, stained to suit owner and finished with hard oil varnish.

COLORS: Shingling on walls, gables and roofs, dipped in and brush coated with moss green stain. Trim, including cornices, veranda posts, rail, outside casings for doors and windows, conductors, etc., dark green. Sashes, blinds and outside doors, dark red. Veranda floor and ceiling, oiled.

ACCOMMODATIONS: The principal rooms and their sizes, closets, etc., are shown by the floor plans. Cellar under the whole house, with inside and outside entrance and concrete floor. Laundry, with two set-tubs in cellar. One servants' room finished in attic, the remainder of attic floored for storage. Bath-room, with complete plumbing, in second story. Stationary wash bowl in tower bedroom. Brick-set range. Fireplaces in hall, dining-room and library. Wide double folding doors connect hall and parlor and hall and library.

COST: $3,500, † not including mantels, range and heater. The estimate is based on ‡ New York prices for materials and labor. In many sections of the country the cost should be less

Price of working plans (with full details drawn to large scale), specifications and * license to build, ... $35.00
Price of †† bill of materials, . . 10.00

FEASIBLE MODIFICATIONS: General dimensions, materials and colors may be changed. Cellar may be reduced in size or wholly omitted. Laundry tubs could be transferred from cellar to kitchen. Two additional rooms may be finished in the attic, or the attic may be left entirely unfinished. Fireplace may be planned in parlor. Veranda may be increased in size. Dining-room bay could be carried up two stories, thus enlarging the bedroom over the dining-room.

The price of working plans, specifications, etc., for a modified design, varies according to the alterations required and will be made known upon application to the Architects.

Address, THE CO-OPERATIVE BUILDING PLAN ASSOCIATION, Architects, 106-108 Fulton Street, New York.

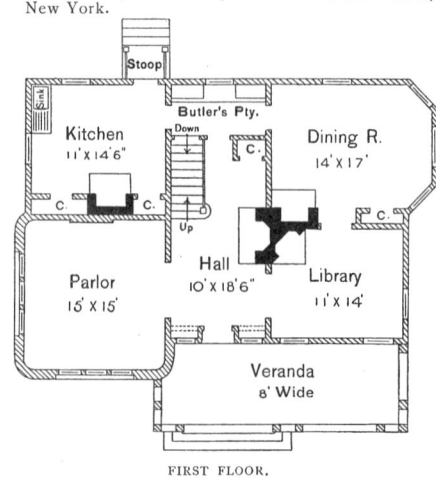

FIRST FLOOR.

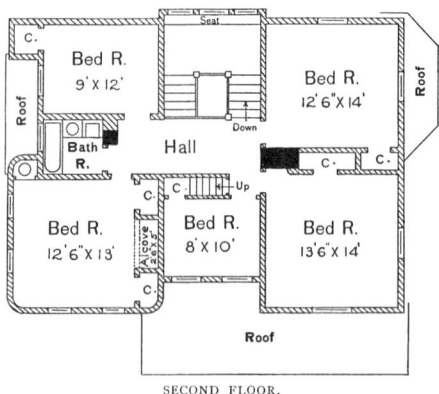

SECOND FLOOR.

NOTES.

Prices for materials and labor, on which all costs of structures are based, are given on page 103.

Many people think it an unnecessary expense to invest in Working Plans, etc.; that their builders can draw up plans or follow rough sketches of their own. This is a great error. It would be true economy to pay even five times as much as our charges for proper drawings, etc. Without them mistakes are sure to occur, and to rectify a single mistake often costs much more than the cost of the plans.

It is also impossible to get a low or correct estimate without the Working Plans and Specifications.

Plans may be returned to us if cost exceeds our estimate. (For terms see page 103.)

Residence, Design No. 1245

PERSPECTIVE.

DESCRIPTION.

GENERAL DIMENSIONS: Extreme width through kitchen and dining-room, 28 ft.; depth, not including veranda, 28 ft. 10 ins.

HEIGHTS OF STORIES: Cellar, 7 ft.; first story, 9 ft.; second story, 8 ft. 6 ins.

EXTERIOR MATERIALS: Foundation, brick; first story, clapboards; second story, gables and roofs, shingles.

INTERIOR FINISH: Two coat plaster, hard white finish. Kitchen and bath-room, wainscoted. Soft wood flooring and trim throughout. Kitchen and dining-room finished in oak; elsewhere white wood. Oak floor in hall and dining-room; elsewhere Georgia pine. Picture molding in parlor, hall and dining-room. Chair-rail in dining-room.

COLORS: Clapboards, Nile green. Trim, including water-table, corner boards, cornices, casings, bands, veranda columns, rail, etc., dark bottle green. Sashes, red. Shingling on side walls and gables dipped in and brush coated with light sienna stain. Shingles on roof dipped in and brush coated with dark sienna stain.

ACCOMMODATIONS: The principal rooms and their sizes, closets, etc., are shown by the floor plans. Cellar under the whole house, with inside and outside entrance and concrete floor. Large veranda across front and around side. Bay-window in parlor. Portière openings connect hall, parlor and dining-room. Entrance to cellar through pantry which contains ample shelving. Flue for portable range in kitchen. Sink and two set-tubs in kitchen. Hat and coat closet in first story hall. Bath-room, with full plumbing, in second story. Enclosed stairs to attic with closet underneath. Attic floored but otherwise unfinished.

COST: $2,560,† not including mantels, range or heater. The estimate is based on ‡ New York prices for materials and labor. In many sections of the country the cost should be less.

Price of working plans (with full details drawn to large scale), specifications and * license to build, ... $25.00

Price of †† bill of materials, ... 10.00

FEASIBLE MODIFICATIONS: General dimensions, material and colors may be changed. Cellar may be reduced in size or entirely omitted and house set upon brick piers. Uncovered part of veranda may be roofed over or veranda may be reduced in size. Brick-set range may be placed in kitchen and open fireplace planned in dining-room. Sliding doors may be substituted for portière openings. Wash-tubs may be transferred to cellar. Tower may be carried up another story and a room planned in attic.

The price of working plans, specifications, etc., for a modified design varies according to the alterations required, and will be made known upon application to the Architects.

Address, THE CO-OPERATIVE BUILDING PLAN ASSOCIATION, Architects, 106–108 Fulton Street, New York.

FIRST FLOOR.

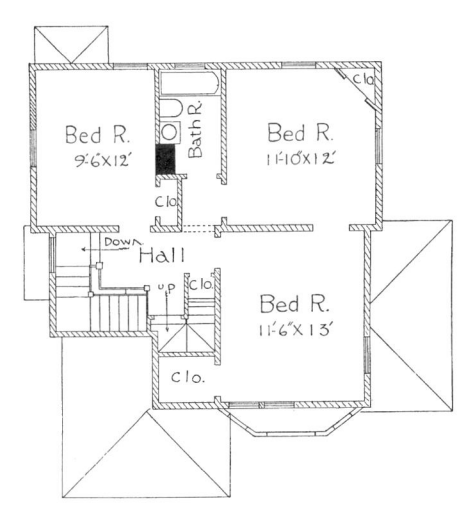

SECOND FLOOR.

Residence, Design No. 1246

PERSPECTIVE.

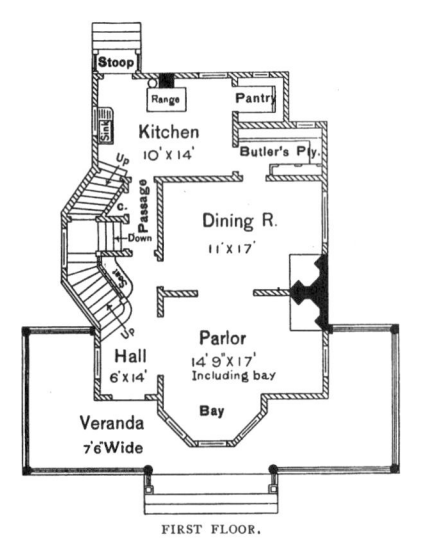

FIRST FLOOR.

SECOND FLOOR.

DESCRIPTION.

GENERAL DIMENSIONS: Width, including veranda, 39 ft. 6 ins.; depth, including veranda, 40 ft. 6 ins.

HEIGHTS OF STORIES: Cellar, 6 ft. 6 ins.; first story, 9 ft.; second story, 8 ft. 6 in.

EXTERIOR MATERIALS: Foundation, brick; side walls, gables and roofs, shingles. Roof over staircase bay, tin.

INTERIOR FINISH: Two coat plaster, hard white finish. Soft wood flooring and trim. Main stairs, ash. Bathroom and kitchen, wainscoted. All interior wood-work finished with hard oil.

COLORS: All shingles on side walls and gables to be left unfinished for weather stain. All roof shingling, dipped and brush coated moss green stain. Trim, sashes and blinds, ivory white. Veranda floor and ceiling, oiled.

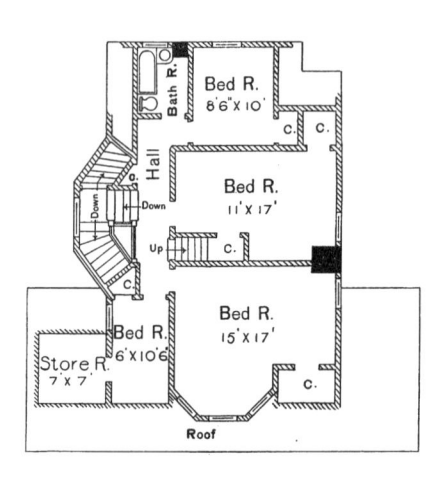

ACCOMMODATIONS: The principal rooms and their sizes, closets, etc., are shown by the floor plans. Cellar under the whole house, with inside and outside entrances. Attic floored for storage. Bath-room with full plumbing in second story. Back stairs from kitchen connect with main stairs at landing. Double folding doors between parlor and hall and parlor and dining-room. Bay window in parlor and bedroom over. Open fireplaces in parlor and dining-room. Numerous and large closets. Large storeroom connecting with small front bedroom.

COST: $2,575, † not including mantels, range and heater. The estimate is based on ‡ New York prices for materials and labor. In many sections of the country the cost should be less.

Price of working plans (with full details drawn to large scale), specifications and * license to build, ... $25.00
Price of †† bill of materials, ... 10.00

FEASIBLE MODIFICATIONS: General dimensions, materials and colors may be changed. Cellar may be reduced in size or wholly omitted. Laundry tubs could be introduced in cellar. A servant's room could be finished off in attic. Double sliding doors could be used between dining-room and parlor. Bath-room may be omitted and the space thrown into the rear bedroom.

The price of working plans, specifications, etc., for a modified design, varies according to the alterations required, and will be made known upon application to the Architects.

Address, THE CO-OPERATIVE BUILDING PLAN ASSOCIATION, Architects, 106–108 Fulton Street, New York.

Residence, Design No. 1247

PERSPECTIVE.

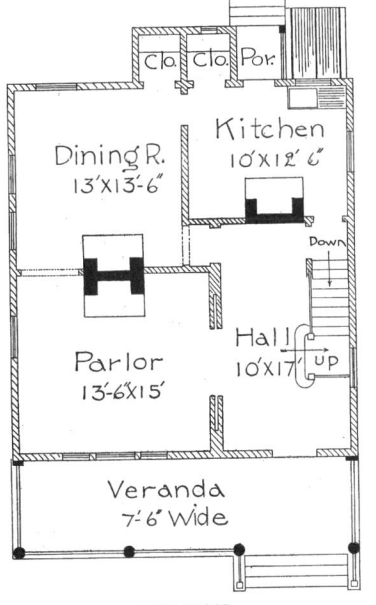

FIRST FLOOR.

SECOND FLOOR.

DESCRIPTION.

GENERAL DIMENSIONS: Width, 27 ft.; depth, 28 ft. 6 ins., not including porch and veranda.

HEIGHTS OF STORIES: Cellar, 7 ft.; first story, 9 ft. 6 ins.; second story, 9 ft.; attic, 8 ft.

EXTERIOR MATERIALS: Foundation, brick; first and second stories, gables and roofs, shingles.

INTERIOR FINISH: Two coat plaster, hard white finish. Soft wood flooring. Trim throughout, N. C. pine. Staircase, ash. Bath room and kitchen, wainscoted. Chair-rail in dining-room. All interior wood-work, grain filled and finished with hard oil varnish.

COLORS: First story shingles, green. Shingling on walls of second story and gables, oiled. Roof shingles stained red. Trim, including water-table, corner boards, casings, cornices, bands, veranda posts, rail, etc., dark bottle green. Sashes, white. Veranda floor, dark brown. Veranda ceiling and brick-work, oiled.

ACCOMMODATIONS: The principal rooms and their sizes, closets, etc., are shown by the floor plans. Cellar under whole house. Attic is floored for storage purposes. One room and hall finished off in attic. Open fireplaces in dining room and parlor. Brick-set range, sink and boiler in kitchen. Bathroom in second story. Linen closet in second story hall. Two set-tubs in cellar. Double sliding doors connect hall and parlor. Portière opening between parlor and dining-room. Large sized veranda with open balcony above.

COST: $2,600, † not including mantels, range or heater. The estimate is based on ‡ New York prices for materials and labor. In many sections of the country the cost should be less.

Price of working plans (with full details drawn to large scale), specifications and * license to build, ... $25.00

Price of †† bill of materials, ... 10.00

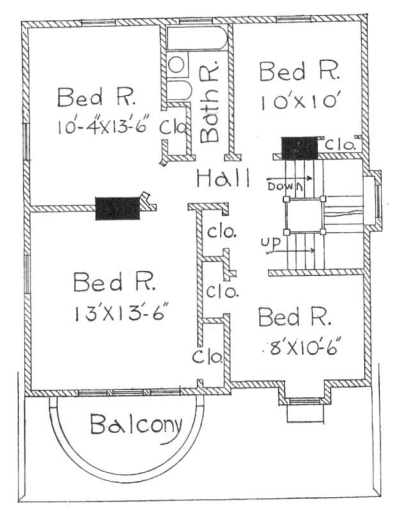

FEASIBLE MODIFICATIONS: General dimensions, materials and colors may be changed. Cellar may be reduced in size or wholly omitted. Any or all fireplaces, sliding doors, and part or all of plumbing may be omitted. Attic may be left unfinished. One chimney will suffice if heating apparatus be used.

The price of working plans, specifications, etc., for a modified design, varies according to the alterations required and will be made known upon application to the Architects.

Address, THE CO-OPERATIVE BUILDING PLAN ASSOCIATION, Architects, 106–108 Fulton Street, New York.

Residence, Design No. 1248

PERSPECTIVE.

FIRST FLOOR.   SECOND FLOOR.

DESCRIPTION.

GENERAL DIMENSIONS: Width, including veranda, 39 ft. 10 ins.; depth, including parlor bay, 38 ft. 6 ins.

HEIGHTS OF STORIES: Cellar, 7 ft.; first story, 9 ft.; second story, 8 ft. 6 ins.

EXTERIOR MATERIALS: Foundation, brick; first story, clapboards; second story, gables and roofs, shingles.

INTERIOR FINISH: Two coat plaster, hard white finish. Plaster centers in parlor, dining-room and first story hall. Picture moulding in parlor, dining-room and hall. Chair-rail in dining-room. Soft wood flooring and trim throughout. All interior wood-work grain filled, stained to suit owner, and finished with hard oil varnish.

COLORS: Clapboards, dark sienna. Trim, including corner boards, cornices, casings, bands, veranda column, rail, etc., white. Shingles in gables dipped in and brush coated with dark sienna stain. Shingles on roofs dipped in and brush coated with moss green stain. Veranda floor and ceiling, oiled. Sashes red.

ACCOMMODATIONS: The principal rooms and their sizes, closets, etc., are shown by the floor plans. Cellar under whole house, with inside and outside entrance and concrete floor. Open fireplace in dining-room. False fireplace in parlor. Flue for portable range in kitchen. Two set-tubs, sink and boiler in kitchen. Portière openings connect hall, parlor and dining-room. Bath-room in second story with full plumbing.

COST: $2,680, † not including mantels, range or heater. The estimate is based on ‡ New York prices for materials and labor. In many sections of the country the cost should be less.

FEASIBLE MODIFICATIONS: General dimensions, materials and colors may be changed. Cellar may be reduced in size or wholly omitted. Laundry may be planned in cellar and tubs transferred from kitchen. Fireplaces may be omitted, or an additional chimney may be built and fireplace introduced in bedrooms and parlor. Sliding doors may be substituted for portière openings. Butler's pantry may be planned in place of closets at rear of kitchen and dining room. Veranda may be reduced in size, or carried around to dining-room bay.

Price of working-plans (with full details drawn to large scale), specifications and * license to build, ... $25.00

Price of †† bill of materials, ... 10.00

The price of working plans, specifications, etc., for a modified design, varies according to the alterations required, and will be made known upon application to the Architects.

Address, THE CO OPERATIVE BUILDING PLAN ASSOCIATION, Architects, 106-108 Fulton Street, New York.

Residence, Design No. 1249

PERSPECTIVE.

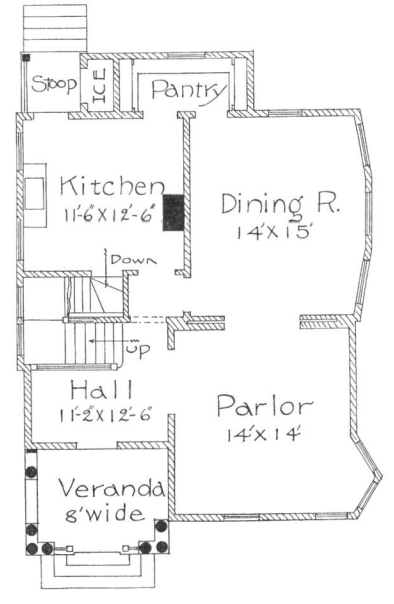

FIRST FLOOR.

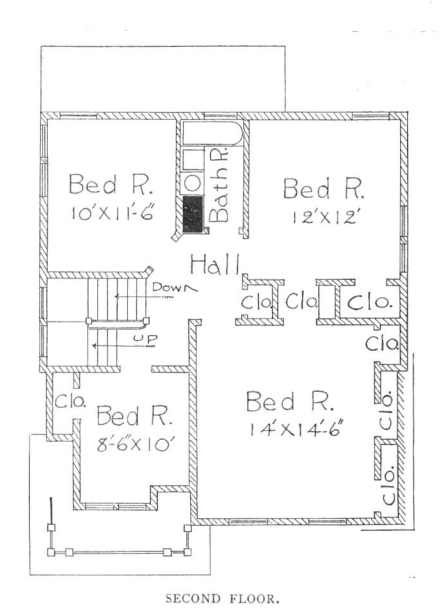

SECOND FLOOR.

DESCRIPTION.

GENERAL DIMENSIONS: Width, 28 ft.; depth, 35 ft. 6 ins., not including veranda.

HEIGHTS OF STORIES: Cellar, 7 ft.; first story, 9 ft.; second story, 8 ft. 6 ins.; attic, 8 ft.

EXTERIOR MATERIALS: Foundation, brick; first story, clapboards; second story, gables, roof and veranda enclosure, shingles.

INTERIOR FINISH: Two coat plaster, hard white finish. Oak floor and staircase in hall; remainder of flooring and trim, soft wood. Kitchen and bath-room, waiscoted. Chair rail in dining room. All interior wood-work grain filled, stained to suit owner and finished with hard oil varnish.

COLORS: Clapboards, light chocolate. Trim, dark chocolate. Shingling on side walls stained umber. Roof shingles stained red. Outside doors, brickwork, veranda floor and ceiling, oiled. Sashes, red.

ACCOMMODATIONS: The principal rooms and their sizes, closets, etc., are shown by the floor plans. Cellar under the whole house. Butler's closet, containing shelving and drawers, connects dining-room and kitchen. Portable range, sink and boiler in kitchen. Bath room in second story, containing wash-bowl, tub and closet. Linen closet in second story. Two set-tubs in laundry placed in cellar. One room finished off in attic, remainder of space floored for storage purposes.

COST: $2,700, † not including mantels, range or heater. The estimate is based on ‡ New York prices for materials and labor. In many sections of the country the cost should be less.

Price of working plans (with full details drawn to large scale), specifications and * license to build, ... $30.00

Price of †† bill of materials, . . 10.00

FEASIBLE MODIFICATIONS: General dimensions, materials and colors may be changed. Cellar may be reduced in size or wholly omitted. Butler's closet and ice-box closet may be omitted and a door between kitchen and dining-room introduced. An additional chimney may be built and a fireplace planned in parlor. Sliding doors may be omitted and portière opening substituted. Attic may be left unfinished. Veranda may be extended across the entire front of house or carried around hall side to kitchen.

The price of working plans, specifications, etc., for a modified design, varies according to the alterations required and will be made known upon application to the Architects.

Address, THE CO-OPERATIVE BUILDING PLAN ASSOCIATION, Architects, 106–108 Fulton Street, New York.

Residence, Design No. 1258

PERSPECTIVE.

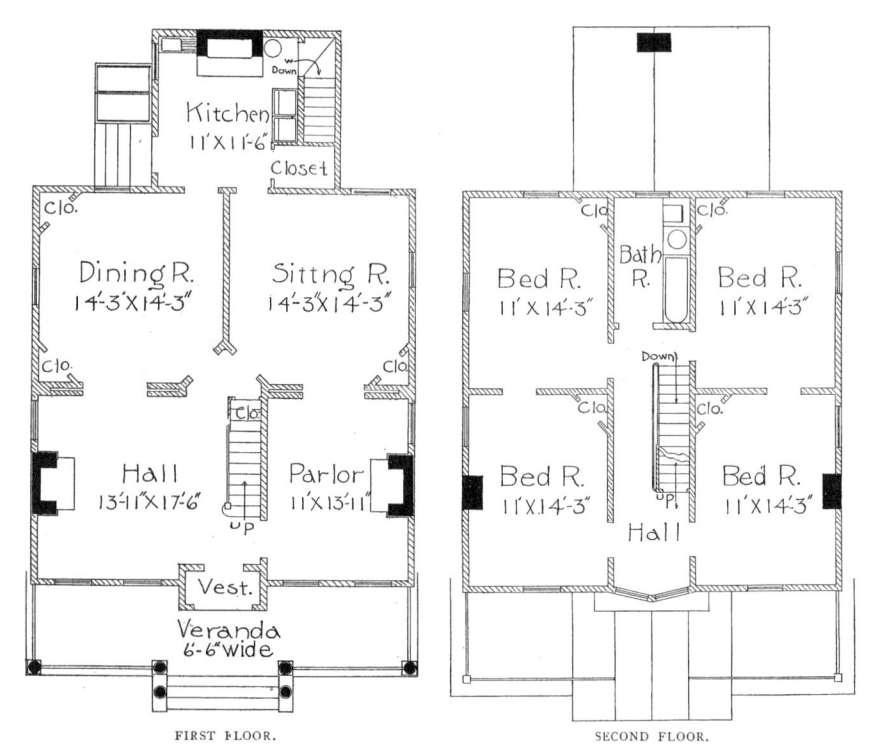

FIRST FLOOR.

SECOND FLOOR.

DESCRIPTION.

GENERAL DIMENSIONS: Width, 30 ft.; depth, including veranda, 48 ft. 6 ins.

HEIGHTS OF STORIES: Cellar, 7 ft.; first story, 9 ft. 6 ins.; second story, 9 ft.; attic, 8 ft. 6 ins.

EXTERIOR MATERIALS: Foundation, brick; first story, clapboards; second story, gables and roof, shingles.

INTERIOR FINISH: Two coat plaster, hard white finish. Plaster centers in parlor, sitting-room, dining-room and hall of first story. Flooring and trim throughout, North Carolina pine. Main staircase, ash. Bath-room and kitchen wainscoted. Chair-rail in dining-room. All interior wood-work, grain filled and finished with hard oil varnish.

COLORS: All clapboards, dark gray. Trim, including water-table, corner boards, casings, cornices, bands, outside blinds, veranda posts, rail, etc., dark green. Shingling on side walls left natural. Shingle roofs dipped and brush coated brown stain. Sashes, white. Veranda floor and ceiling and outside doors, grain filled and finished with hard oil.

ACCOMMODATIONS: The principal rooms and their sizes, closets, etc., are shown by the floor plans. Cellar under the whole house, with inside and outside entrances and concrete floor. Brick-set range, sink, boiler and two set-tubs in kitchen. Sliding doors connect dining-room and hall, and sitting room and parlor. Open fireplace in dining-room and parlor. Hat and coat closet under main staircase.

COST: $2,750, † not including mantels, range or heater. The estimate is based on ‡ New York prices for materials and labor. In many sections of the country the cost should be less.

Price of working plans (with full details drawn to large scale) and specifications, ... $30.00
Price of †† bill of materials, ... 10.00

FEASIBLE MODIFICATIONS: General dimensions, materials and colors may be changed. Cellar may be reduced in size or wholly omitted and house set on brick piers or wooden posts. A laundry may be placed in cellar under kitchen. Kitchen wing may be carried up another story, making an additional bedroom. Any or all fireplaces and part or all of plumbing may be omitted. Double sliding doors may be omitted. Portière openings may be made to connect dining room and parlor with hall. Veranda may extend on both sides.

The price of working plans, specifications, etc., for a modified design, varies according to the alterations required and will be made known upon application to the Architects.

Address, THE CO-OPERATIVE BUILDING PLAN ASSOCIATION, Architects, 106–108 Fulton Street, New York.

Residence, Design No. 1259

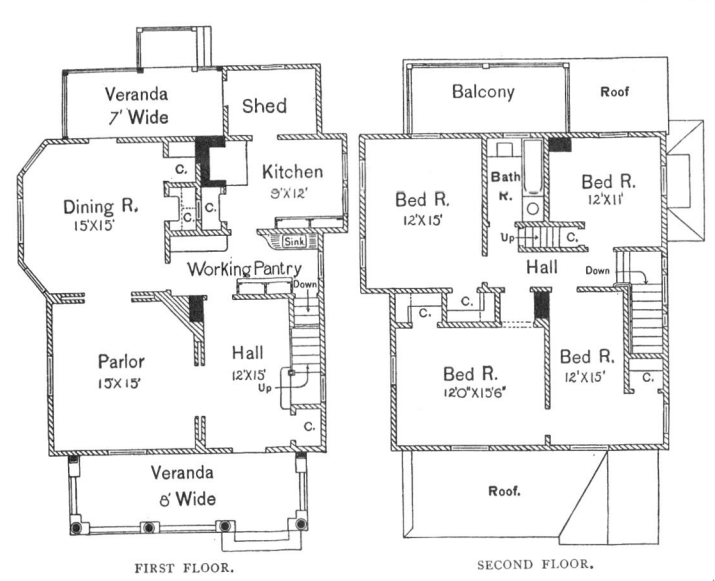

PERSPECTIVE.

FIRST FLOOR.   SECOND FLOOR.

DESCRIPTION.

GENERAL DIMENSIONS: Width, through dining-room and kitchen, 34 ft. 6 ins.; depth, including veranda and shed, 47 ft.

HEIGHTS OF STORIES: Cellar, 7 ft.; first story, 9 ft. 6 ins.; second story, 9 ft.

EXTERIOR MATERIALS: Foundation, brick; first story, clapboards; second story, gables, under portion of veranda railing and roofs, shingles.

INTERIOR FINISH: Three coat plaster, hard white finish throughout. Soft wood flooring and trim. Main staircase, ash. Kitchen and bath-room, wainscoted. All interior wood-work, grain filled, stained to suit owner and finished with hard oil varnish.

COLORS: Clapboards, Colonial yellow. Trim, doors and sashes, white. Shingling on side walls, gables, roofs, etc., left unfinished for weather stain. Veranda floors and ceilings, oiled.

ACCOMMODATIONS: The principal rooms and their sizes, closets, etc., are shown by the floor plans. Cellar under the whole house, with inside and outside entrances and concrete floor. Laundry under dining-room, with two set-tubs. Remainder of cellar is divided into vegetable cellar, furnace-room and coal bins. The attic is floored for storage, but otherwise unfinished. Brick-set range in kitchen. Bath-room with complete plumbing in second story. Balcony over rear veranda. Double sliding doors between dining-room and parlor and parlor and hall. Wide verandas.

COST: $2,800, † not including mantels, range and heater. The estimate is based on ‡ New York prices for materials and labor. In many sections of the country the cost should be less.

Price of working plans (with full details drawn to large scale), specifications and * license to build, - - - - - $30.00

Price of †† bill of materials, - - - - - 10.00

FEASIBLE MODIFICATIONS: General dimensions, materials and colors may be changed. Cellar may be reduced in size or entirely omitted. The laundry tubs may be transferred to the shed, or placed in kitchen. An open fireplace may be introduced in parlor. Three or four rooms may be finished in the attic. Portable range may be used instead of brick-set one. Shed may be omitted or enlarged.

The price of working plans, specifications, etc., for a modified design, varies according to the alterations required and will be made known upon application to the Architects.

Address, THE CO-OPERATIVE BUILDING PLAN ASSOCIATION, Architects, 106-108 Fulton Street, New York.

Residence, Design No. 1260

PERSPECTIVE.

DESCRIPTION.

GENERAL DIMENSIONS: Extreme width, 46 ft. 6 ins.; depth, not including front veranda, 37 ft.

HEIGHTS OF STORIES: Cellar, 7 ft.; first story, 9 ft.; second story, 8 ft. 6 ins.

EXTERIOR MATERIALS: Foundation, brick piers except where cellar occurs, there 12 in. brick walls are to be used; first and second stories, gables and roofs, shingles; balcony floor covered with leaded tin.

INTERIOR FINISH: Two coat plaster, hard white finish. Plaster centres in parlor, dining-room, sitting-room and hall. Soft wood flooring throughout. Trim, N. C. pine. Main staircase, ash. Chair-rail in dining-room. All interior woodwork grain filled, stained to suit owner and finished with hard oil varnish.

COLORS: Trim, including casings, cornices, bands, veranda rail, etc., white. Shingling on side walls to be dipped and brush coated with olive green stain. Shingled roofs, stained red. Sashes, dark bottle green. Blinds, dark bottle green. Veranda floor and ceiling, oiled.

ACCOMMODATIONS: The principal rooms and their sizes, closets, etc., are shown by the floor plans. Cellar under kitchen and hall, with inside entrance and concrete floor. Butler's pantry connects kitchen and dining-room, and contains dresser and shelving. Dish pass between kitchen and dining-room. Open fireplaces in parlor and dining-room. Kitchen closet under main stairs. Piano alcove in parlor. Portière opening connects sitting-room, hall and parlor. Entrance from dining-room to side veranda and from bedroom to balcony. Bathroom with full plumbing in second story.

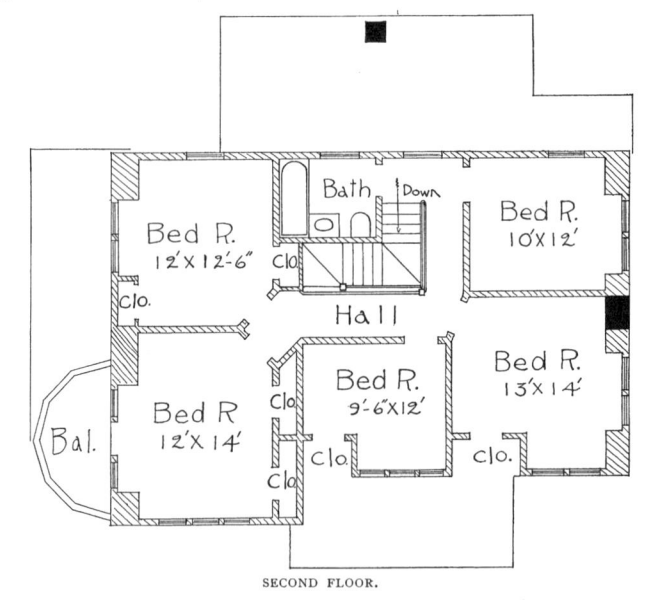

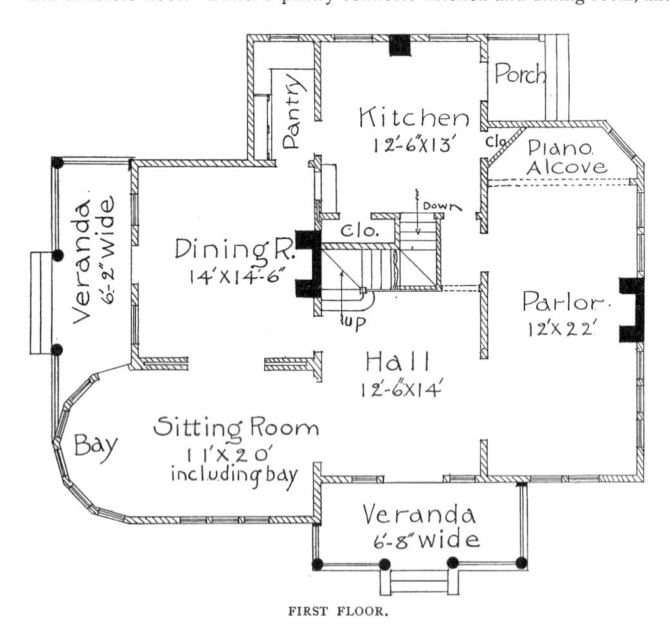

COST: $2,900 † not including plumbing, mantels, range or heater. The estimate is based on ‡ New York prices for materials and labor. In many sections of the country the cost should be less.

Price of working plans (with full details drawn to large scale), specifications and * license to build, ... $30.00
Price of †† bill of materials, ... 10.00

FEASIBLE MODIFICATIONS: General dimensions, materials and colors may be changed. Roof may be raised and one or two rooms finished off in attic, in which case a staircase could be planned to go up over main stairs. Fireplaces and part or all of plumbing may be omitted. Veranda may be extended. Parlor may be divided, thus obtaining an additional room.

The price of working plans, specifications, etc., for a modified design, varies according to the alterations required and will be made known upon application to the Architects.

Address, THE CO-OPERATIVE BUILDING PLAN ASSOCIATION, Architects, 106-108 Fulton Street, New York.

FIRST FLOOR.

SECOND FLOOR.

Two-family Residence, Design No. 1261

PERSPECTIVE.

DESCRIPTION.

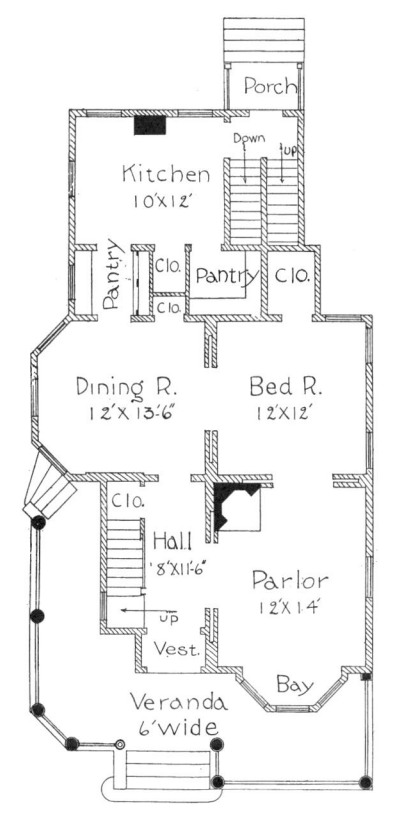

GENERAL DIMENSIONS: Width, through bedroom and dining-room, 27 ft. 6 ins.; depth, not including parlor bay or veranda, 46 ft.

HEIGHTS OF STORIES: Cellar, 7 ft.; first story, 9 ft.; second story, 9 ft.

EXTERIOR MATERIALS. Foundation, brick; first story, clapboards; second story, gables and roof, shingles.

INTERIOR FINISH: Two coat plaster, hard white finish. Plaster cornices and centres in parlors, dining-rooms and halls. Trim and floors throughout, white wood. Kitchens and bath-rooms, wainscoted. All interior wood-work stained to suit owner.

COLORS: Clapboards, fawn brown. Trim, including water-table, corner boards, cornices, casings, etc., white. Shingles in second story and gables, oiled. Roof shingles dipped in and brush coated with dark red stain.

ACCOMMODATIONS: The principal rooms and their sizes, closets, etc., are shown by the floor plans. Cellar under the whole house, with inside and outside entrance and concrete floor. Attic unfinished, but floored for storage purposes. Double sliding doors connect hall, parlor, bedroom and dining-room on first floor, also hall and parlor on second floor. Portière openings in second story between bedroom and dining-room. Bathroom in second story with complete plumbing. Water-closet in cellar. Open fireplaces in parlors. Thimble for portable range in kitchens. Butler's pantry, containing dresser and necessary shelving, connects kitchen and dining-room in first story. Rear stairs to second story, also attractive front staircase with hat and coat closet underneath.

COST: $2,950, † not including plumbing, mantels, ranges, or heater. The estimate is based on ‡ New York prices for materials and labor. In many sections of the country the cost should be less.

Price of working plans (with full details drawn to large scale), specifications and * license to build, ... $30.00
Price of †† bill of materials, ... 10.00

FEASIBLE MODIFICATIONS: General dimensions, materials and colors may be changed. Cellar may be reduced in size or wholly omitted. Fireplaces may be omitted, or additional fireplaces planned in dining-rooms. A bath-room may be planned in first story directly under the present bathroom. One or two rooms may be finished off in attic. Double folding doors or portière openings may be substituted for sliding doors. Brick-set ranges may be used in place of portable ones. This design is planned for two families, but by using the second story for bedrooms, and finishing off two rooms in attic, it would make a commodious residence for a large family.

The price of working plans, specifications, etc., for a modified design, varies according to the alterations required and will be made known upon application to the Architects.

Address, THE CO-OPERATIVE BUILDING PLAN ASSOCIATION, Architects, 106–108 Fulton Street, New York.

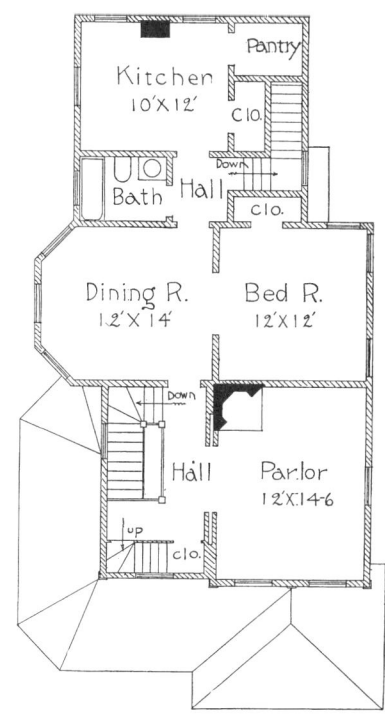

FIRST FLOOR.

SECOND FLOOR.

65

Residence, Design No. 1262

PERSPECTIVE.

FIRST FLOOR.

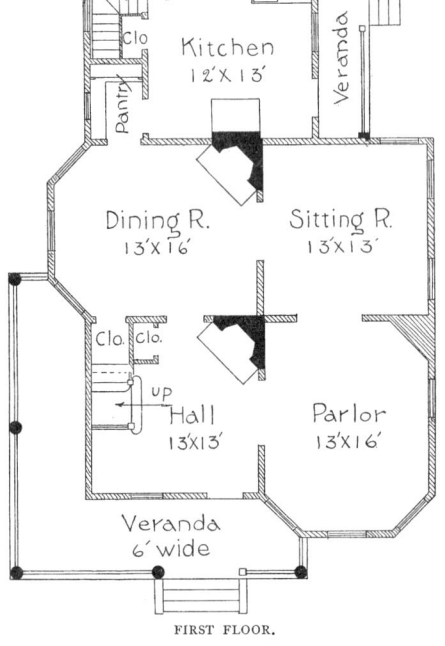

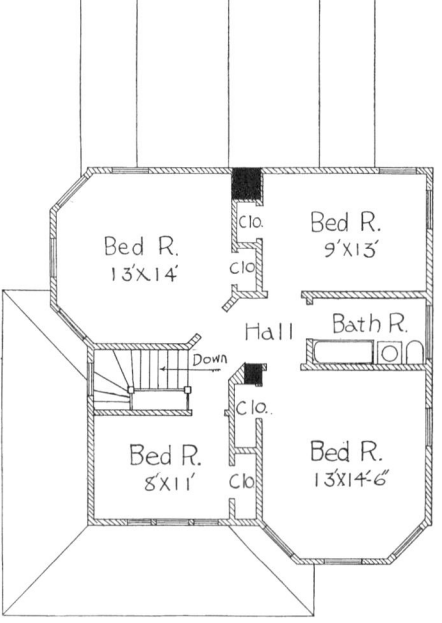

SECOND FLOOR.

DESCRIPTION.

GENERAL DIMENSIONS: Width, through dining-room and back parlor, 33 ft. 6 ins.; depth, including bay-window, 43 ft.

HEIGHTS OF STORIES: Cellar, 7 ft.; first story, 9 ft.; second story, 9 ft.

EXTERIOR MATERIALS: Foundation, stone; first and second stories, clapboards; band between first and second stories, band under eaves, gables, dormers and roofs, shingles.

INTERIOR FINISH: Two coat plaster, hard white finish. Flooring and trim in hall, oak; elsewhere, N. C. pine. Oak staircase. Kitchen walls wainscoted. All interior wood-work grain filled and finished with hard oil varnish.

COLORS: All clapboards, fawn brown. Trim, including water-table, corner boards, cornices, casings, bands, veranda columns, rail, etc., white. Outside doors, varnished. Sashes, red. Veranda floor and ceiling, oiled. Shingles on side walls left natural for weather stain. Shingled roofs stained a deep red.

ACCOMMODATIONS: The principal rooms and their sizes, closets, etc., are shown by the floor plans. Cellar under rear half of house with inside and outside entrance. Portière openings connect hall, parlor, sitting-room and dining-room. Open fireplaces in hall and dining-room. Hat and coat closet in hall. Butler's pantry, containing dresser, connects kitchen and dining-room. False breast in parlor for mantel. Portable range and sink in kitchen. Bath-room in second story, with full plumbing. Ample closet room. Wide veranda across front and around side of house. Deck roof accessible from attic through a scuttle. Attic unfinished, except for storage purposes.

COST: $2,985, † not including plumbing, mantels, range or heater. The estimate is based on ‡ New York prices for materials and labor. In many sections of the country the cost should be less.

Price of working plans (with full details drawn to large scale), specifications and * license to build, ... $30.00

Price of †† bill of materials, . . 10.00

FEASIBLE MODIFICATIONS: General dimensions, materials and colors may be changed. Cellar may be extended under the whole house, or entirely omitted. Fireplaces may be omitted, or additional fireplaces planned for parlor and sitting-room. Brick-set range can be substituted for portable one. Staircase can be planned to attic, and one or two rooms finished off in same. Veranda may be extended across the entire front of house. Kitchen extension may be carried up another story, making an additional bedroom.

The price of working plans, specifications, etc., for a modified design, varies according to the alterations required and will be made known upon application to the Architects.

Address, THE CO-OPERATIVE BUILDING PLAN ASSOCIATION, Architects, 106-108 Fulton Street, New York.

Residence, Design No. 1263

PERSPECTIVE.

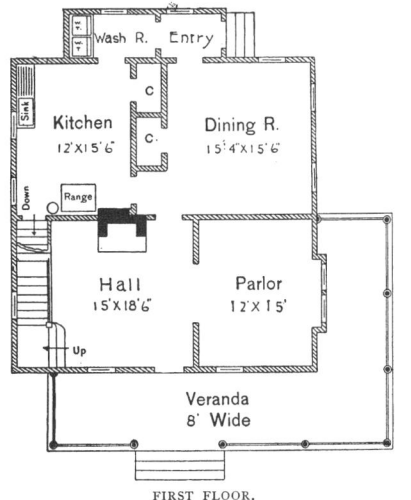

FIRST FLOOR.

SECOND FLOOR.

DESCRIPTION.

GENERAL DIMENSIONS: Width, including veranda, 40 ft.; width through dining-room and kitchen, 32 ft.; depth, including veranda and wash-room extension, 45 ft.

HEIGHTS OF STORIES: Cellar, 6 ft. 6 ins.; first story, 9 ft.; second story, 8 ft 6 ins.; attic, 8 ft.

EXTERIOR MATERIALS: Foundation, stone; first and second stories, clapboards; main roof and sides of dormers, shingles; roofs of outlook and veranda, tin.

INTERIOR FINISH: Three coat plaster, hard white finish. Soft wood flooring and trim. Kitchen and hall wainscoted. Chair-rail in dining-room. Main stairs, Georgia pine. All interior woodwork, grain filled and finished with hard oil.

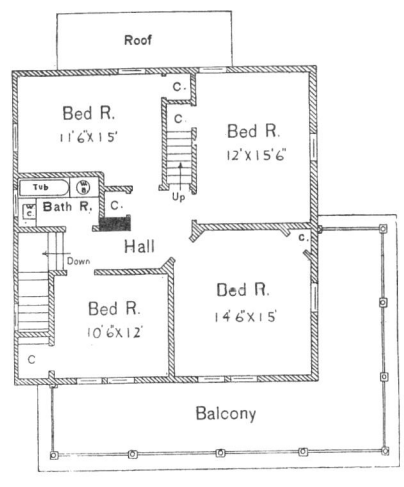

COLORS: All clapboards first and second stories, also blinds and sashes, Colonial yellow. Trim, including water-table, pilasters, casings, cornices, frieze, bands, veranda columns and rails, outside doors, conductors, etc., cream white. Veranda floor and ceiling, oiled. Shingled roofs, dark red.

ACCOMMODATIONS: The principal rooms and their sizes, closets, etc., are shown by the floor plans. Cellar under whole house with inside and outside entrances and concrete floor. Two rooms finished in attic; remainder of attic floored for storage. Access to roof outlook through scuttle. Double doors between hall and parlor. Open fireplace in hall. Balcony over veranda. Separate wash-room off kitchen, with two stationary tubs.

COST: $3,000, † not including mantels, range and heater. The estimate is based on ‡ New York prices for labor and materials.

Price of working plans (with full details drawn to large scale), specifications, and * license to build, . . . $30.00

Price of †† bill of materials, ... 10.00

FEASIBLE MODIFICATIONS: General dimensions, materials and colors may be changed. Cellar may be decreased in size or wholly omitted. One or both of the attic rooms could be omitted. Veranda could be extended around both sides of the house, or the present side veranda could be omitted. Sliding doors could be introduced between hall and parlor and between parlor and dining-room.

The price of working plans, specifications, etc., for a modified design, varies according to the alterations required and will be made known upon application to the Architects.

Address, THE CO-OPERATIVE BUILDING PLAN ASSOCIATION, Architects, 106–108 Fulton Street, New York.

Residence, Design No. 1264

PERSPECTIVE.

DESCRIPTION.

GENERAL DIMENSIONS: Width, including music-room, 36 ft. 6 ins.; depth, including parlor, bay and kitchen, 48 ft. 6 ins.

HEIGHTS OF STORIES: Cellar, 7 ft.; first story, 9 ft.; second story, 8 ft. 6 ins.

EXTERIOR MATERIALS: Foundation, stone; first story, clapboards; second story, gables, roofs and side walls and piers of veranda, shingles.

INTERIOR FINISH: Two coat plaster, hard white finish. Soft wood flooring and trim. Main staircase, oak. Panel backs under windows in parlor, hall and dining-room. Picture molding in principal rooms and hall, first story. Bath-room and kitchen, wainscoted. All interior woodwork finished natural in hard oil varnish.

COLORS: All clapboards, yellow drab. Trim, olive. Rear outside door, bronze green. Front door finished natural with hard oil varnish. Blinds, bronze green. Sashes and conductors, bright red.

ACCOMMODATIONS: The principal rooms and their sizes, closets, etc., are shown by the floor plans. Cellar under the whole house with inside and outside entrances. Attic floored for storage purposes. Bath-room with complete plumbing in second story. Sink in kitchen. Open fireplace in hall. Attractive main staircase with lounging seat. Large butler's pantry and dining-room closet. Balcony in second story over porch.

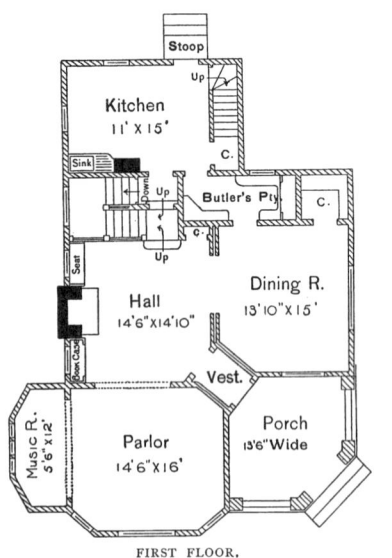

COST: $3,000, † not including mantels, range and heater.

The estimate is based on ‡ New York prices for materials and labor. In many sections of the country the cost should be less.

Price of working plans (with full details drawn to large scale), specifications and * license to build, . . . $35.00

Price of †† bill of materials, . . . 10.00

FEASIBLE MODIFICATIONS: General dimensions, materials and colors may be changed. A• laundry could be planned in cellar under kitchen. Music-room may be omitted. Parlor and hall may be divided by double sliding doors. Additional veranda could be added at the front or side. Cellar may be reduced in size.

The price of working plans, specifications, etc., for a modified design, varies according to the alterations required, and will be made known upon application to the Architects.

Address, THE CO-OPERATIVE BUILDING PLAN ASSOCIATION, Architects, 106–108 Fulton Street, New York.

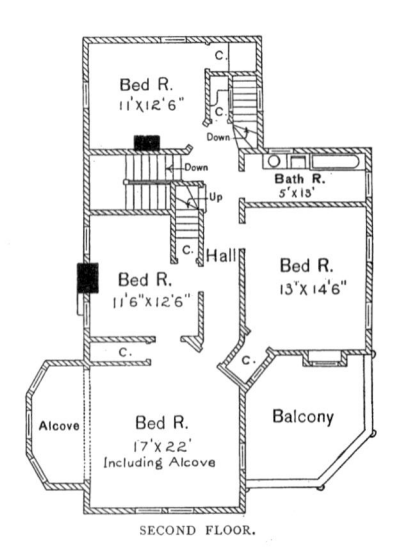

FIRST FLOOR.

SECOND FLOOR.

Residence, Design No. 1265

PERSPECTIVE.

DESCRIPTION.

GENERAL DIMENSIONS: Width, 33 ft.; depth, including veranda, 43 ft. 6 ins.

HEIGHTS OF STORIES: Cellar, 6 ft. 6 ins.; first story, 9 ft.: second story, 8 ft.

EXTERIOR MATERIALS: Foundation, stone; first story, clapboards; second story, gables and roofs, shingles.

INTERIOR FINISH: Hard white plaster throughout. First floor double, with paper between. Finished flooring, first story, hard pine; second story flooring, soft wood. Attic has a rough floor for storage purposes. Trim, white pine. Main staircase, ash. Bath-room, wainscoted. Chair-rail in kitchen. All interior woodwork, grain filled and finished with hard oil varnish.

COLORS: All clapboards, gray. Trim, including water-table, corner boards, casings, cornices, bands, veranda posts, rail, etc., olive drab. Outside doors, light olive drab. Sashes, dark red. Veranda and porch floors and ceilings, oiled. Shingling on side walls and roofs, left natural for weather stain.

ACCOMMODATIONS: The principal rooms and their sizes, closets, etc., are shown by the floor plans. Cellar under the whole house, with inside and outside entrances and concrete floor. Laundry with three set-tubs under parlor. Attic unfinished, except laying floor. Bath-room with complete plumbing in the second story. Rear stairway from kitchen, connecting at platform with main staircase. Broad veranda. Fireplaces in reception room and parlor. Portière openings between reception-room and dining-room and parlor and reception-room.

COST: $3,000, † not including mantels, range and heater. The estimate is based on ‡ New York prices for materials and labor. In many sections of the country the cost should be less.

Price of working plans (with full details drawn to large scale), specifications and * license to build, ... $25.00

Price of †† bill of materials, . . 10.00

FEASIBLE MODIFICATIONS: General dimensions, materials and colors may be changed. Cellar may be reduced in size or entirely omitted. Laundry in cellar may be omitted and the tubs transferred to the kitchen. Two or three large rooms may be finished in the attic. Fireplace may be introduced in the dining-room. A portion or all the plumbing may be omitted. Hall may be separate from reception-room. This change would reduce the size of the reception-room to 12 ft. by 13 ft. 2 ins.

The price of working plans, specifications, etc., for a modified design, varies according to the alterations required and will be made known on application to the Architects.

Address, THE CO-OPERATIVE BUILDING PLAN ASSOCIATION, Architects, 106-108 Fulton Street, New York.

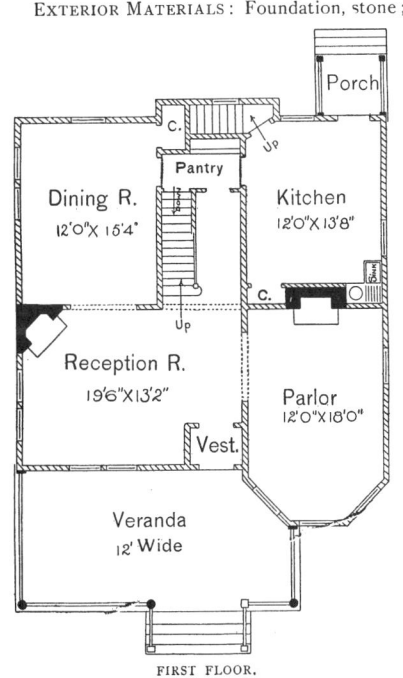

FIRST FLOOR.

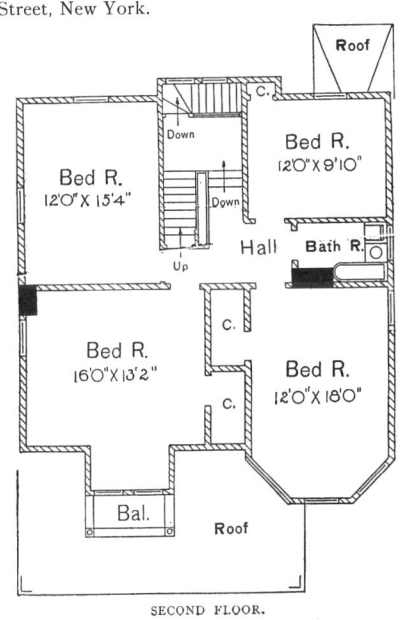

SECOND FLOOR.

Residence, Design No. 1266

PERSPECTIVE.

DESCRIPTION.

GENERAL DIMENSIONS: Width, not including veranda, 32 ft. 6 ins.; depth, not including veranda, 35 ft. 7 ins.

HEIGHTS OF STORIES: Cellar, 7 ft.; first story, 9 ft. 6 ins.; second story, 9 ft.; attic, 8 ft.

EXTERIOR MATERIALS: Foundation, brick; first story, clapboards; second story, gables, roofs and balcony enclosure, shingles.

INTERIOR FINISH: Two coats plaster, hard white finish. Plaster centres in parlor, hall and dining-room. Flooring and trim throughout, N. C. pine. Bath-room and kitchen, wainscoted. Chair-rail in dining-room. Picture molding in principal rooms and hall of first story. Staircase, yellow pine. All interior wood-work grain filled and finished with hard oil varnish.

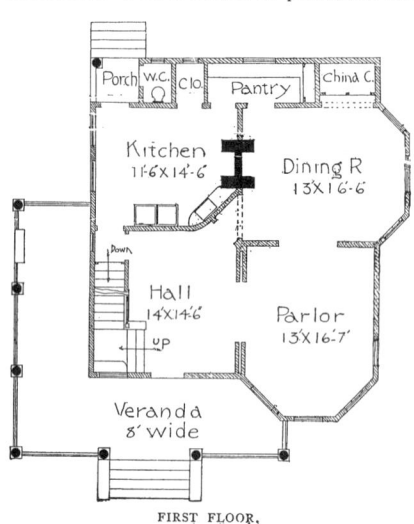

COLORS: Body of work, all clapboards, white. Trim, including water-table, corner boards, casings, cornices, veranda posts, rail, etc., dark bottle green. Outside doors, varnished. Outside blinds, dark bottle green. Sashes, dark red. Veranda floor and ceiling, oiled. All shingles left natural for weather stain.

ACCOMMODATIONS: The principal rooms and their sizes, closets, etc., are shown by the floor plans. Cellar under the whole house, with inside and outside entrances, and concrete floor. One room finished off in attic, remainder of space floored for storage purposes. Double sliding doors connect parlor and hall. Open fireplace in dining-room. China closet in dining-room and dresser in butler's pantry. Sink, boiler and two set-tubs in kitchen. Water-closet off rear porch. Alcove in second story, in connection with front bedroom. Bath-room with full plumbing in second story. Large-sized veranda with small balcony above. Front door glazed.

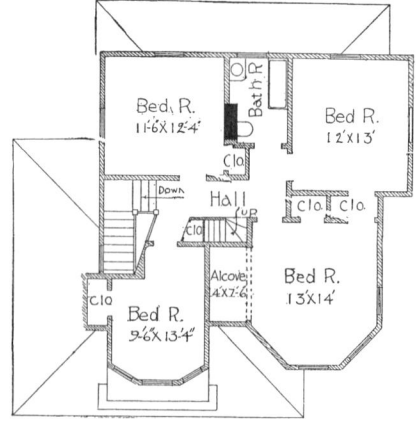

COST: $3,100, † not including mantel, range or heater. The estimate is based on ‡ New York prices for materials and labor. In many sections of the country the cost should be less.

Price of working plans (with full details drawn to large scale), specifications and * license to build, ... $30.00

Price of †† bill of materials, . . 10.00

FEASIBLE MODIFICATIONS: General dimensions, materials and colors may be changed. Cellar may be reduced in size or wholly omitted. Attic may be left unfinished. Sliding doors may be omitted and portière openings substituted. Fireplace may be omitted, or chimney may be transferred and additional fireplaces introduced. China-closet, butler's pantry and kitchen closet may be omitted, making the depth of house 4 ft. 6 ins. less. Set-tubs may be removed from kitchen and placed in cellar. Alcove in large bedroom may be dispensed with and space used to enlarge small hall room.

The price of working plans, specifications, etc., for a modified design, varies according to the alterations required and will be made known upon application to the Architects.

Address, THE CO-OPERATIVE BUILDING PLAN ASSOCIATION, Architects, 106-108 Fulton Street, New York.

FIRST FLOOR.

SECOND FLOOR.

Residence, Design No. 1267

PERSPECTIVE.

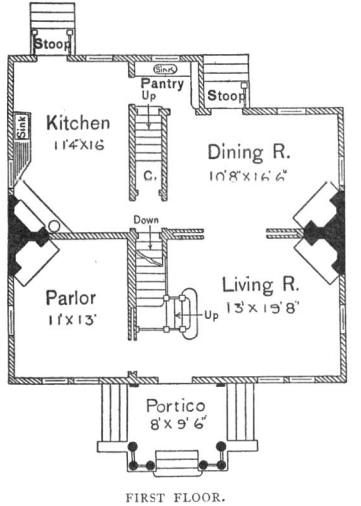

FIRST FLOOR.

SECOND FLOOR.

DESCRIPTION.

GENERAL DIMENSIONS: Width, 32 ft. 6 ins.; depth, including portico, 38 ft. 6 ins.

HEIGHTS OF STORIES: Cellar, 7 ft.; first story, 9 ft.; second story, 8 ft.; attic, 8 ft.

EXTERIOR MATERIALS: Foundation, stone; first and second stories, clapboards; balcony floor covered with canvas; deck and extension roofs, tin; main roof, shingles.

INTERIOR FINISH: Hard white plaster. Georgia pine flooring, first and second stories; spruce in attic. Trim to be Georgia pine in main part of first story; elsewhere, North Carolina pine. Main stairs, white oak. Wooden cornice and picture molding in three principal rooms. Chair-rail in dining and living-rooms.

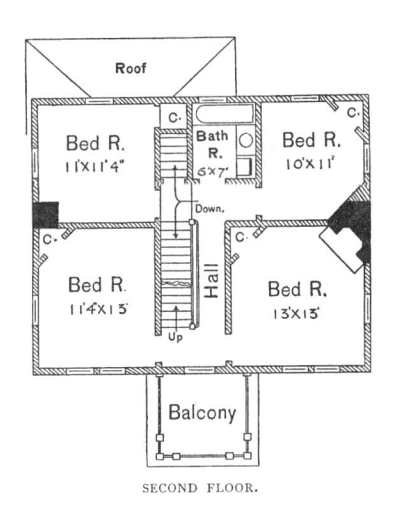

COLORS: Clapboards and blinds, Colonial yellow. Trim, papier-maché work and outside doors, cream white. Portico floor and ceiling to be oiled. Shingles on roofs, dipped and brush coated red stain. Tin roofs, dark red.

ACCOMMODATIONS: The principal rooms and their sizes, closets, etc., are shown by the floor plans. Cellar under the whole house, with inside and outside entrances and concrete floor. Servants' water-closet and laundry with three set-tubs in cellar. Two bedrooms and hall finished in attic. Access to deck roof by scuttle from attic hall. Open fireplaces in parlor, living-room, dining-room and one bedroom. Brick-set range in kitchen. Balcony over portico. Sliding doors between living-room and dining room and between parlor and living room.

COST: $3,100, † not including mantels, range and heater. The estimate is based on ‡ New York prices for materials and labor. In many sections of the country the cost should be less.

Price of working plans (with full details drawn to large scale), specifications and * license to build, . . . $30.00
Price of †† bill of materials, ... 10.00

FEASIBLE MODIFICATIONS: General dimensions, materials and colors may be changed. Attic may be left unfinished. Portico may be extended to form veranda across entire front and around either or both sides. Brick-set range may be omitted and portable range substituted. A portion or all plumbing may be omitted and the small bedroom enlarged at the expense of the bath-room.

The price of working plans, specifications, etc., for a modified design, varies according to the alterations required and will be made known upon application to the Architects.

Address, THE CO-OPERATIVE BUILDING PLAN ASSOCIATION, Architects, 106–108 Fulton Street, New York.

Residence, Design No. 1268.

PERSPECTIVE.

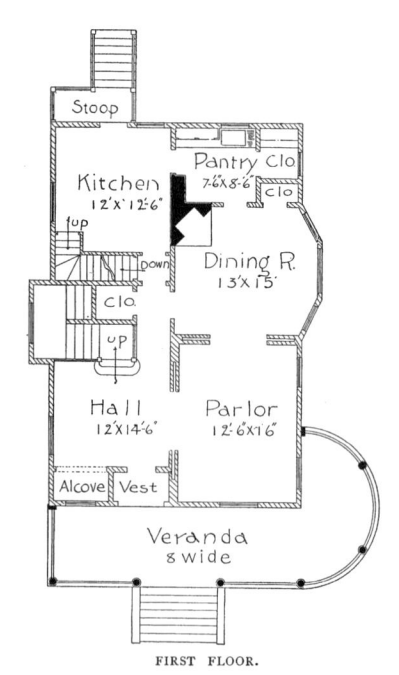

DESCRIPTION.

GENERAL DIMENSIONS: Extreme width, 36 ft. 6 ins.; depth, exclusive of rear porch, 47 ft.

HEIGHTS OF STORIES: Cellar, 7 ft.; first story, 9 ft. 6 ins.; second story, 9 ft.

EXTERIOR MATERIALS: Foundation, stone; first story, clapboards; second story, gables, roof and veranda, shingles.

INTERIOR FINISH: Two coat plaster, hard white finish. Plaster centres in parlor, dining-room and hall of first story. Flooring and trim, N. C. pine throughout. Main staircase, ash. Bath-room and kitchen wainscoted. Chair-rail in dining-room. Picture molding in principal rooms and hall of first story. All interior wood-work grain filled and finished with hard oil varnish.

COLORS: All clapboards, light terra-cotta. Trim, dark terra-cotta. Shingling on second story, gables, etc., stained red. Roof shingles, oiled. Outside doors and sashes, also veranda floor and ceiling, finished with hard oil. Brickwork, painted red.

ACCOMMODATIONS: The principal rooms and their sizes, closets, etc., are shown by the floor plans. Cellar under the whole house. Sink and boiler in kitchen. Bath-room, with complete plumbing. Laundry, with two set wash-tubs in cellar. Open fireplace in dining-room. Double sliding doors connect dining-room, parlor and hall. Hall contains very pretty staircase. Butler's pantry connecting kitchen and dining-room, contains sink, dresser and china closet. Two rooms and hall finished off in attic.

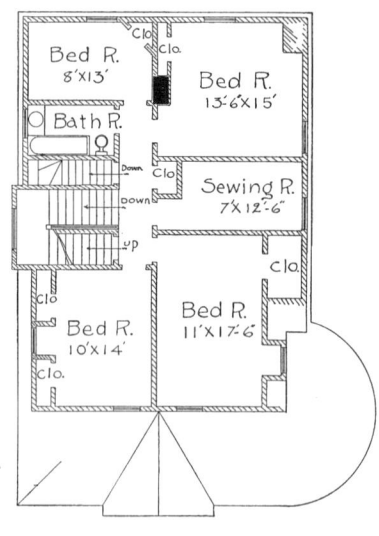

FIRST FLOOR.

SECOND FLOOR.

COST: $3,100, † not including mantels, range or heater. The estimate is based on ‡ New York prices for materials and labor. In many sections of the country the cost should be less.

Price of working plans (with full details drawn to large scale), specifications and *license to build $30.00

Price of †† bill of materials, ... 10.00

FEASIBLE MODIFICATIONS: General dimensions, materials and colors may be changed. Cellar may be reduced in size or wholly omitted. Laundry may be omitted and tubs transferred to kitchen. Brick-set range may be introduced in kitchen. Sliding doors may be omitted and portière openings substituted. Attic may be left unfinished and floored for storage only.

The price of working plans, specifications, etc., for a modified design, varies according to the alterations required and will be made known upon application to the Architects.

Address, THE CO-OPERATIVE BUILDING PLAN ASSOCIATION, Architects, 106–108 Fulton Street, New York.

Residence, Design No. 1269

PERSPECTIVE.

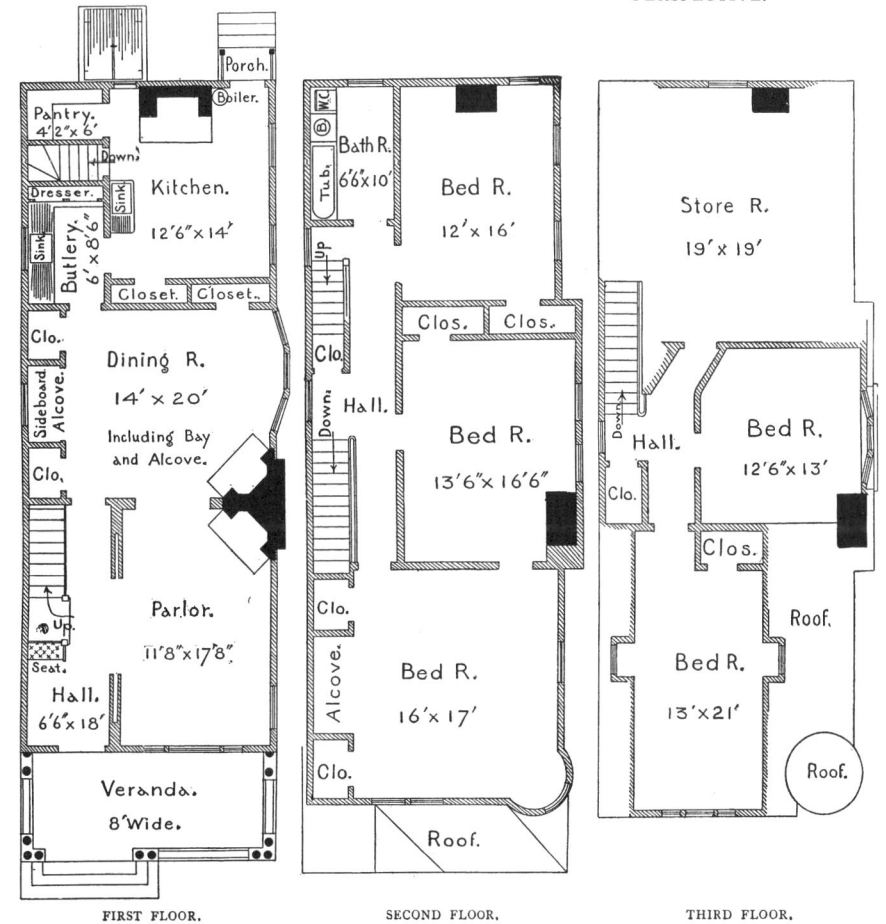

FIRST FLOOR.   SECOND FLOOR.   THIRD FLOOR.

DESCRIPTION.

GENERAL DIMENSIONS: Width through dining-room, including bay, 21 ft.; depth, including veranda, 58 ft.

HEIGHTS OF STORIES: Cellar, 7 ft.; first story, 9 ft.; second story, 9 ft.; attic, 8 ft.

EXTERIOR MATERIALS: Foundation, stone and brick; first story, clapboards; second story, front and side gables, dormers and roofs, shingles.

INTERIOR FINISH: Hard white plaster. Soft wood flooring and trim. Ash staircase. Interior wood-work stained to suit owner and finished with hard oil.

COLORS: All first story clapboards and veranda posts, balusters and flooring, and all paneling, light brown. All outside trim, cornices and other moldings, veranda rails and caps and bases of posts, seal brown. Sashes, white. Outside doors finished with hard oil. All wall shingles dipped in and brush coated with silver gray stain. Clapboards above first story treated with silver gray stain. Roof shingles dipped in and brush coated with dark red stain. Veranda ceiling, oiled. Brickwork, oiled.

ACCOMMODATIONS: The principal rooms and their sizes, closets, etc., are shown by the floor plans. Cellar under whole house, with inside and outside entrance and concrete floor. Two rooms and hall finished in the attic. Laundry and servant's water-closet in basement. Sink in butlery and kitchen. Full plumbing in bath-room. Sideboard alcove in dining-room. Bed alcove and circular bay in front bedroom. Portière between parlor and dining-room. Sliding doors between hall and parlor. Box seat in hall. Open fireplaces in parlor and dining-room. Linen closet in second story hall. House piped throughout for gas.

COST: $3,200, † not including plumbing, mantels, range and heater. The estimate is based on ‡ New York prices for materials and labor. In many sections of the country the cost should be less.

Price of working plans (with full details drawn to large scale), specifications and * license to build, . $30.00
Price of †† bill of materials, . . . 10.00

FEASIBLE MODIFICATIONS: General dimensions, materials and colors may be changed. Part or all of plumbing, fireplaces, sliding doors and attic finish, except flooring, may be omitted. Kitchen range may be portable, instead of brick-set. Cellar may be reduced in size or omitted. Dining-room closets and alcove may be omitted.

The price of working plans, specifications, etc., for a modified design, varies according to the alterations required and will be made known upon application to the Architects.

Address, THE CO-OPERATIVE BUILDING PLAN ASSOCIATION, Architects, 106–108 Fulton Street, New York.

Residence, Design No. 1278

PERSPECTIVE.

DESCRIPTION.

GENERAL DIMENSIONS: Width, including veranda, 79 ft. 6 ins.; depth, including veranda, 31 ft. 6 ins.

HEIGHTS OF STORIES: Cellar, 6 ft. 6 ins.; first story, 9 ft.; second story, 9 ft. 6 ins.

EXTERIOR MATERIALS: Foundation, brick walls and piers; first and second stories, balcony fronts, gables and roofs, shingles.

INTERIOR FINISH: All walls and ceilings throughout first and second stories covered with hard pine ceiling boards, with wooden cornices in all rooms. Yellow pine flooring, trim and staircase. Interior woodwork finished with varnish.

COLORS: All wall shingles, veranda posts, veranda floor, and shingles of kitchen porch roof, olive drab. Outside doors varnished. Trim, including casings, cornices, bands, veranda rails, etc., light drab. Sashes, olive. Veranda ceiling oiled. Rain conductors, balcony floor, roof of bay and all brickwork, red. Plaster panel on front, buff. Shingled roofs left natural.

ACCOMMODATIONS: The principal rooms and their sizes, closets, etc., are shown by the floor plans. Cellar under kitchen. Attic floored, but unfinished; space in attic for three or four rooms, to be lighted by dormers. Extensive balcony and veranda. Rear hall in first story is open on one side, forming a porch passage between kitchen and dining-room.

COST: $3,250, † not including plumbing, mantels, range or heater. The estimate is based on ‡ New York prices for materials and labor. In many sections of the country the cost should be less.

Prices of working plans (with full details drawn to large scale), specifications and * license to build, $30.00

Price of †† bill of materials, 10.00

FEASIBLE MODIFICATIONS: Heights of stories, sizes of rooms, materials and colors may be changed. Part of the balcony and veranda and all fireplaces and sliding doors may be omitted. The porch and hall may be enclosed with glass, either straight or in bay form, and serve as a conservatory for wintering plants. The two end bedrooms may be connected either directly or through closets.

The price of working plans, specifications, etc., for a modified design, varies according to the alterations required and will be made known upon application to the Architects.

Address, THE CO-OPERATIVE BUILDING PLAN ASSOCIATION, Architects, 106–108 Fulton Street, New York.

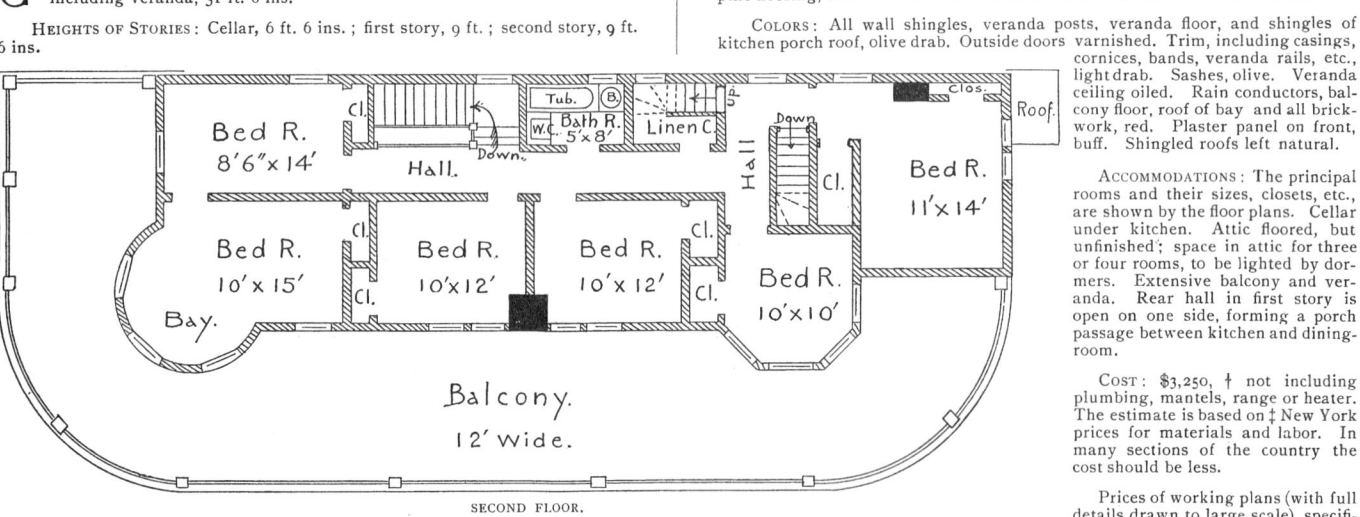

SECOND FLOOR.

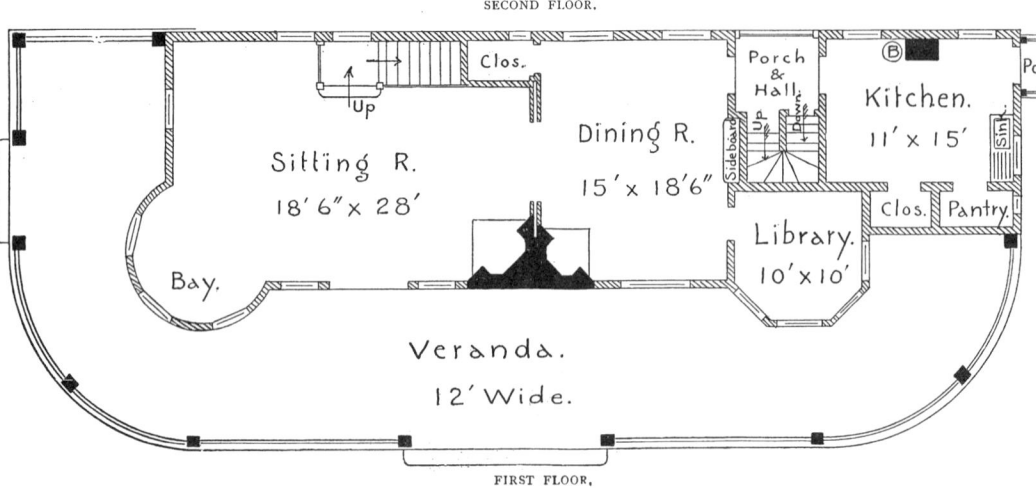

FIRST FLOOR.

74

Residence, Design No. 1279

PERSPECTIVE.

DESCRIPTION.

GENERAL DIMENSIONS: Width over all, 38 ft. 6 ins.; depth, including veranda, 48 ft. HEIGHTS OF STORIES: Cellar, 7 ft.; first story, 9 ft.; second story, 8 ft. 6 ins.

EXTERIOR MATERIALS: Foundation, stone; first story, clapboards; second story, gables, dormers and roofs, shingles.

INTERIOR FINISH: Three coat plaster, hard white finish. Plaster centers in parlor and dining-room. Double floors throughout first and second stories, with paper between. Top floors in kitchen pantry and bath-room to be yellow pine, elsewhere to be soft wood. Soft wood trim throughout finished with hard oil. Main stairs, oak. Paneled backs under windows in parlor. Wooden cornice in hall, parlor and dining-room. Picture molding in principal rooms and hall of first story. Chair-rail in dining-room. Bath-room and kitchen wainscoted.

COLORS: Clapboards, Colonial yellow. Trim, including cornices, veranda posts, rail, etc., ivory white. Outside doors, blinds and sashes, ivory white. Veranda floor and ceiling to be oiled. Shingles on sides to be stained light sienna. Shingles on roofs to be stained green.

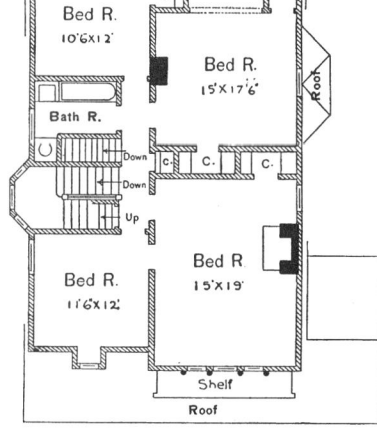

ACCOMMODATIONS: The principal rooms and their sizes, closets, etc., are shown by the floor plans. Cellar under the whole house with concrete floor, and is accessible from the kitchen and from the outside of house. Laundry with three set-tubs and servants' water-closet in cellar. Attic floored for storage only. Attractive staircase with bay and seat at landing. There is an ingenious arrangement of kitchen entrance which gives a convenient and cool place for the refrigerator, and access to cellar from the kitchen or from the outside without entering the kitchen. Bay and conservatory off dining-room. Wide double doors between hall and parlor and parlor and dining-room. Open fireplaces in parlor and bedroom over. Spacious veranda. Bath room with complete plumbing.

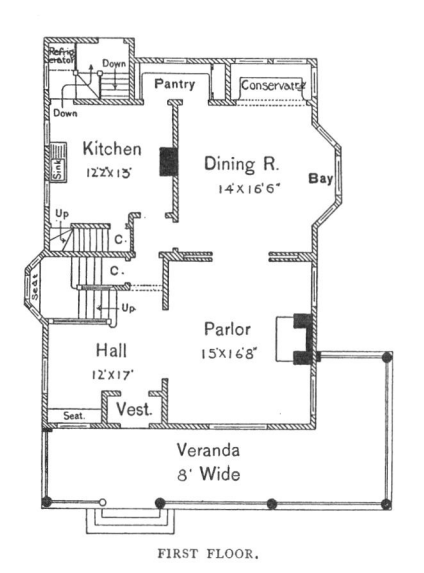

COST: $3,300, † not including mantels, range and heater. The estimate is based on ‡ New York prices for materials and labor. In many sections of the country the cost should be less.

Price of working plans (with full details drawn to large scale), specifications and
* license to build, ... $35.00
Price of †† bill of materials, ... 10.00

FEASIBLE MODIFICATIONS: General dimensions, materials and colors may be changed. Cellar may be reduced in size or wholly omitted. One large room may be finished in attic. The arrangement of kitchen entrance may be changed and a kitchen porch introduced, in which case the cellar stairs could go under the rear stairs to second story. Fireplaces may be added in dining-room and bedroom above.

The price of working plans, specifications, etc., for a modified design varies according to the alterations required and will be made known upon application to the Architects.

Address, THE CO-OPERATIVE BUILDING PLAN ASSOCIATION, Architects, 106–108 Fulton Street, New York.

FIRST FLOOR.

SECOND FLOOR.

Residence, Design No. 1280

PERSPECTIVE.

DESCRIPTION.

GENERAL DIMENSIONS: Width, through dining-room and kitchen, 30 ft.; depth over all, 48 ft. 6 ins.

HEIGHTS OF STORIES: Cellar, 7 ft.; first story, 9 ft. 6 ins.; second story, 9 ft.; third story, 8 ft.

EXTERIOR MATERIALS: Foundations, stone; first story, clapboards; second story and gables, dormers, roofs, and veranda enclosure, shingles.

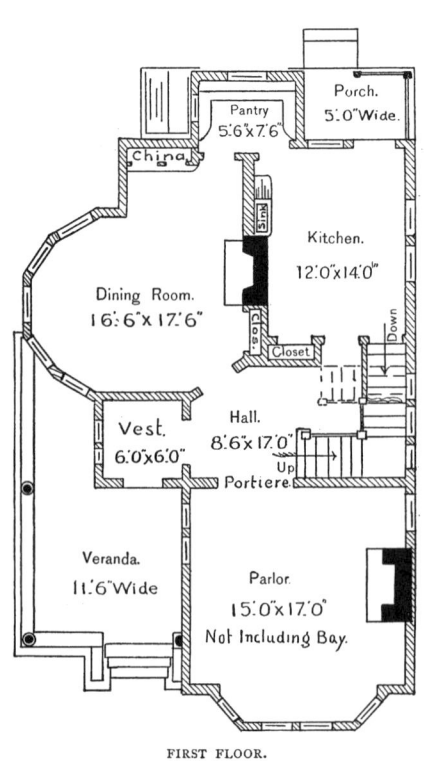

INTERIOR FINISH: Hard white plaster throughout and plaster cornices and centers in hall, parlor and dining-room. Trim, yellow pine. Staircase of cherry. Bath-room and kitchen wainscoted. All wood-work finished in hard oil. Flooring in kitchen, pantry and bath-room, yellow pine, and in attic, spruce; elsewhere, white pine.

COLORS: All clapboards, brown. Trim and rain conductors, orange red. Outside doors, blinds and sashes, dark green. Veranda floor, tan color. Veranda ceiling, varnished. Wall shingles dipped in and brush coated with dark red stain.

ACCOMMODATIONS: The principal rooms and their sizes, closets, etc., are shown by the plans. Cellar under whole house. One room finished in attic and space for one more. Colonial in style and regarded as a very pleasing design.

COST: $3,300, † not including mantels, range and heater. The estimate is based on ‡ New York prices for materials and labor. In many sections of the country the cost should be less.

Price of working plans (with full details drawn to large scale), specifications and * license to build, . $35.00

Price of †† bill of materials, . 10.00

Address, THE CO-OPERATIVE BUILDING PLAN ASSOCIATION, Architects, 106–108 Fulton Street, New York.

FEASIBLE MODIFICATIONS: Heights of stories, sizes of rooms, materials and colors may be changed. Cellar may be reduced in size. Fireplaces may be omitted. If heating apparatus be used parlor chimney may be omitted. Front door may be placed in vestibule where windows are now shown. Sliding doors may be introduced between parlor and hall.

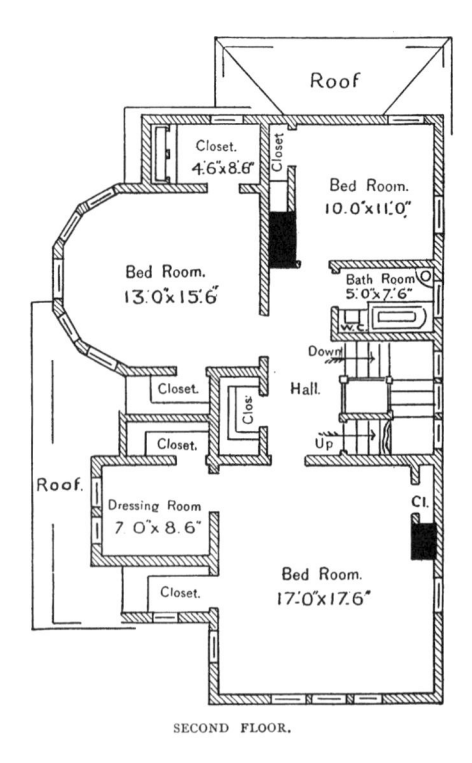

The price of working plans, specifications, etc., for a modified design, varies according to the alterations required and will be made known upon application to the Architects.

FIRST FLOOR.

SECOND FLOOR.

Residence, Design No. 1281

PERSPECTIVE.

DESCRIPTION.

GENERAL DIMENSIONS: Width, through sitting-room and dining-room, 31 ft. 6 ins.; depth, including veranda, 53 ft.

HEIGHTS OF STORIES: Cellar, 7 ft. 6 ins.; first story, 9 ft. 6 ins.; second story, 9 ft.; attic, 7 ft.

EXTERIOR MATERIALS: Foundation, stone; first story, clapboards; second story, gables and roofs, shingles.

INTERIOR FINISH: Hard white plaster; plaster cornices and centers in parlor, dining and sitting-rooms. Double floor in first story with paper between; finished floors, soft wood. Trim in hall and vestibule, quartered oak. Main staircase, oak. Panel-backs under windows in parlor, dining-room and sitting-room. Picture molding in principal rooms and hall of first story. Chair-rail in dining-room. Bathroom and kitchen, wainscoted. Interior wood-work stained to suit owner and finished in hard oil.

COLORS: Clapboards, seal brown. Trim, including watertable, corner boards, cornices, casings, bands, veranda posts and rails, outside blinds, rain conductors, etc., chocolate. Outside doors finished with hard oil. Sashes, Pompeiian red. Veranda floor and ceiling and all brickwork, oiled. Wall shingles dipped in and brush coated with light sienna stain. Roof shingles dipped in and brush coated dark red stain.

ACCOMMODATIONS: The principal rooms and their sizes, closets, etc., are shown by the floor plans. Cellar under the whole house, with inside and outside entrances and concrete floor. One room finished in attic; space for two more. Attractive main staircase. Sliding doors connect hall and parlor, dining-room and sitting-room. Attractive circular bay in second story.

COST: $3,400, † not including mantels, range or heater. The estimate is based on ‡ New York prices for materials and labor. In many sections of the country the cost should be less.

Prices of working plans (with full details drawn to large scale), specifications and * license to build, . . $35.00

Price of †† bill of materials, ... 10.00

FEASIBLE MODIFICATIONS: General dimensions, materials and colors may be changed. Cellar may be reduced in size, or omitted. Attic may be left unfinished. Sliding doors, open fireplaces, and part or all of plumbing may be omitted. Circular bay may be carried down through first story and up through attic to form a tower. Veranda may be extended to dining-room bay. Another bedroom may be planned over kitchen and porch. Portable range may be substituted for brick-set one. Wash tubs may be transferred to cellar, or laundry may be added to rear of kitchen.

The price of working plans, specifications, etc., for a modified design, varies according to the alterations required and will be made known upon application to the Architects.

Address, THE CO-OPERATIVE BUILDING PLAN ASSOCIATION, Architects, 106-108 Fulton Street, New York.

FIRST FLOOR.

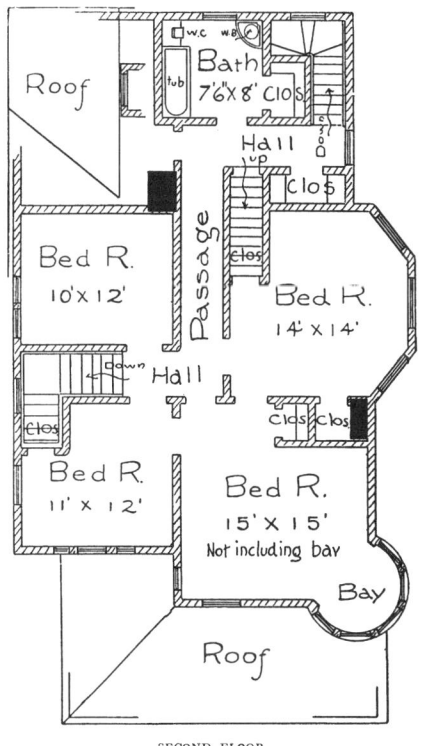

SECOND FLOOR.

Residence, Design No. 1282

PERSPECTIVE.

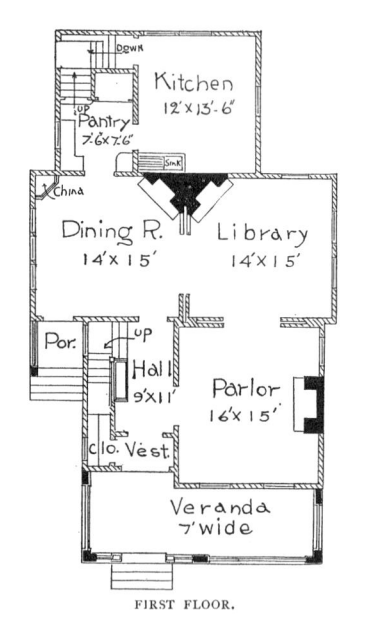

FIRST FLOOR.

SECOND FLOOR.

DESCRIPTION.

GENERAL DIMENSIONS: Width, through library and dining-room, 31 ft. 10 ins.; depth, including veranda, 52 ft. 10 ins.

HEIGHTS OF STORIES: Cellar, 7 ft.; first story, 10 ft.; second story, 9 ft.

EXTERIOR MATERIALS: Foundation, brick; first story, clapboards; second story and gables, shingles; roof, slate.

INTERIOR FINISH: Hard white plaster; cellar ceiling plastered one heavy coat. Soft wood flooring throughout. Trim in hall and bedroom, oak; in library and dining-room, cherry; elsewhere, soft wood. Main staircase, oak. Picture molding in principal rooms and hall of first story. Panel backs under windows in parlor, library and dining-room. Bath-room and kitchen wainscoted. Front entrance doors, oak. Interior wood-work finished with hard oil; soft wood stained to suit owner.

COLORS: All clapboards and sashes, buff. Trim, including water-table, cornices, corner boards, casings, bands, rain conductors, also front and rear outside doors and outside blinds, Tuscan yellow. Veranda ceiling and floor, oiled. Brick-work, dark red. Veranda columns, all moldings and balusters, buff. Pedestals of columns and top and bottom rail of balusters, Tuscan yellow. Wall shingles dipped in and brush coated with sienna stain.

ACCOMMODATIONS: The principal rooms and their sizes, closets, etc., are shown by the floor plans. Cellar under the whole house, with inside and outside entrances and concrete floor. Laundry under kitchen. Furnace cellar under library and dining-room. Vegetable cellar under parlor and hall, separated by brick partition wall. Attic floored but unfinished; space for three rooms and storage. Sliding doors connect parlor, library and dining-room. Open fireplaces in parlor, library, dining-room and two bedrooms. Hat and coat closet off vestibule.

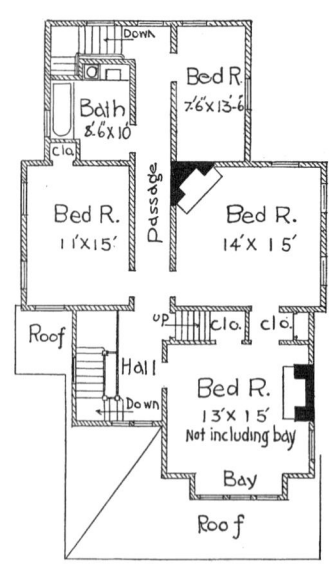

COST: $3,450, † not including mantels, range or heater. The estimate is based on ‡ New York prices for materials and labor. In many sections of the country the cost should be less.

Price of working plans (with full details drawn to large scale), specifications and * license to build, ... $35.00

Price of †† bill of material, ... 10.00

FEASIBLE MODIFICATIONS: General dimensions, materials and colors may be changed. Cellar may be reduced in size or wholly omitted. Cellar partition walls may be omitted. Sliding doors, fireplaces and part or all of plumbing may be omitted. Hat and coat closet may be made accessible from hall instead of from vestibule.

The price of working plans, specifications, etc., for a modified design, varies according to the alterations required and will be made known upon application to the Architects.

Address, THE CO-OPERATIVE BUILDING PLAN ASSOCIATION, Architects, 106–108 Fulton Street, New York.

Residence, Design No. 1283

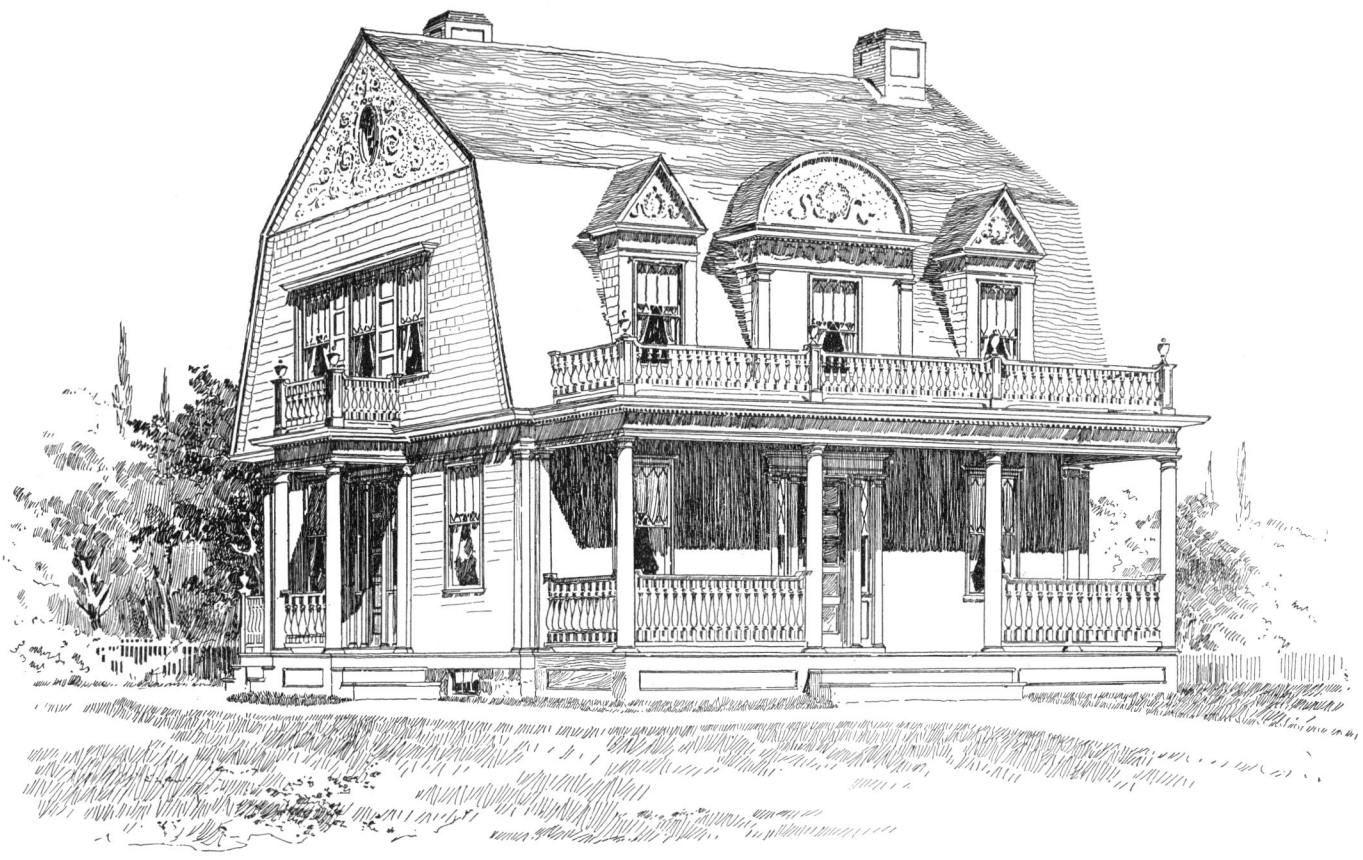

PERSPECTIVE.

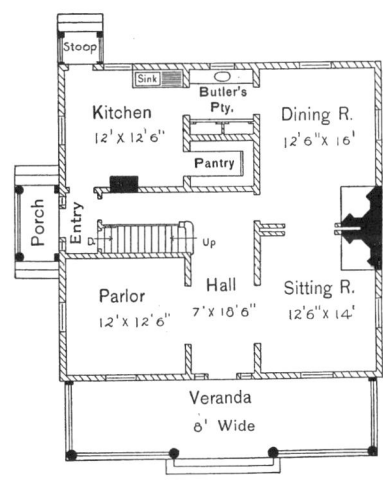

FIRST FLOOR.

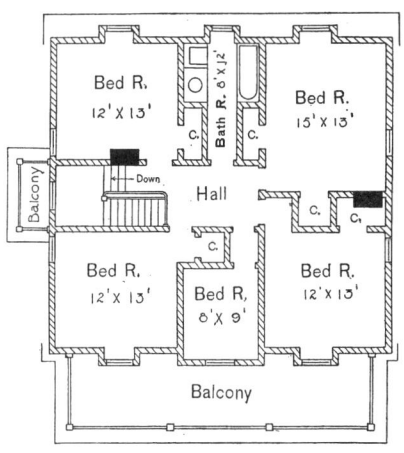

SECOND FLOOR.

DESCRIPTION.

GENERAL DIMENSIONS: Depth, including veranda, 40 ft.; width, not including side porch, 34 ft.; width, including side porch, 38 ft. 6 ins.

HEIGHTS OF STORIES: Cellar, 7 ft.; first story, 9 ft. 6 ins.; second story, 8 ft. 6 ins.

EXTERIOR MATERIALS: Foundation, stone; first story, clapboards; gables, ornamented with papier-maché and shingles; pediments of dormers and frieze of large dormer, ornamented with papier-maché; main roof, shingles; balcony floors, tin.

INTERIOR FINISH: Hard white plaster throughout. Soft wood flooring and trim. Main staircase, ash. Kitchen and bath-room wainscoted. All interior wood-work, grain filled, stained to suit owner and finished with hard oil.

COLORS: All clapboards, Colonial yellow. Trim, white. All shingles, left natural for weather stain. Veranda and porch floors and ceilings, oiled.

ACCOMMODATIONS: The principal rooms and their sizes, closets, etc., are shown by the floor plans. Cellar under the whole house, with inside and outside entrances and concrete floor. Attic floored for storage. Laundry under kitchen, with two set-tubs. Sink in kitchen, butler's sink in butler's pantry, and complete plumbing in bathroom. Open fireplaces in sitting-room and dining-room. Double sliding doors between sitting-room and dining-room. Wide portière openings between parlor and hall and sitting-room and hall. Large pantries and closets. Balconies over veranda and side porch.

COST: $3,500, † not including mantels, range and heater. The estimate is based on ‡ New York prices for materials and labor. In many sections of the country the cost should be less.

Price of working plans (with full details drawn to large scale), specifications and * license to build, . . . $35.00

Price of †† bill of materials, . 10.00

FEASIBLE MODIFICATIONS: General dimensions, materials and colors may be changed. Cellar may be reduced in size or wholly omitted. The amount of plumbing may be reduced. Double sliding or folding doors may be used between parlor and hall and sitting room and hall, instead of portière openings. Bay-window may be planned at side of dining-room. Side porch may be omitted.

The price of working plans, specifications, etc., for a modified design, varies according to the alterations required and will be made known upon application to the Architects.

Address, THE CO OPERATIVE BUILDING PLAN ASSOCIATION, Architects, 106–108 Fulton Street, New York.

Residence, Design No. 1284

PERSPECTIVE.

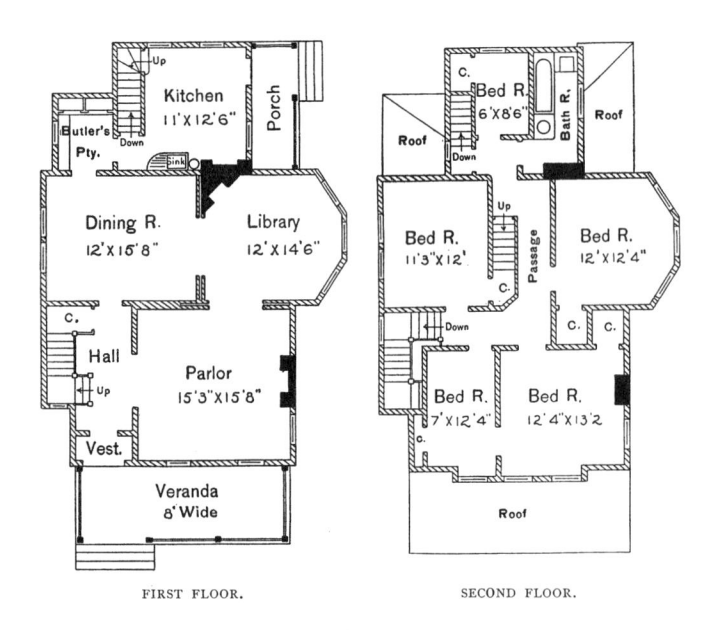

FIRST FLOOR.

SECOND FLOOR.

DESCRIPTION.

GENERAL DIMENSIONS: Width, through dining-room and library, 32 ft.; depth, including veranda, 50 ft. 6 ins.

HEIGHTS OF STORIES: Cellar, 7 ft.; first story, 9 ft. 8 ins.; second story, 8 ft. 10 ins.

EXTERIOR MATERIALS: Foundations, stone and brick; first story, clapboards; second story and roofs, shingles; gables, panels and shingles. Outside blinds to all windows, except those of the cellar and attic.

INTERIOR FINISH: Hard white plaster; plaster cornices and centers in parlor, hall, library and dining-room. Soft wood flooring and trim. Panels under windows in parlor, library and dining-room. Stairs, ash. Bath-room and kitchen wainscoted. Interior woodwork finished in hard oil.

COLORS: Clapboards, seal brown. Trim, outside doors, blinds and veranda floor, maroon. Sashes and rain conductors, dark green. Veranda ceiling, varnished. Brick work, Indian red. Panels in gables, seal brown; frames around panels, maroon. Wall shingles, dipped and brush coated light sienna stain. Roof shingles, dipped and brush coated Indian red stain.

ACCOMMODATIONS: The principal rooms and their sizes, closets, etc., are shown by the plans. Cellar under kitchen, dining and sitting-rooms; walls extended under whole house. Attic floored but unfinished; space for three fine rooms. Sliding doors connect parlor, library and dining-room. Fireplaces and mantels in library and parlor. Double front door, with glazed single vestibule door. Hat and coat closet under main stairs.

COST: $3,507, † not including mantels, range and heater. The estimate is based on ‡ New York prices for materials and labor. In many sections of the country the cost should be less.

Price of working plans (with full details drawn to large scale), specifications and * license to build, ... $30.00

Price of †† bill of materials, ... 10.00

FEASIBLE MODIFICATIONS: General dimensions, materials and colors may be changed. Cellar may be reduced in size. Two front bedrooms may be combined, or the smaller form an alcove off the larger. Fireplaces and mantels may be omitted. Rear chimney will suffice if heating apparatus be used. Veranda may be extended at either side.

The price of working plans, specifications, etc., for a modified design, varies according to the alterations required and will be made known upon application to the Architects.

Address, THE CO-OPERATIVE BUILDING PLAN ASSOCIATION, Architects, 106–108 Fulton Street, New York.

Residence, Design No. 1286

PERSPECTIVE.

FIRST FLOOR.

DESCRIPTION.

GENERAL DIMENSIONS: Extreme width, 34 ft. 6 ins.; depth, including verandas, 50 ft 4 ins.

HEIGHTS OF STORIES: Cellar, 7 ft.; first story, 9 ft. 6 ins.; second story, 9 ft.; attic, 8 ft.

EXTERIOR MATERIALS: Foundation, stone; first story, clapboards; second story, gables and roof, shingles.

INTERIOR FINISH: Three coat plaster, hard white finish. Plaster centers and cornices in hall, parlor and dining-room of first story. First story floor double, with paper between. Floor in dining-room and bath-room, yellow pine; elsewhere, white pine. Trim throughout, N. C. pine. Chair-rail in dining-room. Bath-room and kitchen wainscoted. Hard wood mantel in dining-room. Windows of staircase bay, glazed with stained Cathedral glass.

COLORS: Clapboards, light bronze green. Trim, including water-table, corner boards, cornices, casings, bands, veranda columns, rail, etc., dark bronze green. Shingles on roof, dark red. Sashes, red.

ACCOMMODATIONS: The principal rooms and their sizes, closets, etc., are shown by the floor plans. Cellar under whole house, with inside and outside entrance. One room finished off in attic, remainder floored for storage. Portière opening between parlor and hall. Sliding doors connect parlor with dining-room. Attractive window seat in parlor. Brick-set range, dresser, sink and two tubs in kitchen. Entry off kitchen, opening on to rear veranda. Two large closets in connection with the dining-room and kitchen contain ample shelving. Bath-room in second story, containing full plumbing. Linen closet in second story hall. Wash-bowl in bedroom closet.

COST: $3,548, † not including mantels, range or heater. The estimate is based on ‡ New York prices for materials and labor. In many sections of the country the cost should be less.

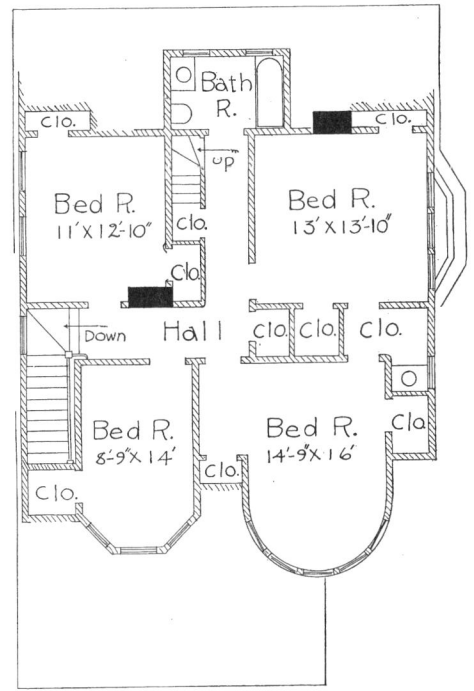

SECOND FLOOR.

Price of working plans (with full details drawn to large scale), specifications and * license to build, ... $35.00

Price of †† bill of materials, ... 10.00

FEASIBLE MODIFICATIONS: General dimensions, materials and colors may be changed. Cellar may be reduced in size. Attic may be left unfinished. Portière opening between hall and parlor may be omitted and sliding doors introduced. Brick-set range in kitchen may be omitted and portable one substituted. A laundry may be planned in cellar and wash-tubs transferred from kitchen.

The price of working plans, specifications, etc., for a modified design, varies according to the alterations required and will be made known upon application to the Architects.

Address, THE CO-OPERATIVE BUILDING PLAN ASSOCIATION, Architects, 106–108 Fulton Street, New York.

Residence, Design No. 1452

PERSPECTIVE.

DESCRIPTION.

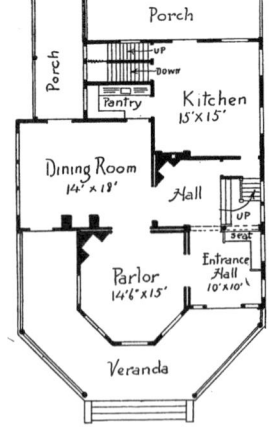

GENERAL DIMENSIONS: Width, through kitchen and dining-room, 34 ft. 6 ins.; depth, not including porch and veranda, 41 ft. 6 ins.

HEIGHTS OF STORIES: Cellar, 7 ft.; first story, 9 ft. 6 ins.; second story, 9 ft.; attic, 8 ft.

EXTERIOR MATERIALS: Foundation, brick; first and second stories, gables and roofs, shingles.

INTERIOR FINISH: Hard white plaster; plaster centers in parlor, dining-room and hall. Double floor in first story with paper between; finished floors, soft wood. Trim, white wood. Main staircase, oak. Panel-backs under windows in parlor and dining-room. Two wash-tubs in cellar. Picture molding in principal rooms and hall of first story. Chair-rail in dining-room. Bath-room and kitchen, wainscoted. Interior wood-work stained to suit owner and finished in hard oil varnish.

COLORS: Trim, including cornices, casings, bands, veranda posts and rails, outside blinds, rain conductors, etc., chocolate. Outside doors finished with hard oil. Sashes, Pompeian red. Veranda floor and ceiling and all brick-work, oiled. Wall shingles dipped in and brush coated with light sienna stain. Roof shingles dipped in and brush coated dark red stain.

ACCOMMODATIONS: The principal rooms and their sizes, closets, etc., are shown by the floor plans. Cellar under the whole house, with inside and outside entrances and concrete floor. One room finished in attic; space for two more. Attractive main staircase. Sliding doors connect hall, parlor and dining-room. Attractive staircase has columns and spindle arch.

COST: $3,375, † not including mantels, range or heater. The estimate is based on ‡ New York prices for materials and labor. In many sections of the country the cost should be less.

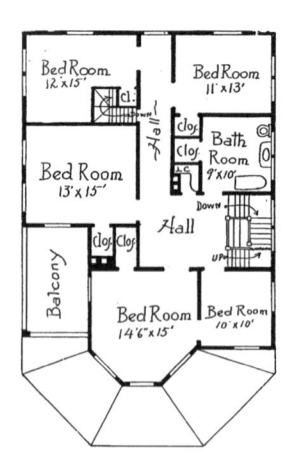

FIRST FLOOR.

SECOND FLOOR.

Price of working plans (with full details drawn to large scale), specifications and * license to build, ... $35.00

Price of †† bill of materials, . . 10.00

FEASIBLE MODIFICATIONS: General dimensions, materials and colors may be changed. Cellar may be reduced in size or omitted. Attic may be left unfinished. Sliding doors, open fireplaces and part or all of plumbing may be omitted. Veranda may be extended. Portable range may be omitted and brick-set one substituted. Wash-tubs may be transferred to kitchen, or laundry may be introduced in cellar.

The price of working plans, specifications, etc. for a modified design, varies according to the alterations required and will be made known upon application to the Architects.

Address, THE CO-OPERATIVE BUILDING PLAN ASSOCIATION, Architects, 106–108 Fulton Street, New York.

Residence, Design No. 1453

PERSPECTIVE

DESCRIPTION.

GENERAL DIMENSIONS : Width through dining-room and kitchen, including stoop and dining-room bay, 34 ft.; depth, including veranda, 47 ft. 6 ins.

HEIGHTS OF STORIES : Cellar, 7 ft.; first story, 9 ft. 6 ins.; second story, 9 ft.; attic, 8 ft.

EXTERIOR MATERIALS : Foundation, brick ; first and second stories, gables and roofs, shingles.

INTERIOR FINISH : Hard white plaster. Hard wood flooring and trim. Ash staircase. Interior wood-work stained to suit owner and finished with hard oil varnish.

COLORS : Veranda columns, balusters and flooring, light brown. All outside trim, cornices and other moldings, veranda rails and caps and bases of columns, seal brown. Sashes, white. Outside doors finished with hard oil. All wall shingles dipped in and brush coated with silver gray stain. Roof shingles dipped in and brush coated with dark red stain. Veranda ceiling, oiled.

ACCOMMODATIONS: The principal rooms and their sizes, closets, etc., are shown by the floor plans. Cellar under whole house, with inside and outside entrance and concrete floor. Two rooms and hall finished in the attic. Laundry and servant's water-closet in cellar. Sink in butlery and kitchen. Full plumbing in bath-room. Two angle china closets in dining-room. Alcove in front bedroom. Sliding doors between hall and parlor and parlor and dining-room. Box seat in hall. Open fireplaces in parlor and hall. Linen closet in second story hall. House piped throughout for gas.

COST : $3,600, † including plumbing, mantels, range and heater. The estimate is based on ‡ New York prices for materials and labor. In many sections of the country the cost should be less.

Price of working plans (with full details drawn to large scale), specifications and * license to build, . . . $35.00
Price of †† bill of materials, . . . 10.00

FEASIBLE MODIFICATIONS : General dimensions, materials and colors may be changed. Part or all of plumbing, fireplaces, sliding doors and attic finish, except flooring, may be omitted. Kitchen range may be brick-set. Cellar may be reduced in size or omitted.

The price of working plans, specifications, etc., for a modified design, varies according to the alterations required and will be made known upon application to the Architects.

Address, THE CO-OPERATIVE BUILDING PLAN ASSOCIATION, Architects, 106–108 Fulton Street, New York.

Residence, Design No. 1307

PERSPECTIVE.

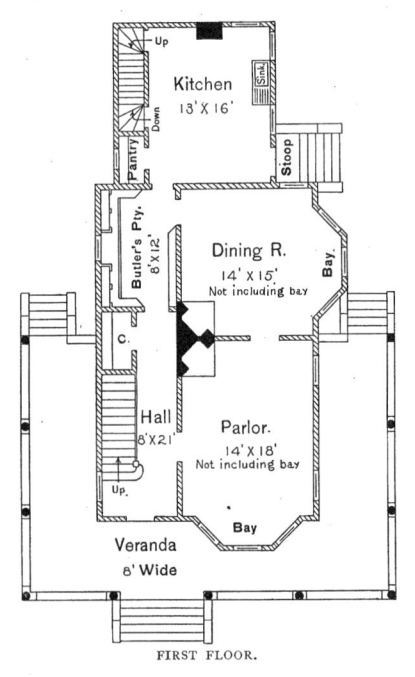

DESCRIPTION.

GENERAL DIMENSIONS: Width, including veranda, 39 ft. 6 ins.; depth, including veranda, 59 ft.

HEIGHTS OF STORIES: Cellar, 7 ft.; first story, 10 ft.; second story, 9 ft.

EXTERIOR MATERIALS: Foundation, stone or brick. First story, clapboards. Second story, gables, roofs and lower portion of veranda, shingles.

INTERIOR FINISH: Two coat plaster, hard white finish. Soft wood flooring and trim. Main staircase, ash. Picture molding in principal rooms and hall, first story. All interior wood-work grain filled, stained to suit owner and finished with hard oil varnish.

COLORS: All clapboards, first story, yellow drab. Trim, buff. Outside doors, blinds and sashes, bronze green. Shingling on side walls stained sienna. Shingles on roofs stained dark red.

ACCOMMODATIONS: The principal rooms and their sizes, closets, etc., are shown by the floor plans. Cellar under kitchen, dining-room and butler's pantry with inside and outside entrances and concrete floor. Attic floored for storage, otherwise left unfinished. Open fireplaces in dining-room and parlor. Spacious veranda. Ample closet and pantry room.

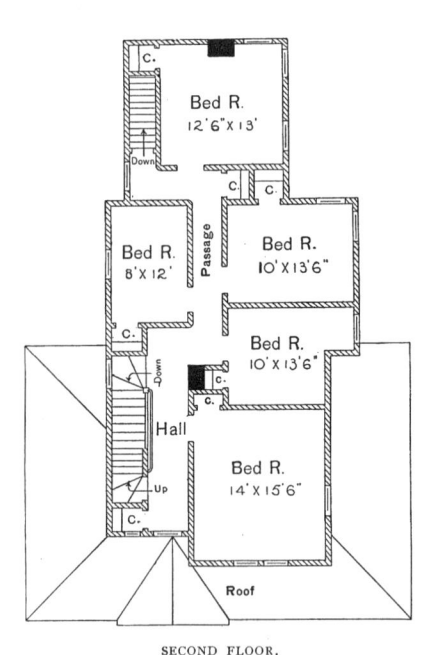

FIRST FLOOR.

SECOND FLOOR.

COST: $3,650, † not including mantels, range and heater. The estimate is based on ‡ New York prices for materials and labor. In many sections of the country the cost should be less.

Price of working plans (with full details drawn to large scale), specifications, and * license to build, . . . $40.00
Price of †† bill of materials, ... 15.00

FEASIBLE MODIFICATIONS: General dimensions, materials and colors may be changed. Cellar may be increased in size or wholly omitted. Three rooms may be finished in attic. The small bedroom in second story may be re-planned for a bath-room. Laundry tubs may be introduced in kitchen or a separate laundry planned in the cellar. Double folding or sliding doors may be used between hall and parlor and parlor and dining-room. Veranda may be decreased in size.

The price of working plans, specifications, etc., for a modified design, varies according to the alterations required and will be made known upon application to the Architects.

Address, THE CO-OPERATIVE BUILDING PLAN ASSOCIATION, Architects, 106–108 Fulton Street, New York.

Residence, Design No. 1454

PERSPECTIVE.

DESCRIPTION.

GENERAL DIMENSIONS: Width over all, 36 ft. 6 ins.; depth, including veranda, 33 ft. 6 ins.

HEIGHTS OF STORIES: Cellar, 7 ft.; first story, 9 ft. 6 ins.; second story, 8 ft. 6 ins.

EXTERIOR MATERIALS: Foundation, brick; first story, mitered clapboards; second story, gables, dormers and roofs, shingles.

INTERIOR FINISH: Three coat plaster, hard white finish. Plaster centers in parlor and dining-room. Double floors throughout first and second stories, with paper between. Top floors in kitchen, pantry and bath-room to be yellow pine, elsewhere to be soft wood. Oak trim throughout finished with hard oil. Main stairs, oak. Paneled backs under windows in parlor. Wooden cornice in hall, parlor and dining-room. Picture molding in principal rooms and hall of first story. Chair-rail in dining-room. Bath-room and kitchen wainscoted.

COLORS: Clapboards, Colonial yellow. Trim, including cornices, veranda posts, rail, etc., ivory white. Outside doors, blinds and sashes, ivory white. Veranda floor and ceiling to be oiled. Shingles on sides to be stained light sienna. Shingles on roofs to be stained green.

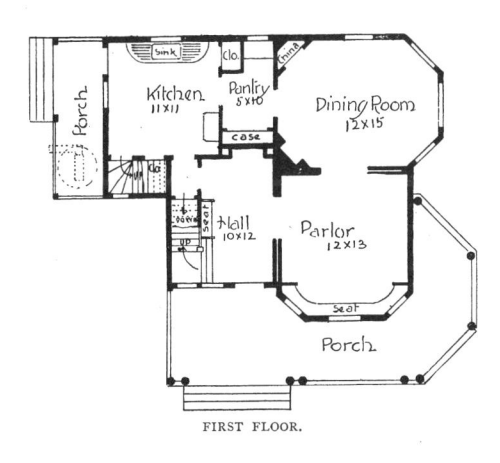

FIRST FLOOR.

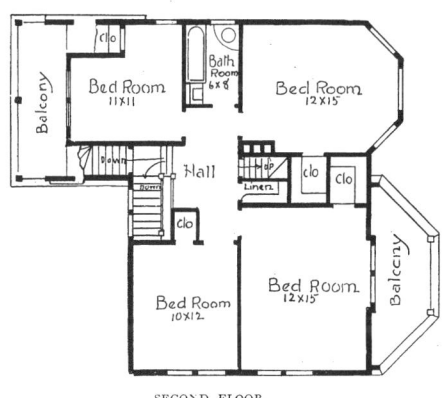

SECOND FLOOR.

ACCOMMODATIONS: The principal rooms and their sizes, closets, etc., are shown by the floor plans. Cellar under the whole house with concrete floor, and is accessible from the kitchen and from the outside of house. Laundry, with three set-tubs and servants' water-closet, in cellar. Combination front and rear stairway. Two rooms and hall in attic. Box seat in hall and parlor. China closet in dining-room. Wide doors between hall and parlor and parlor and dining-room. Open fireplace in dining-room. Spacious veranda. Bath room with complete plumbing.

COST: $3,690, † not including mantels, range and heater. The estimate is based on ‡ New York prices for materials and labor. In many sections of the country the cost should be less.

Price of working plans (with full details drawn to large scale), specifications and * license to build, . . . $35.00

Price of †† bill of materials, ... 10.00

FEASIBLE MODIFICATIONS: General dimensions, materials and colors may be changed. Cellar may be reduced in size or wholly omitted. Fireplace may be added in parlor. Attic may be left unfinished.

The price of working plans, specifications, etc., for a modified design, varies according to the alterations required and will be made known upon application to the Architects.

Address, THE CO-OPERATIVE BUILDING PLAN ASSOCIATION, Architects, 106–108 Fulton Street, New York.

Residence, Design No. 1456

PERSPECTIVE.

DESCRIPTION.

GENERAL DIMENSIONS: Width, including veranda, 37 ft.; depth, including front veranda and porch, 55 ft. 6 ins.

HEIGHTS OF STORIES: Cellar, 7 ft. 6 ins.; first story, 9 ft. 6 ins.; second story, 9 ft.; attic, 8 ft.

EXTERIOR MATERIALS: Foundation and portion of first story, stone; remainder of first story, second story, gables and roofs, shingles.

INTERIOR FINISH: Three coat plaster, hard white finish. Plaster centers in parlor, dining-room and hall of first story. Flooring throughout, N. C. pine. Trim, white wood. Main staircase, ash. Kitchen and bath-room, wainscoted. Chair-rail in dining-room. All interior wood-work grain filled, stained to suit owner and finished in hard oil varnish.

COLORS: Trim, including cornices, casings, veranda posts, rail, etc., white. Sashes, dark green. Outside doors, varnished. Veranda floor and ceiling, oiled. Shingles on side walls stained light sienna. Roof shingles stained dark red.

ACCOMMODATIONS: The principal rooms and their sizes, closets, etc., are shown by the floor plans. Cellar under the whole house, with inside and outside entrance and concrete floor. Laundry under kitchen contains two set-tubs and servant's closet. One room finished off in attic, remainder of space floored for storage purposes. Open fireplace in hall and dining-room. Sliding doors connect hall parlor and dining-room. Butler's pantry, containing dressers and shelving, connects kitchen with dining-room. Nook, with seat, in hall. Bath-room, in second story, containing full plumbing. Brick-set range in kitchen.

COST: 3,850, † not including mantels, range or heater. The estimate is based on ‡ New York prices for materials and labor. In many sections of the country the cost should be less.

Price of working plans (with full details drawn to large scale), specifications and * license to build, . . $40.00
Price of †† bill of materials, 15.00

FEASIBLE MODIFICATIONS: General dimensions, materials and colors may be changed. Cellar may be reduced in size. Laundry may be omitted and tubs transferred to kitchen. Brick-set range may be omitted. Butler's pantry may be omitted and space used to enlarge kitchen. Sliding doors may be omitted and portière openings substituted. Fireplace may be planned in parlor. One or two additional rooms may be finished off in attic or attic may be left entirely unfinished. Veranda may be reduced in size.

The price of working plans, specifications, etc., for a modified design, varies according to the alterations required and will be made known upon application to the Architects.

Address, THE CO-OPERATIVE BUILDING PLAN ASSOCIATION, Architects, 106-108 Fulton Street, New York.

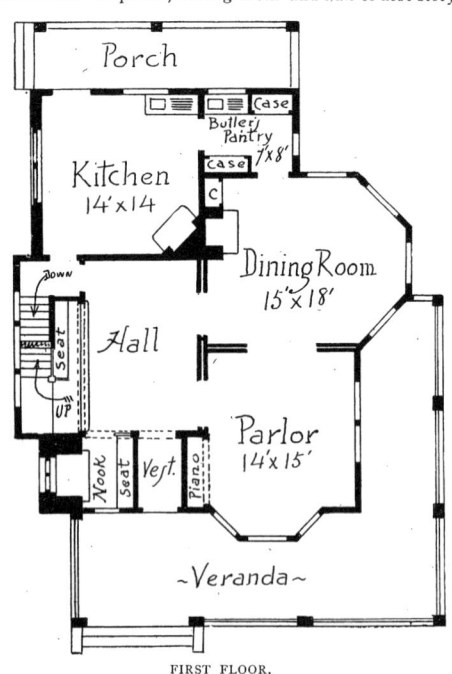

FIRST FLOOR.

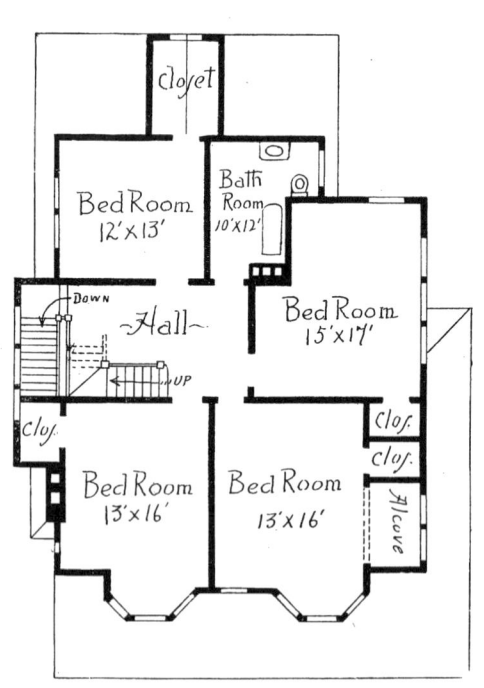

SECOND FLOOR.

Residence, Design No. 1309

PERSPECTIVE.

DESCRIPTION.

GENERAL DIMENSIONS: Width through dining-room and kitchen, 35 ft. 6 ins.; depth, including veranda porch, 54 ft.
HEIGHTS OF STORIES: Cellar, 7 ft.; first story, 9 ft.; second story, 8 ft. 6 ins.; attic, 8 ft.
EXTERIOR MATERIALS; Foundations, stone; first story, clapboards; second story, gables and veranda roofs, shingles; main roofs, metallic shingles. Outside blinds to kitchen and pantry windows, inside folding blinds to all other windows in first and second stories.
INTERIOR FINISH: Hard white plaster. Soft wood trim and floors throughout. Hard wood main stairs. Windows in parlor have panels below. All interior wood-work finished in hard oil and stained to imitate hard woods.
COLORS: Clapboards, light golden brown. Trim, veranda posts, rail, etc., brown. Outside doors, blinds and veranda floor, seal brown. Sashes, dark brown. Wall shingles and veranda and porch roof shingles dipped in yellow stain. Metallic shingles painted dark red.
ACCOMMODATIONS: The principal rooms and their sizes, closets, etc., are shown by the plans. Cellar under whole house, with outside and inside entrances and concrete floor. Wash-bowls in closets of two bedrooms and in bath-room. Five fireplaces, with hard wood mantels, are included in the estimate. Extensive front and rear verandas. Well-lighted halls—no dark corners. Two rooms finished in attic, leaving ample storage space.
COST: $3,900, † not including heater and range. The estimate is based on ‡ New York prices for materials and labor. In many sections of the country the cost should be less.
Price of working plans (with full details drawn to large scale), specifications and * license to build, . . $40.00
Price of †† bill of materials, ... 10.00
Address, THE CO-OPERATIVE BUILDING PLAN ASSOCIATION, Architects, 106-108 Fulton Street, New York.

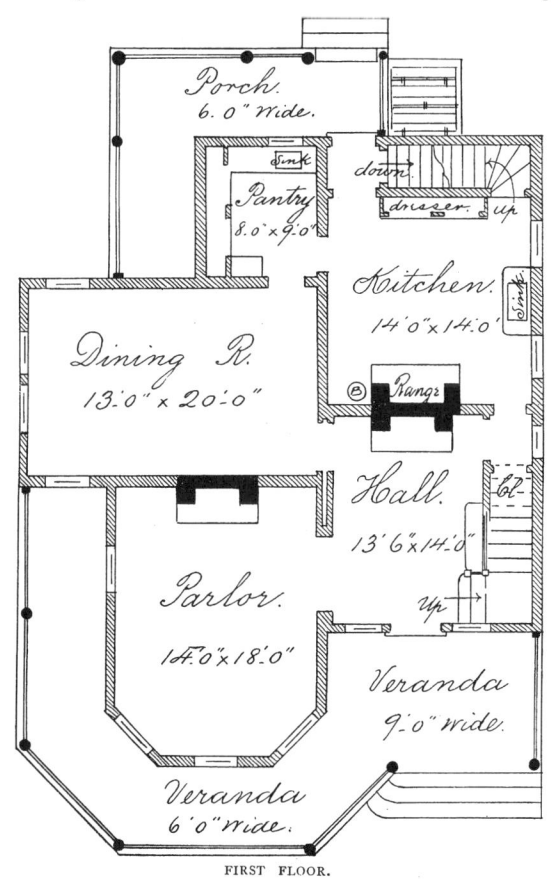

FIRST FLOOR.   87   SECOND FLOOR.

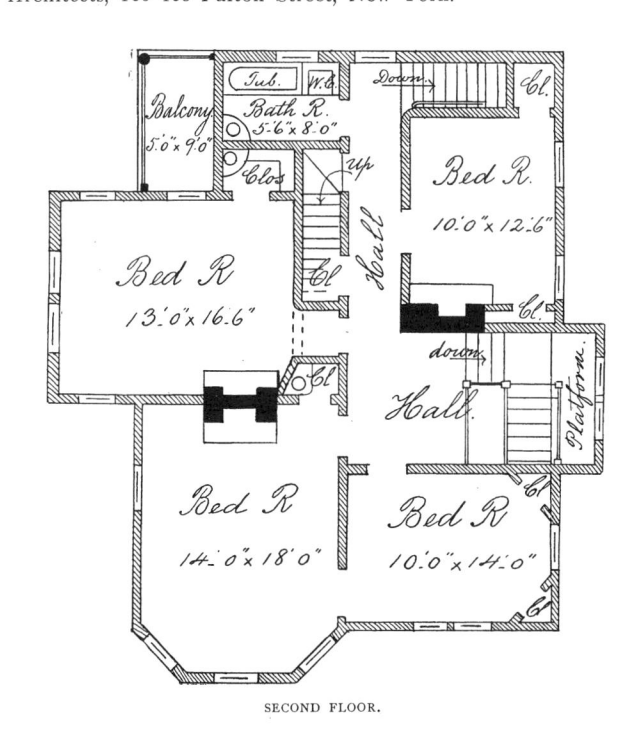

Residence, Design No. 1462

PERSPECTIVE.

DESCRIPTION.

GENERAL DIMENSIONS: Width, 42 ft. 4 ins.; depth, not including veranda, 34 ft. 2 ins.

HEIGHTS OF STORIES: Cellar, 7 ft.; first story, 10 ft.; second story, 9 ft.

EXTERIOR MATERIALS: Foundation, first story, veranda piers and chimneys, field stone; second story, gables and roofs, shingles.

INTERIOR FINISH: Hard white plaster throughout. First floor double, with paper between. Finished flooring, first story, hard pine; second story flooring, soft wood. Attic floored for storage purposes. Trim, white pine. Main staircase, ash. Bathroom and kitchen, wainscoted. Chair-rail in kitchen. All interior wood-work grain filled and finished with hard oil varnish.

COLORS: All clapboards, gray. Casings, cornices, bands, porch posts, rail, etc., olive drab. Outside doors, light olive drab. Sashes, dark red. Veranda and porch floors and ceilings, oiled. Shingling on side walls and roofs left natural for weather stain.

ACCOMMODATIONS: The principal rooms and their sizes, closets, etc., are shown by the floor plans, Cellar under the whole house, with inside and outside entrances and concrete floor. Brick set range, sink and boiler in kitchen. Butler's sink in pantry. Laundry, with three set-tubs, in cellar. Attic unfinished, except laying floor. Bath-room, with complete plumbing, in the second story. Broad veranda. Fireplaces in library, dining-room, hall and parlor. Portière openings between library and parlor, parlor and hall, and hall and dining-room.

COST: $4,790, † not including mantels, range and heater. The estimate is based on ‡ New York prices for materials and labor. In many sections of the country the cost should be less.

Price of working plans (with full details drawn to large scale), specifications and * license to build, ... $50.00

Price of †† bill of materials, . 15.00

FEASIBLE MODIFICATIONS: General dimensions, materials and colors may be changed. Cellar may be reduced in size or entirely omitted. Laundry in cellar may be omitted and the tubs transferred to the kitchen. Two or three large rooms may be finished in the attic. Fireplaces may be omitted. A portion or all of the plumbing may be omitted.

The price of working plans, specifications, etc., for a modified design, varies according to the alterations required and will be made known upon application to the Architects.

Address, THE CO-OPERATIVE BUILDING PLAN ASSOCIATION, Architects, 106–108 Fulton Street, New York.

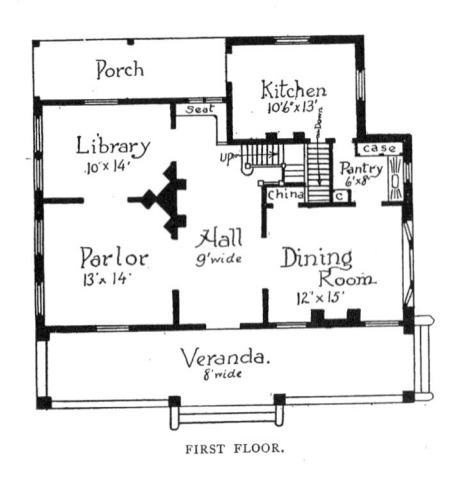

FIRST FLOOR.

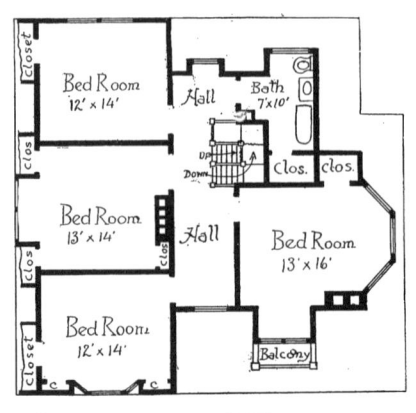

SECOND FLOOR.

Residence, Design No. 1469

PERSPECTIVE.

DESCRIPTION.

GENERAL DIMENSIONS: Width, including veranda and porte cochere, 69 ft.; depth, including veranda, 58 ft.

HEIGHTS OF STORIES: Cellar, 7 ft.; first story, 10 ft.; second story, 9 ft.; attic, 8 ft.

EXTERIOR MATERIALS: Foundation, brick; the entire building, sides, gables, dormers and roofs, shingles; balcony floors, tin.

INTERIOR FINISH: Hard white plaster in first and second stories; skim white coat in attic and laundry. Double floors in first and second stories, all top floors, North Carolina pine. Soft wood trim and ash stairs, finished with hard oil. Wainscot in bath-room, water-closet and kitchen. Picture molding in principal rooms and hall of first story. Panel backs for windows of parlor and dining-room.

COLORS: All shingles on side wall stained sienna. Roof shingles painted red. Trim, outside doors and blinds, bronze green. Sashes, Pompeian red. Veranda floor and ceiling to be oiled.

ACCOMMODATIONS: The principal rooms and their sizes, closets, etc. are shown by the floor plans. Cellar under whole house, with inside and outside entrances and concrete floor. Laundry with three set-tubs in cellar. Two bedrooms, closets and hall finished in third story, remainder of third story floored for storage. Spacious veranda with porte cochere. Open fireplaces in hall, parlor, dining-room and principal bedroom. Large hall with attractive staircase and window seat. Bath-room with complete plumbing. Water-closet separate from bath-room. Brick-set range. Balconies in second story front and rear. Numerous bay windows.

COST: $5,500, † not including mantels, range and heater. The estimate is based on ‡ New York prices for materials and labor. In many sections of the country the cost should be less.

Price of working plans (with full details drawn to large scale), specifications and * license to build, . . . $55.00
Price of †† bill of materials, ... 15.00

FEASIBLE MODIFICATIONS: General dimensions, materials and colors may be changed. Servants' water-closet may be introduced in cellar. One more room may be finished in third story, or the entire third story may be left unfinished. Veranda space may be reduced and porte cochere omitted. Fireplaces may be reduced in number or another may be introduced in bedroom over kitchen. Dining-room may be enlarged at expense of study.

The price of working plans, specifications, etc., for a modified design, varies according to the alterations required and will be made known upon application to the Architects.

Address, THE CO-OPERATIVE BUILDING PLAN ASSOCIATION, Architects, 106–108 Fulton Street, New York.

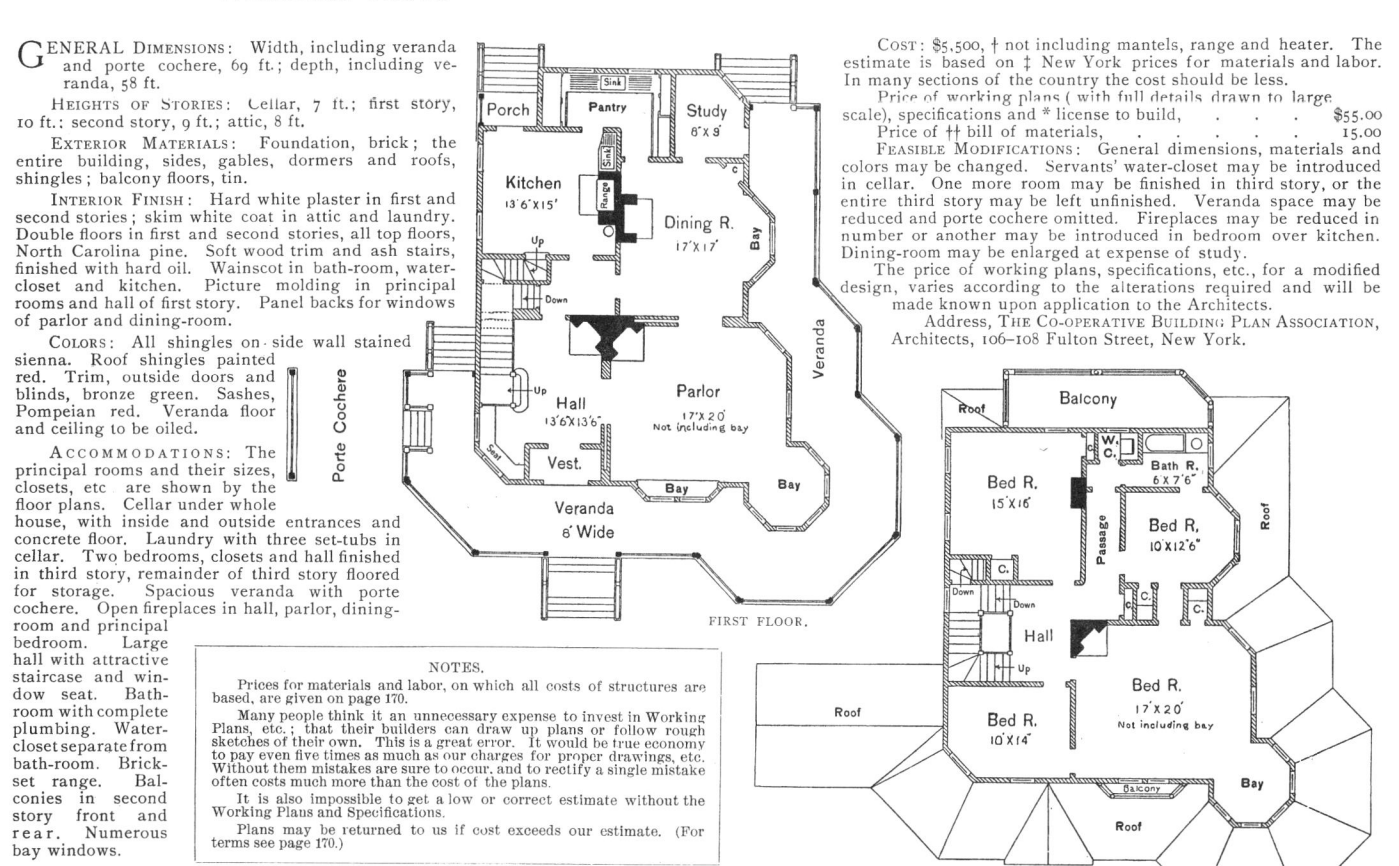

FIRST FLOOR.

SECOND FLOOR.

NOTES.

Prices for materials and labor, on which all costs of structures are based, are given on page 170.

Many people think it an unnecessary expense to invest in Working Plans, etc.; that their builders can draw up plans or follow rough sketches of their own. This is a great error. It would be true economy to pay even five times as much as our charges for proper drawings, etc. Without them mistakes are sure to occur, and to rectify a single mistake often costs much more than the cost of the plans.

It is also impossible to get a low or correct estimate without the Working Plans and Specifications.

Plans may be returned to us if cost exceeds our estimate. (For terms see page 170.)

Residence, Design No. 1470

PERSPECTIVE.

DESCRIPTION.

GENERAL DIMENSIONS: Width through dining and sitting rooms, 37 ft. 10 ins.; depth, including veranda, 62 ft. 8 ins.

HEIGHTS OF STORIES: Cellar, 7 ft.; first story, 10 ft.; second story, 9 ft. 6 ins.; attic, 8 ft. 6 ins.

EXTERIOR MATERIALS: Foundations, stone; first story, clapboards; second story, gables, veranda and balcony rails, and all roofs, shingles.

INTERIOR FINISH: Ceilings, hard white plaster; walls plastered two coats and tinted to suit owner; plaster cornices in parlor, dining and sitting rooms, front hall, and four principal bedrooms. Double floors in hall, vestibule, dining-room, sitting-room and study, the finished floor to be of oak; all other floors, single. Floors in kitchen, laundry and pantries, maple; elsewhere, soft wood. Oak trim in vestibule, hall, dining-room and study; cherry in sitting-room and parlor; Georgia pine in kitchen, laundry, pantries and bath-room; cedar in bedrooms over parlor and hall; ash in dressing-room and bedroom over sitting-room; elsewhere, white pine. Panels under windows in parlor, dining and sitting rooms. Staircase, oak. Wainscot in hall, dining-room, bath-room and kitchen. Walls and ceiling of first story main hall, paneled with oak. Wood-work finished with hard oil, except attic, which is painted to suit owner.

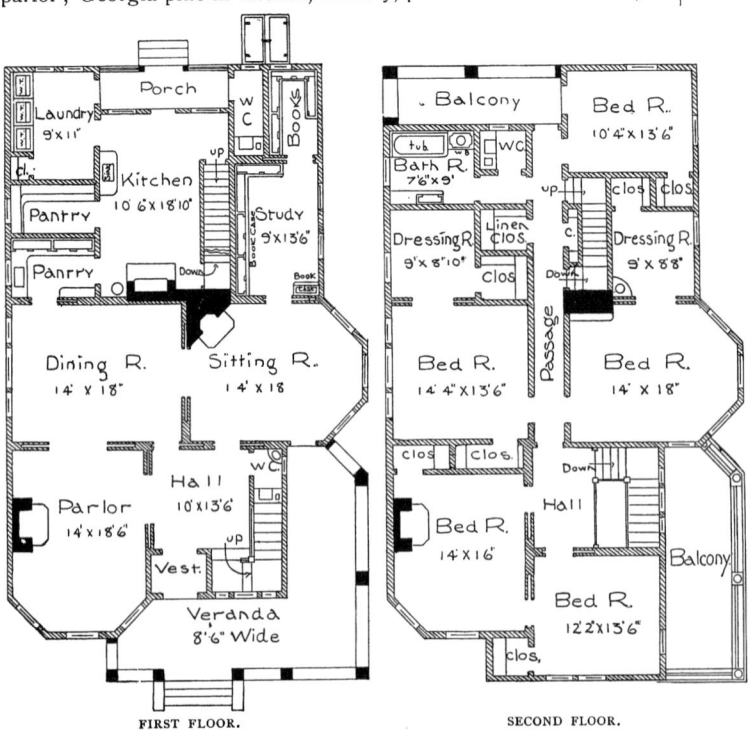

COLORS: Clapboards, light olive. Trim, water-table, corner boards, casings, cornices, bands, rails, sashes and rain conductors, light red. Front door finished with hard oil; other outside doors and outside blinds, painted dark green. Veranda floor and all exposed brick work, oiled. Veranda ceiling, light drab. Wall shingles dipped and brush coated sienna stain. Roof shingles dipped and brush coated dark red stain.

ACCOMMODATIONS: The principal rooms and their sizes, closets, etc., are shown by the floor plans. Cellar under whole house, with inside and outside entrance and concrete floor. Three rooms and hall finished in attic. Open fireplaces in parlor, sitting-room and one bedroom. Sliding doors connect hall, parlor, study, dining and sitting rooms, hall and bedrooms, and dressing-rooms with main bedrooms. Water closet separated from bath-room. Water closet off kitchen porch, and one in closet under main stairs. Bookcases built in study. Large linen closet. Sink in kitchen and butler's sink in pantry. Closet in study fitted up for particularly valuable books (this may readily be made a fireproof vault). Stationary wash bowls in closet under main stairs, in bath-room and in dressing-room over study.

COST: $5,500, † not including mantels, range and heater. The estimate is based on ‡ New York prices for materials and labor. In many sections of the country the cost should be less.

Price of working plans (with full details drawn to large scale), specifications, and * license to build, . $55.00
Price of †† bill of materials, ... 15.00

FEASIBLE MODIFICATIONS: General dimensions, materials, and colors may be changed. Sliding doors and fireplaces may be reduced in number or all omitted. Plumbing may be greatly reduced or omitted entirely. Laundry may be placed in cellar. Dressing-room next to bath-room may be re-planned for a bedroom and connected with hall by omitting linen and other closet. Balconies may be omitted. Rear balcony may be enclosed with glass for sun parlor. Attic may be left unfinished except flooring.

Address, THE CO-OPERATIVE BUILDING PLAN ASSOCIATION, Architects, 106–108 Fulton Street, New York.

FIRST FLOOR. SECOND FLOOR.

Residence, Design No. 1471

PERSPECTIVE.

DESCRIPTION.

GENERAL DIMENSIONS: Width through bedroom and sitting-room, including bay, 35 ft.; depth, including kitchen extension and front veranda, 69 ft. 6 ins.

HEIGHTS OF STORIES: Cellar, 7 ft.; first story, 10 ft.; second story, 9 ft.

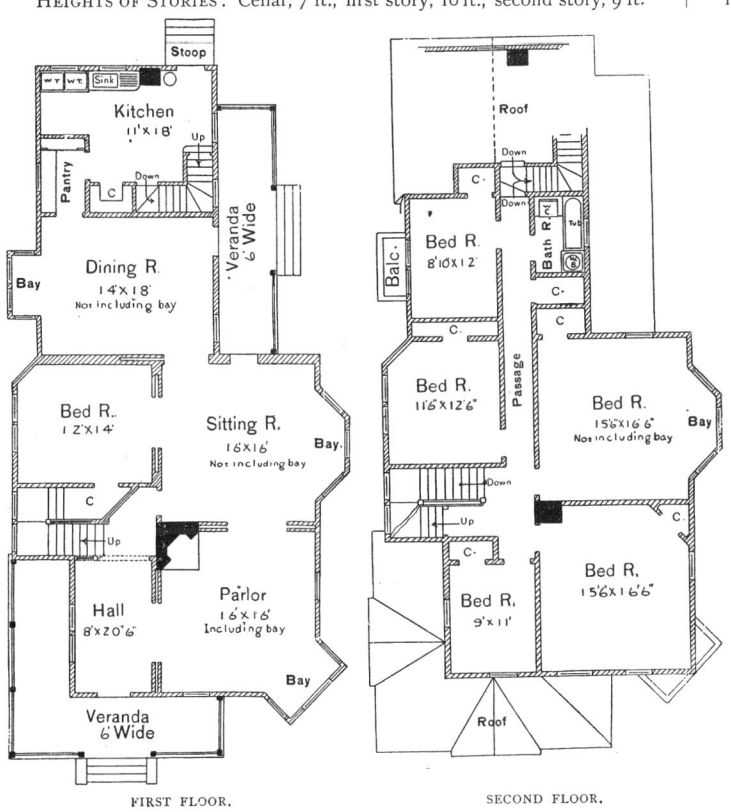

EXTERIOR MATERIALS: Brick foundation; clapboards for first story (except parlor bay); shingles for parlor bay, second story and roofs.

INTERIOR FINISH: Three coat plaster, hard white finish. Plaster cornices and centers in hall, parlor, sitting-room, dining-room, and bedroom of first story. Flooring throughout first and second stories, white pine; attic floor, spruce. Trim throughout, white pine. Panel backs under windows in hall, parlor and sitting-room. Picture moulding in hall and principal rooms of first story. Chair-rail in dining-room. Main stairs, ash. Bathroom and kitchen, wainscoted. All wood-work grain-filled and finished with hard oil.

COLORS: All clapboards of first story, yellow stone shade. Trim, including water table, corner boards, casings, cornices, bands, veranda posts, rails, outside doors and blinds, bronze green. Sashes, dark green. Veranda floors, light brown. Veranda ceilings, oiled. Shingles on side walls, sienna. Roof shingles, dark red.

ACCOMMODATIONS: The principal rooms and their sizes, closets, etc., are shown by the floor plans. Cellar under whole house; cellar has concrete floor and inside and outside entrances. Attic floored for storage use. Sliding doors between dining-room and sitting-room, parlor and sitting-room, bedroom and sitting-room, and parlor and hall. Bay window in dining-room, sitting-room, parlor, and bedroom over sitting-room. Bath-room with full plumbing. Two set-tubs in kitchen. Storage-room over kitchen.

COST: $5,500, † not including mantels, range and heater. The estimate is based on ‡ New York prices for labor and materials.

Price of working plans (with full details drawn to large scale), specifications, and * license to build, ... $55.00
Price of †† bill of materials, ... 15.00

FEASIBLE MODIFICATIONS: General dimensions, materials and colors may be changed. Laundry tubs may be transferred to cellar. Sliding doors may be omitted. Three bedrooms may be finished in attic. Additional veranda may be planned or present veranda made wider. Brick set range may be used instead of portable. Dining-room bay window may be omitted. First story bedroom may be used as library, and double doors may be built between it and dining-room. Additional fireplaces may be introduced.

The price of working plans, specifications, etc., for a modified design, varies according to the alterations required and will be made known upon application to the Architects.

Address, THE CO-OPERATIVE BUILDING PLAN ASSOCIATION, Architects, 106–108 Fulton Street.

FIRST FLOOR.   SECOND FLOOR.

Residence, Design No. 1472

PERSPECTIVE.

DESCRIPTION.

GENERAL DIMENSIONS: Extreme width, including parlor bay, 79 ft. 6 ins.; depth, including porch and veranda, 53 ft.

HEIGHTS OF STORIES: Cellar, 8 ft.; first story, 10 ft.; second story, 9 ft.

EXTERIOR MATERIALS: Foundation, stone; first and second story, gables and roofs, shingles.

INTERIOR FINISH: Hard white plaster. Plaster cornices and centers in hall, parlor, study and dining-room. Oak floor and trim in hall and dining-room. Oak main staircase. Soft wood flooring and trim elsewhere stained to suit owner. Interior wood-work finished with hard oil.

COLORS: All wall shingles dipped and brush coated silver stain. Trim, cornices, veranda and porch posts, rails, balusters and all mouldings, light red. Sashes, white. Outside doors finished with hard oil. Veranda and porch floors and ceilings, oiled. Brick-work, red. Roof shingles dipped and brush coated dark red stain.

ACCOMMODATIONS: The principal rooms and their sizes, closets, etc., are shown by the floor plans. Cellar under whole house, with inside and outside entrance and concrete floor. Attic floored for storage only; space for three rooms. Sliding doors connect hall, dining room, study and parlor. Open fireplace in hall, dining-room and large bedroom. Lavatory convenient to main hall.

COST: $6,000, † not including mantels, range and heater. The estimate is based on ‡ New York prices for materials and labor. In many sections of the country the cost should be less.

Price of working plans (with full details drawn to large scale), specifications and * license to build, $60.00

Price of †† bill of materials, ... 20.00

FEASIBLE MODIFICATIONS: General dimensions, materials and colors may be changed. Cellar may be reduced in size or omitted. Sliding doors and open fireplaces may be reduced in number or all may be omitted. Part or all of the plumbing may be omitted. Study, parlor and passage may be combined to form a parlor 19 x 25. Veranda may be reduced in size or omitted. Balconies may be omitted.

The price of working plans, specifications, etc., for a modified design, varies according to the alterations required and will be made known upon application to the Architects.

Address, THE CO-OPERATIVE BUILDING PLAN ASSOCIATION, Architects, 106–108 Fulton Street, New York.

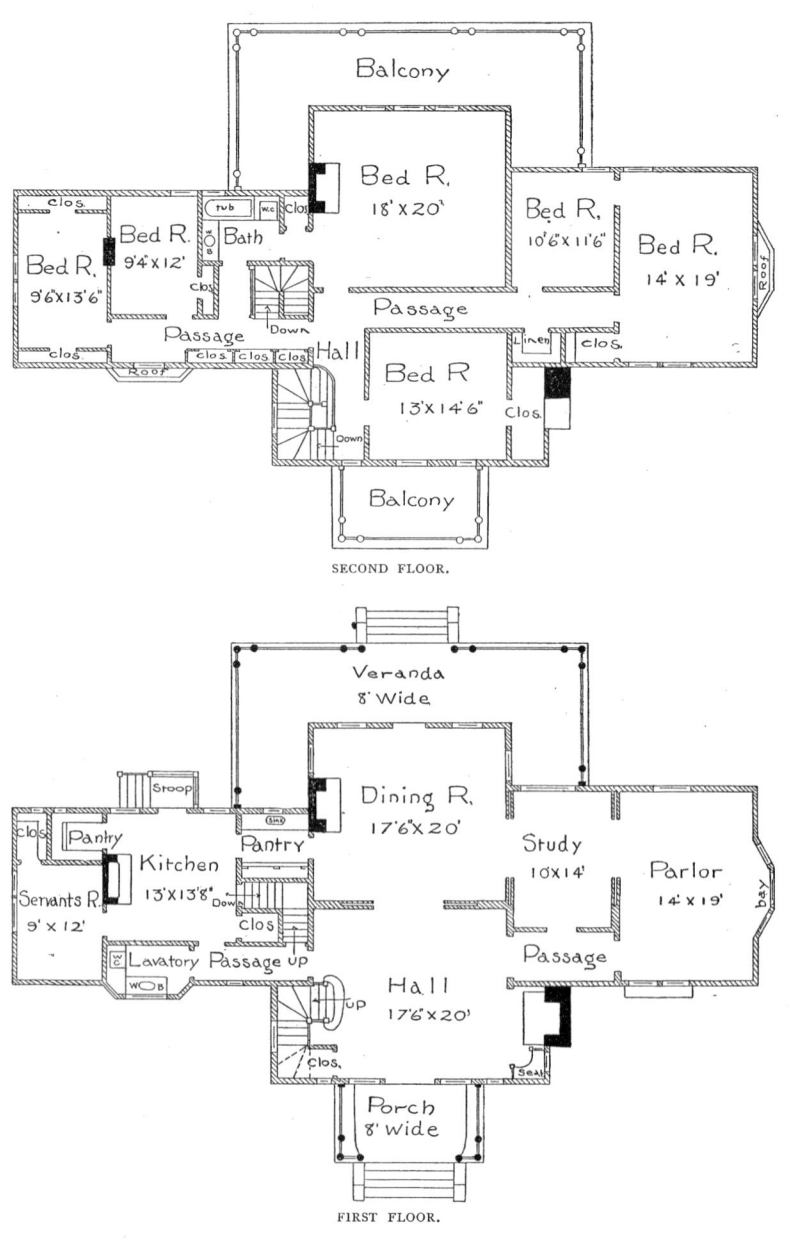

SECOND FLOOR.

FIRST FLOOR.

Residence, Design No. 1474

PERSPECTIVE.

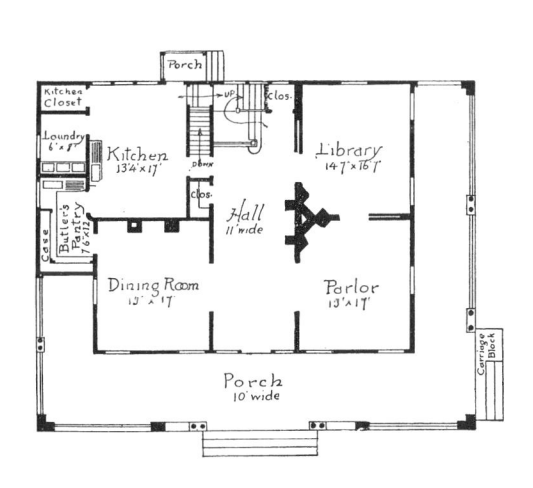

FIRST FLOOR.

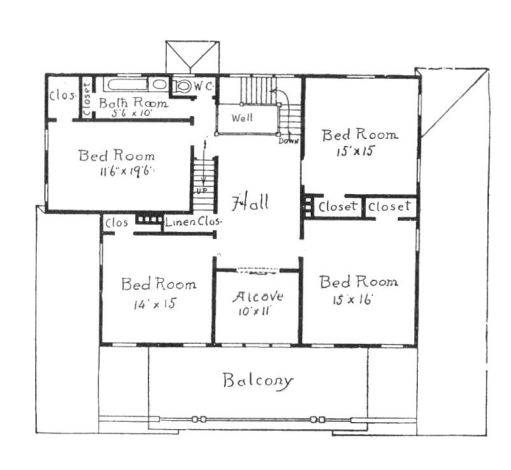

SECOND FLOOR.

DESCRIPTION.

GENERAL DIMENSIONS: Width, 51 ft. 6 ins., not including veranda; depth, not including veranda, 35 ft. 7 ins.

HEIGHTS OF STORIES: Cellar, 7 ft.; first story, 10 ft.; second story, 9 ft. 6 ins.

EXTERIOR MATERIALS: Foundation, brick; veranda parapet, first story, second story, gables and roof, shingles.

INTERIOR FINISH: Three coat plaster, hard white finish. Plaster centers in parlor, library, dining-room and hall of first story. Flooring and trim in first story, hard wood throughout. Main staircase, ash. Bath-room and kitchen, wainscoted. Chair-rail in dining-room. All interior wood-work, grain filled and finished with hard oil varnish.

COLORS: Trim, including water-table, casings, cornices, bands, outside blinds, veranda posts, rail, etc., dark green. Shingling on side walls left natural. Shingle roofs dipped and brush coated brown stain. Sashes, white. Veranda floor and ceiling and outside doors, grain filled and finished with hard oil.

ACCOMMODATIONS: The principal rooms and their sizes, closets, etc., are shown by the floor plans. Cellar under the whole house, with inside and outside entrances and concrete floor. Portable range, sink, boiler and two set-tubs in laundry in cellar. Sliding doors connect hall, library and parlor, and portiere openings dining-room, hall and library. Open fireplace in dining-room, hall, library and parlor. Hat and coat closet in hall.

COST: $6,000, † not including mantels, range or heater. The estimate is based on ‡ New York prices for materials and labor. In many sections of the country the cost should be less.

Price of working plans (with full details drawn to large scale), specifications and * license to build, ... $60.00

Price of †† bill of materials, ... 20.00

FEASIBLE MODIFICATIONS: General dimensions, materials and colors may be changed. Cellar may be reduced in size or wholly omitted. Any or all fireplaces and part or all of plumbing may be omitted. Sliding doors may be omitted. Veranda may be reduced in size. One or two bedrooms may be finished off in attic.

The price of working plans, specifications, etc., for a modified design, varies according to the alterations required and will be made known upon application to the Architects.

Address, THE CO-OPERATIVE BUILDING PLAN ASSOCIATION, Architects, 106–108 Fulton Street, New York.

Residence, Design No. 1475

DESCRIPTION.

GENERAL DIMENSIONS: Width through dining-room and sitting-room, 39 ft.; depth, including veranda, 54 ft. 6 ins.

HEIGHTS OF STORIES: Cellar, 7 ft.; first story, 10 ft.; second story, 9 ft.; attic, 8 ft.

EXTERIOR MATERIALS: Stone for foundation and first and second stories; shingles and cement panels for gables; shingles for roof.

INTERIOR FINISH: Three coat plaster, hard white finish. Cellar ceiling, plastered. Laundry (under kitchen), plastered two coats, brown finish. Plaster cornices and centers in parlor, hall, sitting-room and dining-room. Flooring throughout, North Carolina pine. Trim throughout, white pine. Paneled backs under windows in parlor, sitting-room and dining-room. Main staircase, oak. Bath-room and kitchen wainscoted. Picture moulding in hall and principal rooms of first story. All wood-work grain-filled and finished with hard oil.

COLORS: Veranda columns, blue stone, Trim, including casings, cornices, bands, veranda rail, sashes and conductors, dark terra cotta. Outside doors, blue stone color. Veranda floors and ceilings, oiled. Panels and shingles in gables, buff. Roof shingles, dark red.

ACCOMMODATIONS: The principal rooms and their sizes, closets, etc., are shown by the floor plans. Cellar, with concrete floor, under whole house. Laundry, with three tubs, under kitchen. One bedroom, 12 x 16, finished in attic; space for two additional rooms in attic if required, and ample storage room. Sliding doors between hall and parlor, and sitting-room and dining-room.

COST: $6,224, † not including range and heater. The estimate is based on ‡ New York prices for labor and materials.

Price of working plans (with full details drawn to large scale), complete specifications, and * license to build, ... $65.00
Price of †† bill of materials, . 20.00

FEASIBLE MODIFICATIONS: General dimensions, materials and colors may be changed. Cellar may be reduced in size. Open fire places may be introduced in parlor, dining-room and sitting-room, and bedrooms over parlor and dining-room. Sliding doors may be placed between hall and sitting-room, and between parlor and dining-room.

The price of working plans, specifications, etc., for a modified design varies according to the alterations required and will be made known upon application to the Architects.

Address, THE CO-OPERATIVE BUILDING PLAN ASSOCIATION, Architects, 106-108 Fulton Street, New York.

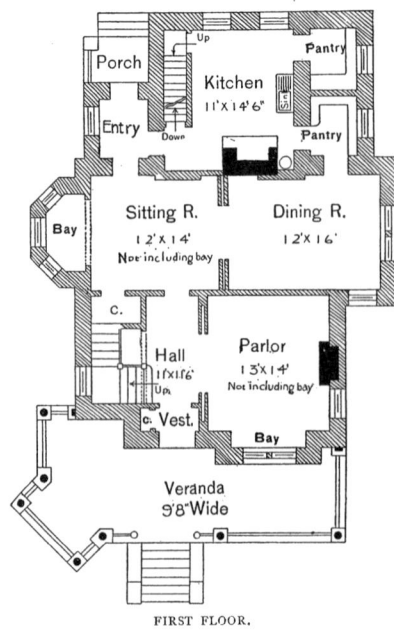

FIRST FLOOR.

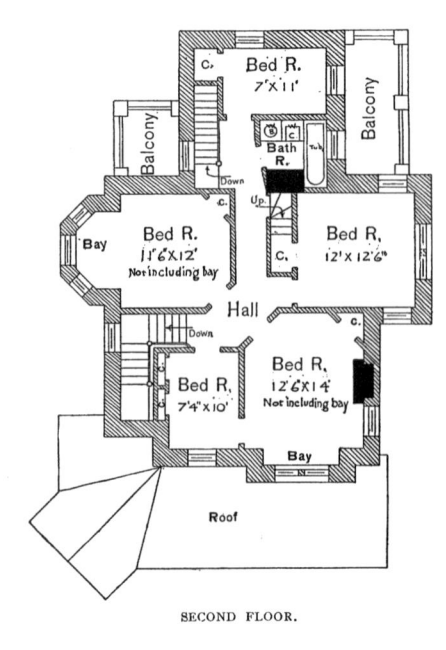

SECOND FLOOR.

94

Residence, Design No. 1476

PERSPECTIVE.

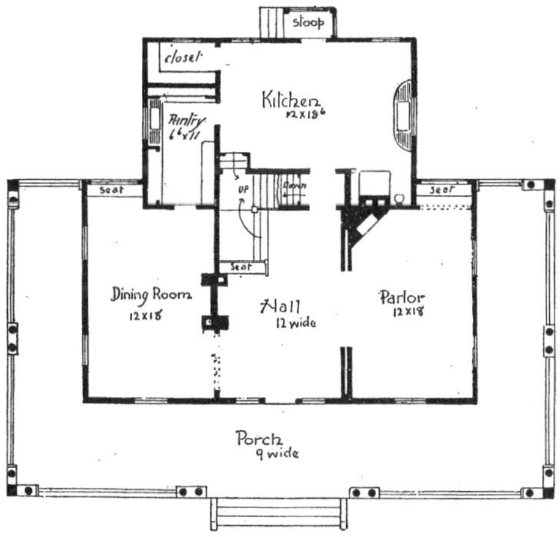

FIRST FLOOR.

NOTES.

Prices for materials and labor, on which all costs of structures are based, are given on page 170.

Many people think it an unnecessary expense to invest in Working Plans, etc.; that their builders can draw up plans or follow rough sketches of their own. This is a great error. It would be true economy to pay even five times as much as our charges for proper drawings, etc. Without them mistakes are sure to occur, and to rectify a single mistake often costs much more than the cost of the plans.

It is also impossible to get a low or correct estimate without the Working Plans and Specifications.

Plans may be returned to us if cost exceeds our estimate. (For terms see page 170.)

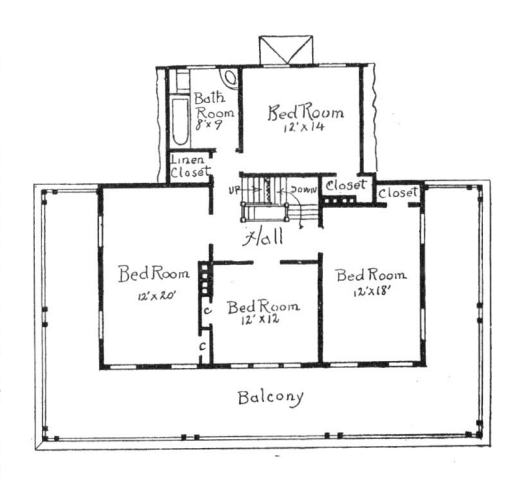

DESCRIPTION.

GENERAL DIMENSIONS: Width, 38 ft. 6 ins., not including porch; depth, not including veranda, 34 ft.

HEIGHTS OF STORIES: Cellar, 7 ft.; first story, 10 ft.; second story, 9 ft. 6 ins.; attic, 8 ft. 6 ins.

EXTERIOR MATERIALS: Foundation, brick; first story, clapboards; second story, gables and roofs, shingles.

INTERIOR FINISH: Hard white plaster throughout. First floor double, with paper between. Finished flooring, first story, hard pine; second story, soft wood. Hard wood trim in first story. Main staircase, ash. Bath-room and kitchen, wainscoted. Chair-rail in dining-room. All interior wood-work, grain filled, stained to suit owner, and finished with hard oil varnish.

COLORS: All clapboards, gray. Trim, including water-table, corner boards, casings, cornices, bands, veranda columns, rail, etc., olive drab. Outside doors, light olive drab. Sashes, dark red. Veranda and porch floors and ceilings, oiled. Shingling on side walls and roofs, left natural for weather stain.

ACCOMMODATIONS: The principal rooms and their sizes, closets, etc., are shown by the floor plans. Cellar under the whole house, with inside and outside entrances and concrete floor. Three set-tubs in cellar. Portable range, boiler and sink in kitchen. Bath-room, with complete plumbing, in the second story. Rear stairway from kitchen, connecting at platform with main staircase. Broad veranda. Fireplaces in hall, parlor and dining-room. Portiere opening connects dining-room and hall. Attractive staircase has upholstered seat. One room finished in attic. Sliding doors between hall and parlor.

COST: $6,400, † not including mantels, range and heater. The estimate is based on ‡ New York prices for materials and labor. In many sections of the country the cost should be less.

Price of working plans (with full details drawn to large scale), specifications and * license to build, ... $65.00

Price of †† bill of materials, . . . 20.00

FEASIBLE MODIFICATIONS: General dimensions, materials and colors may be changed. Cellar may be reduced in size or entirely omitted. Two additional rooms may be finished in the attic. Fireplace may be introduced in the dining-room. A portion or all the plumbing may be omitted. Laundry may be introduced in cellar.

The price of working plans, specifications, etc., for a modified design, varies according to the alterations required and will be made known upon application to the Architects.

Address, THE CO-OPERATIVE BUILDING PLAN ASSOCIATION, Architects, 106-108 Fulton Street, New York.

SECOND FLOOR.

Residence, Design No. 1477

DESCRIPTION.

GENERAL DIMENSIONS: Width, including veranda, 80 ft.; depth, not including front veranda or alcove, 17 ft. 8 ins.

HEIGHTS OF STORIES: Cellar, 7 ft.; first story, 9 ft. 4 ins.; second story, 9 ft. 2 ins.; attic, 9 ft.

EXTERIOR MATERIALS: Foundation, stone; first story, brick; second story, gables, dormers, roofs and veranda and balcony enclosures, shingles.

INTERIOR FINISH: Three coat plaster, hard white finish. Plaster centers and cornices in parlor, dining-room and hall of first story. Flooring throughout, N. C. pine. Trim, white wood. Main staircase, ash. Kitchen and bathroom, wainscoted. Chair-rail in dining-room. All interior wood-work grain filled, stained to suit owner and finished in hard oil varnish.

COLORS: Trim, including cornices, casings, veranda posts, rail, etc., white. Sashes, dark green. Outside doors, varnished. Veranda floor and ceiling, oiled. Shingles on side walls stained dark sienna. Roof shingles stained dark red.

ACCOMMODATIONS: The principal rooms and their sizes, closets, etc., are shown by the floor plans. Cellar under the whole house, with inside and outside entrance and concrete floor. Laundry under kitchen contains two set-tubs and servants' closet. One room finished off in attic, remainder of space floored for storage purposes. Open fireplaces in parlor, dining-room and hall. Hat and coat closet in main hall. Bath-room in second story. Linen closet in second story hall.

COST: $6,500, † not including mantels, range or heater. The estimate is based on ‡ New York prices for materials and labor. In many sections of the country the cost should be less.

Price of working plans (with full details drawn to large scale), specifications, and * license to build, ... $65.00

Price of †† bill of materials, . . 20.00

FEASIBLE MODIFICATIONS: General dimensions, materials and colors may be changed. Cellar may be reduced in size. Laundry may be omitted and tubs transferred to kitchen. Sliding doors may be introduced between hall and parlor. Fireplace may be planned in dining-room. One or two additional rooms may be finished off in attic, or attic may be left entirely unfinished.

The price of working plans, specifications, etc., for a modified design, varies according to the alterations required and will be made known upon application to the Architects.

Address, THE CO-OPERATIVE BUILDING PLAN ASSOCIATION, Architects, 106–108 Fulton Street, New York.

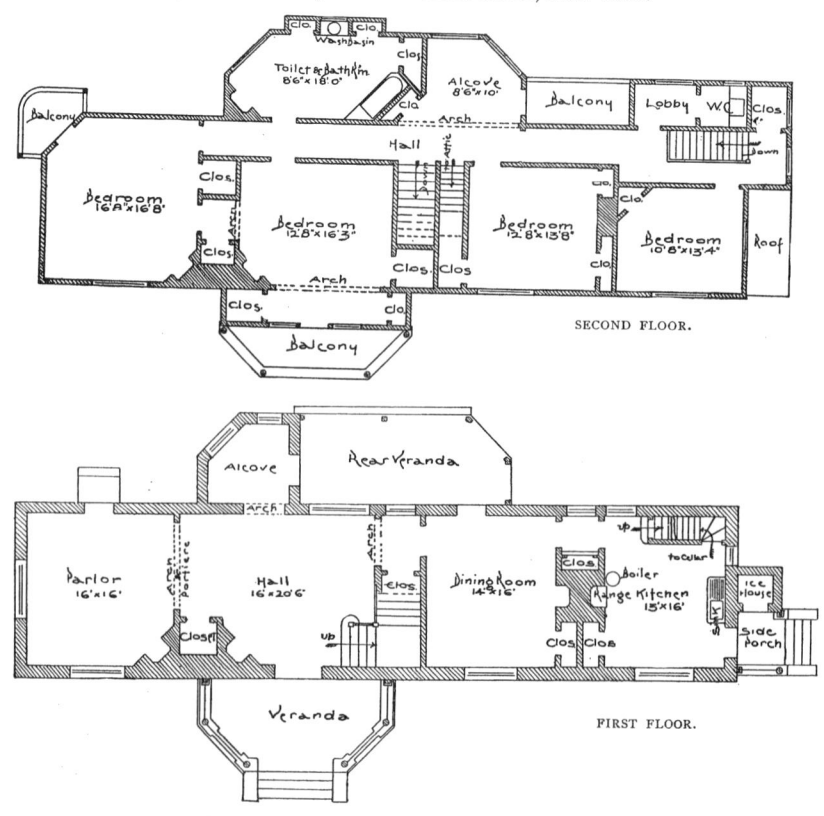

Residence, Design No. 1478

DESCRIPTION.

GENERAL DIMENSIONS: Width, not including veranda and dining-room bay, 42 ft. 2 ins.; depth, not including veranda, 35 ft. 6 ins.

HEIGHTS OF STORIES: Cellar, 7 ft.; first story, 10 ft.; second story, 9 ft.; attic, 8 ft. 6 ins.

EXTERIOR MATERIALS: Foundation, stone and brick; first story, second story, gables and roof, shingles.

INTERIOR FINISH: Hard white plaster; plaster cornices and centers in parlor, dining room and library. Double floor in first story with paper between; finished floors, soft wood. Trim in hall and vestibule, quartered oak. Main staircase, oak. Panel-backs under windows in parlor, dining-room and library. Picture moulding in principal rooms and hall of first story. Chair rail in dining-room. Bath-room and kitchen, wainscoted. Interior wood work stained to suit owner and finished in hard oil varnish.

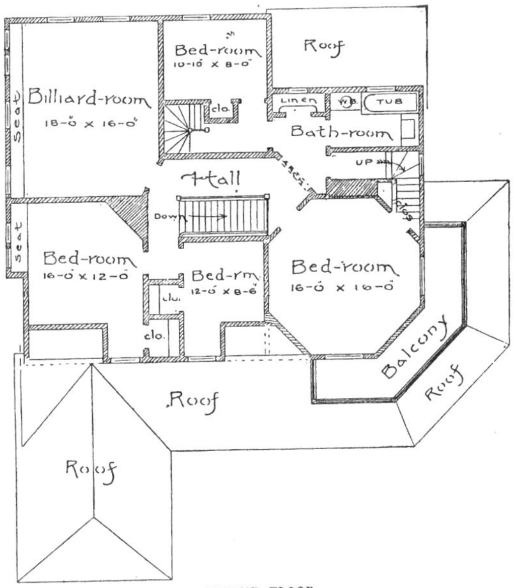

COLORS: Trim, including corner boards, cornices, casings, bands, veranda posts and rails, outside blinds, rain conductors, etc., chocolate. Outside doors finished with hard oil. Sashes, Pompeiian red. Veranda floor and ceiling and all brick-work, oiled. Wall shingles dipped in and brush coated with light sienna stain. Roof shingles dipped in and brush coated dark green stain.

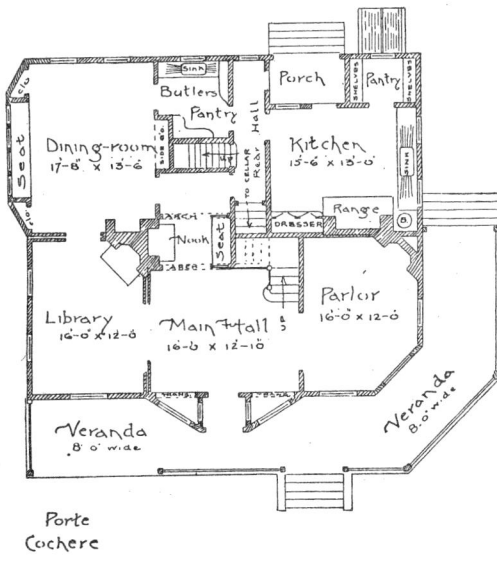

ACCOMMODATIONS: The principal rooms and their sizes, closets, etc., are shown by the floor plans. Cellar under the whole house, with inside and outside entrances and concrete floor. One room finished in attic; space for two more. Attractive main staircase. Sliding doors connect dining-room, library and hall and portiere, hall and parlor.

COST: $7,000, † not including mantels, range or heater. The estimate is based on ‡ New York prices for materials and labor. In many sections of the country the cost should be less.

Price of working plans (with full details drawn to large scale), specifications and * license to build, ... $70.00
Price of †† bill of materials, ... 20.00

FEASIBLE MODIFICATIONS: General dimensions, materials and colors may be changed. Cellar may be reduced in size, or omitted. Attic may be left unfinished. Sliding doors, open fireplaces, and part or all of plumbing, may be omitted. Veranda may be extended to dining-room bay. Portable range may be substituted for brick-set one. Wash-tubs may be transferred from cellar to kitchen, or a laundry may be added at rear of kitchen.

The price of working plans, specifications, etc., for a modified design, varies according to the alterations required and will be made known upon application to the Architects.

Address, THE CO-OPERATIVE BUILDING PLAN ASSOCIATION, Architects, 106–108 Fulton Street, New York.

FIRST FLOOR.

SECOND FLOOR.

Residence, Design No. 1479

PERSPECTIVE.

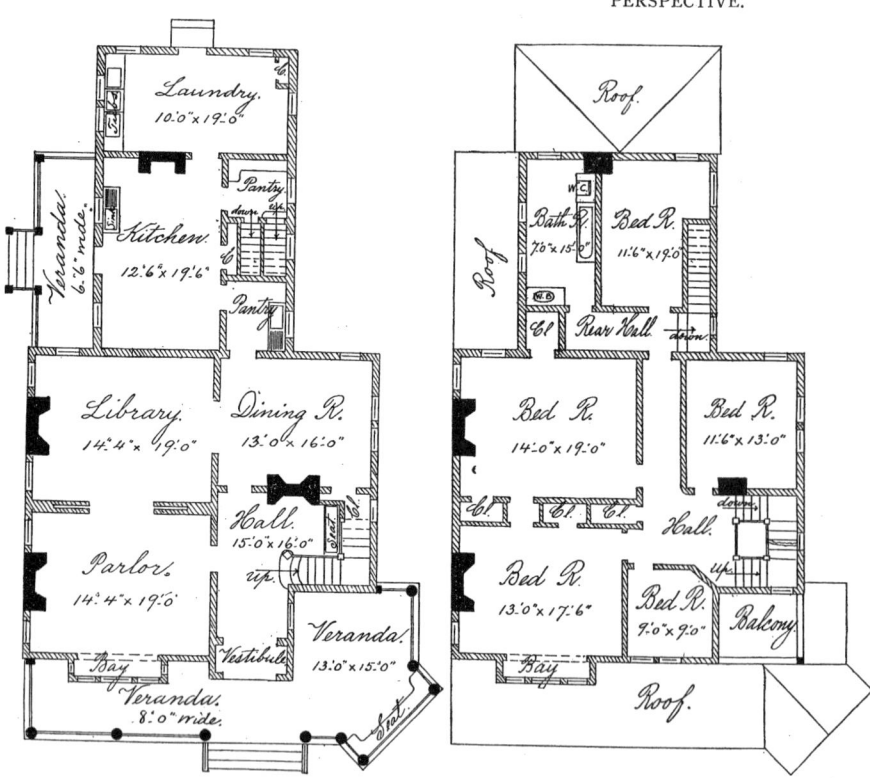

FIRST FLOOR.   SECOND FLOOR.

DESCRIPTION.

GENERAL DIMENSIONS: Width, including veranda, 42 ft. 8 ins.; depth, including veranda, 72 ft. 6 ins.

HEIGHTS OF STORIES: Cellar, 7 ft. 6 ins.; first story, 10 ft. 6 ins.; second story, 9 ft. 6 ins.; attic, 8 ft. 6 ins.

EXTERIOR MATERIALS: Foundations, stone and brick; first story, clapboards; second story, shingles; gables are paneled bracketed and shingled; roof, slate.

INTERIOR FINISH: Hard wood main staircase; Three coat hard white plaster throughout; plaster cornices and centers in parlor, library, dining-room and hall. Hard wood trim in halls (both stories), parlor, library and dining-room; other rooms throughout trimmed with soft woods of handsome design. Halls wainscoted with hard wood. Hard wood floors throughout first story. All wood-work finished in hard oil. House piped for gas, and wired for electric bells from front door to kitchen and from front second story and attic halls to kitchen. All large window panes plate glass.

COLORS: All clapboards, light yellow. Trim, cornices, veranda and balcony posts, rails, balusters gable brackets, and framing of panels, white. Second story shingles dipped in and brush coated with yellowish red stain. Shingles in gables and veranda pediment, panels in gables, and cheeks of dormers painted light yellow. Slate on roof oiled. Brick-work of foundation and veranda piers painted red. Brick-work of chimneys painted yellow. Cresting and finials painted red. Veranda floors and ceilings, oiled. All sashes, dark green.

ACCOMMODATIONS: The principal rooms and their sizes, closets, etc., are shown by the plans. Cellar under the whole house. Three rooms and hall finished in attic besides ample storage room. Fireplaces in parlor, library, dining-room, hall and two bedrooms of second story. Handsome stairway and seat in hall. Tile floor in vestibule.

COST: $7,500, † not including mantels, range and heater. The estimate is based on ‡ New York prices for materials and labor. In many sections of the country the cost should be less.

Price of working plans (with full details drawn to large scale), specifications and * license to build, ... $75.00
Price of †† bill of materials, . . . 20.00

FEASIBLE MODIFICATIONS: General dimensions, materials and colors may be changed. First story may be brick or stone. Small front bedroom may be connected with larger bedroom and serve as a dressing room. The number of fireplaces and chimneys may be reduced if heating apparatus be used, and one chimney will suffice. Gas piping, a portion or all of plumbing, electric bells, and all hard wood may be omitted

Address, THE CO-OPERATIVE BUILDING PLAN ASSOCIATION, Architects, 106–108 Fulton Street, New York.

Residence, Design No. 1481

PERSPECTIVE.

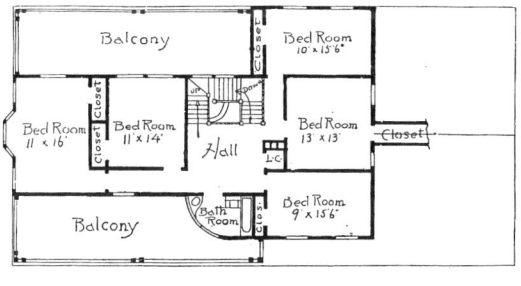

DESCRIPTION.

GENERAL DIMENSIONS: Extreme width, not including veranda, 57 ft. 6 ins.; depth, including veranda, 37 ft.

HEIGHTS OF STORIES: Cellar, 8 ft.; first story, 10 ft.; second story, 9 ft. 6 ins.; attic, 8 ft.

EXTERIOR MATERIALS: Foundation, stone; first story, clapboards; second story, gables and roof, shingles. Outside blinds to all windows, except those of the cellar and bay.

INTERIOR FINISH: Hard white plaster; plaster cornices and centers in main hall (first story), parlor, sitting and dining-room. Hard pine flooring in laundry, pantry, water closet and kitchen; remainder of flooring, soft wood, except in hall, dining-room and sitting-room where oak is used. Ash trim in first story, soft wood trim in remainder. Ash staircase. Panels under windows in sitting-room, parlor and dining-room. Wainscot in bath-room, laundry, pantry and kitchen. Interior wood-work finished in hard oil, except attic, which is painted colors to suit owner.

COLORS: All clapboards, olive drab. Trim, blinds, rain conductors and balcony posts, olive green. Outside doors dark green with olive green panels. Sashes, dark red. Veranda floor and ceiling, varnished. Wall shingles oiled and stained a little darker than natural color of wood. Roof shingles dipped and brush coated in red stain.

ACCOMMODATIONS: The principal rooms and their sizes, closets, etc., are shown by the plans. Cellar under whole house, with concrete floor and inside and outside entrance. Three bedrooms finished in attic. Laundry under kitchen. Sliding doors connect principal rooms of first story. Three open fireplaces and portable range. Balconies in second and attic story.

COST: $7,900, † not including mantels, range or heater. The estimate is based on ‡ New York prices for materials and labor. In many sections of the country the cost should be less.

Price of working plans (with full details drawn to large scale), specifications and * license to build, ... $80.00

Price of †† bill of materials, ... 25.00

SECOND FLOOR.

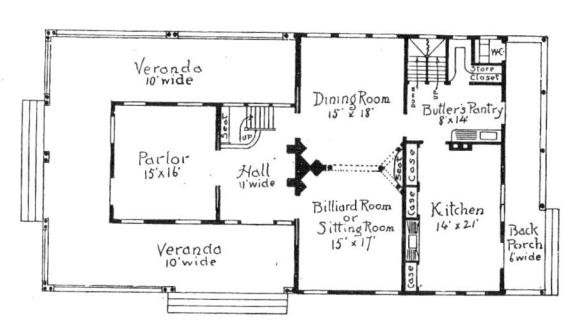

FIRST FLOOR.

FEASIBLE MODIFICATIONS: General dimensions, materials and colors may be changed. Cellar may be reduced in size and concrete floor omitted. Attic finish, open fireplaces and mantels, sliding doors, and a part or all of plumbing may be omitted.

The price of working plans, specifications, etc., for a modified design, varies according to the alterations required and will be made known upon application to the Architects.

Address, THE CO-OPERATIVE BUILDING PLAN ASSOCIATION, Architects, 106–108 Fulton Street, New York.

Residence, Design No. 1482

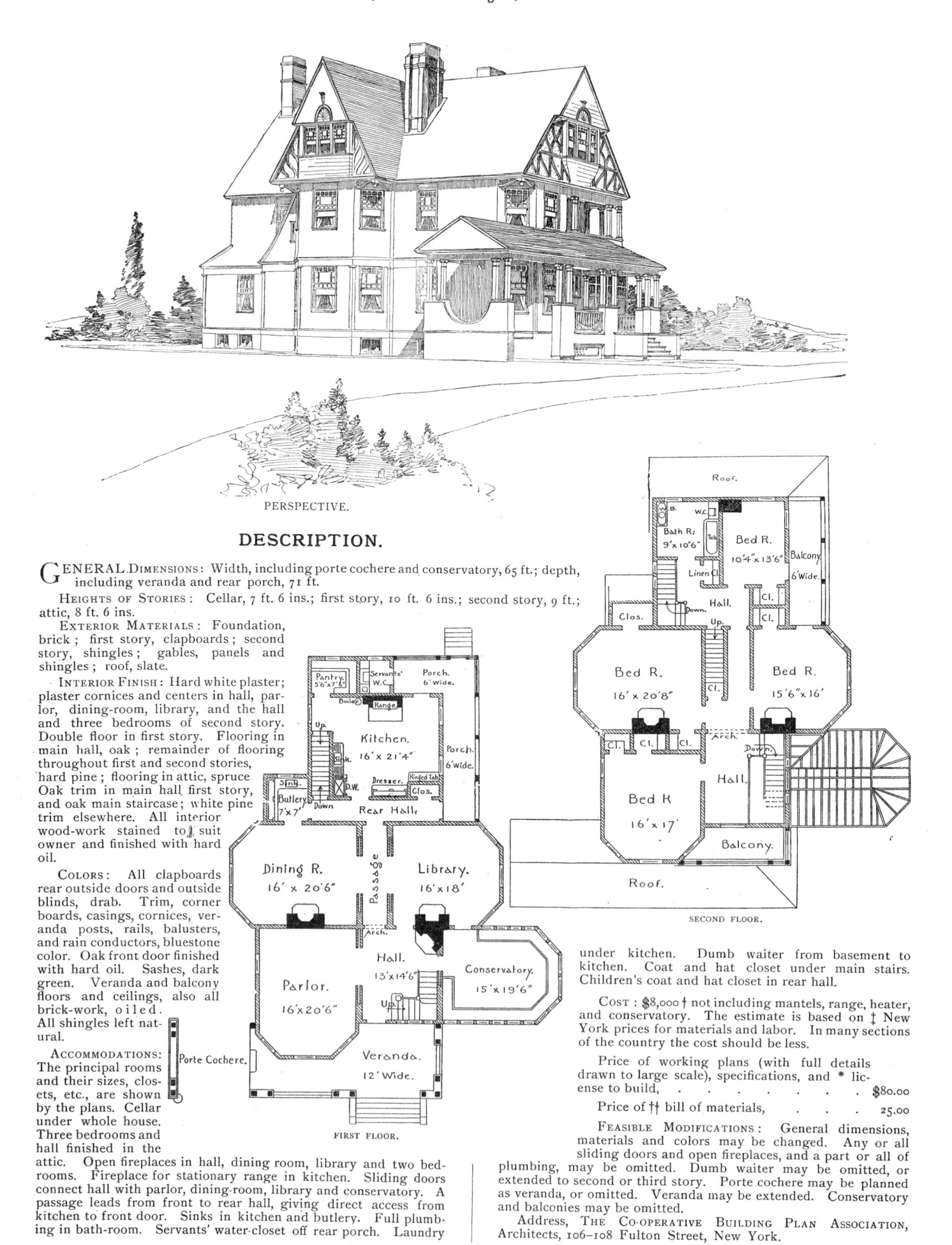

PERSPECTIVE.

DESCRIPTION.

GENERAL DIMENSIONS: Width, including porte cochere and conservatory, 65 ft.; depth, including veranda and rear porch, 71 ft.

HEIGHTS OF STORIES: Cellar, 7 ft. 6 ins.; first story, 10 ft. 6 ins.; second story, 9 ft.; attic, 8 ft. 6 ins.

EXTERIOR MATERIALS: Foundation, brick; first story, clapboards; second story, shingles; gables, panels and shingles; roof, slate.

INTERIOR FINISH: Hard white plaster; plaster cornices and centers in hall, parlor, dining-room, library, and the hall and three bedrooms of second story. Double floor in first story. Flooring in main hall, oak; remainder of flooring throughout first and second stories, hard pine; flooring in attic, spruce. Oak trim in main hall, first story, and oak main staircase; white pine trim elsewhere. All interior wood-work stained to suit owner and finished with hard oil.

COLORS: All clapboards rear outside doors and outside blinds, drab. Trim, corner boards, casings, cornices, veranda posts, rails, balusters, and rain conductors, bluestone color. Oak front door finished with hard oil. Sashes, dark green. Veranda and balcony floors and ceilings, also all brick-work, oiled. All shingles left natural.

ACCOMMODATIONS: The principal rooms and their sizes, closets, etc., are shown by the plans. Cellar under whole house. Three bedrooms and hall finished in the attic. Open fireplaces in hall, dining room, library and two bedrooms. Fireplace for stationary range in kitchen. Sliding doors connect hall with parlor, dining-room, library and conservatory. A passage leads from front to rear hall, giving direct access from kitchen to front door. Sinks in kitchen and butlery. Full plumbing in bath-room. Servants' water-closet off rear porch. Laundry under kitchen. Dumb waiter from basement to kitchen. Coat and hat closet under main stairs. Children's coat and hat closet in rear hall.

COST: $8,000 † not including mantels, range, heater, and conservatory. The estimate is based on ‡ New York prices for materials and labor. In many sections of the country the cost should be less.

Price of working plans (with full details drawn to large scale), specifications, and * license to build, ... $80.00

Price of †† bill of materials, . . . 25.00

FEASIBLE MODIFICATIONS: General dimensions, materials and colors may be changed. Any or all sliding doors and open fireplaces, and a part or all of plumbing, may be omitted. Dumb waiter may be omitted, or extended to second or third story. Porte cochere may be planned as veranda, or omitted. Veranda may be extended. Conservatory and balconies may be omitted.

Address, THE CO-OPERATIVE BUILDING PLAN ASSOCIATION, Architects, 106–108 Fulton Street, New York.

Residence, Design No. 1483

PERSPECTIVE.

DESCRIPTION.

GENERAL DIMENSIONS: Width, 48 ft. 6 ins., not including porch; depth, not including veranda, 53 ft.

HEIGHTS OF STORIES: Cellar, 8 ft.; first story, 10 ft.; second story, 9 ft. 6 ins.

EXTERIOR MATERIALS: Foundation and portion of first story, field stone; first and second stories, gables and roofs, shingles.

INTERIOR FINISH: Three coat plaster, hard white finish. Plaster centers in parlor, dining-room, library and hall. Main staircase, oak. Chair-rail in dining-room. Hardwood trim and floor in dining-room, library and hall. All interior wood-work grain filled, stained to suit owner and finished with hard oil varnish.

COLORS: Trim, including casings, cornices, bands, veranda rail, etc., white. Shingling on side walls to be dipped and brush coated with olive green stain. Shingled roofs, stained red. Sashes, dark bottle green. Veranda floor and ceiling, oiled.

ACCOMMODATIONS: The principal rooms and their sizes, closets, etc., are shown by the floor plans. Cellar under whole house, with inside entrance and concrete floor. Butler's pantry connects kitchen and dining-room, and contains dresser, sink and shelving. Open fireplace in dining-room, library and parlor. Two rooms and hall finished in attic. Sliding doors connect hall, parlor, dining-room and library. Bath-room, with full plumbing, in second story.

COST: $8,000, † not including plumbing, mantels, range or heater. The estimate is based on ‡ New York prices for materials and labor. In many sections of the country the cost should be less.

Price of working plans (with full details drawn to large scale), specifications and * license to build, ... $80.00

Price of †† bill of materials, ... 20.00

FEASIBLE MODIFICATIONS: General dimensions, materials and colors may be changed. Fireplace and part or all of plumbing may be omitted. Veranda may be extended or be partly omitted.

The price of working plans, specifications, etc., for a modified design, varies according to the alterations required and will be made known upon application to the Architects.

Address, THE CO-OPERATIVE BUILDING PLAN ASSOCIATION, Architects, 106-108 Fulton Street, New York.

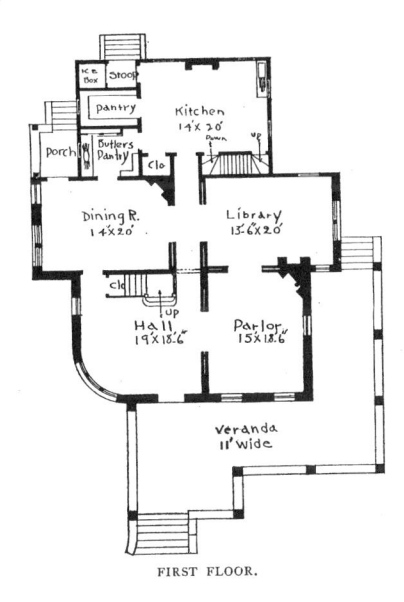

FIRST FLOOR.

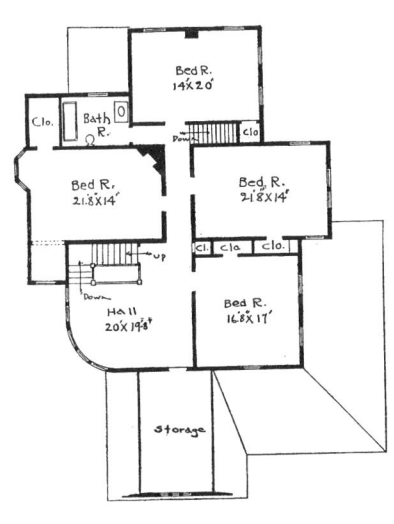

SECOND FLOOR.

Residence, Design No. 1484

PERSPECTIVE.

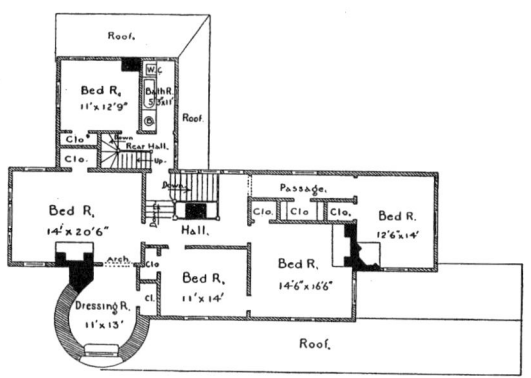

SECOND FLOOR.

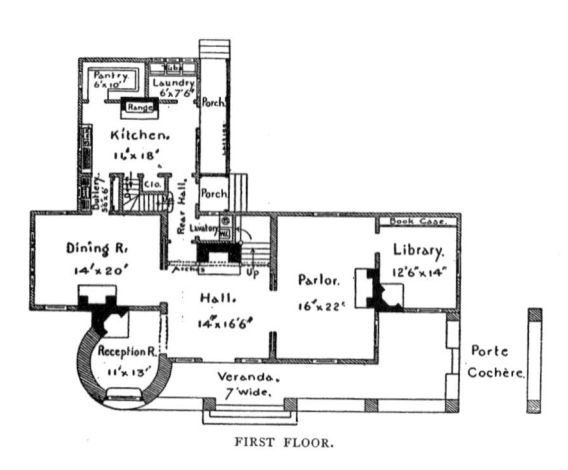

FIRST FLOOR.

DESCRIPTION.

GENERAL DIMENSIONS: Width, including porte cochere, 81 ft. 6 ins.; depth, including veranda, 54 ft.

HEIGHTS OF STORIES: Cellar, 8 ft.; first story, 10 ft.; second story, 9 ft.; attic, 8 ft.

EXTERIOR MATERIALS: Foundation, porte cochere, veranda, and part of first and second stories, stone; remainder of walls and all roofs, shingles.

INTERIOR FINISH: Hard white plaster. Main stairs and first story hall finished with oak; remainder of house floored and trimmed with soft woods, stained to suit owner. All wood-work finished with hard oil rubbed to a dull gloss.

COLORS: All wall shingles left natural. Trim and all cornices and other mouldings, white. Sashes, red. Veranda floor and ceiling, oiled. Outside doors finished with hard oil. Roof shingles dipped and brush coated red stain.

ACCOMMODATIONS: The principal rooms and their sizes, closets, etc., are shown by the floor plans. Cellar under whole house. Two rooms and hall finished in attic. Sliding doors connect hall with dining-room and parlor. Open fireplaces in reception-room, dining-room, hall, parlor, library, and three bedrooms. Stationary range in kitchen. Stationary tubs in laundry. Sinks in kitchen and butlery. Wash-bowl and water-closet in lavatory under main stairs. Full plumbing in bath-room. Handsome staircase and fireplace. Kitchen porch enclosed by lattice. Bookcase built in the wall of library.

COST: $8,500, † not including mantels, range and heater. The estimate is based on ‡ New York prices for materials and labor. In many sections of the country the cost should be less.

Price of working plans (with full details drawn to large scale), specifications
and * license to build, ... $85.00
Price of †† bill of materials, ... 25.00

FEASIBLE MODIFICATIONS: General dimensions, materials and colors may be changed. Size of cellar may be reduced. Two more rooms may be finished in attic. Porte cochere may be re-planned as veranda. Veranda may be reduced or extended Laundry may be placed in basement. Reception-room projection may be carried up to form tower. Any or all sliding doors and open fireplaces and a part or all of plumbing may be omitted.

Address, THE CO-OPERATIVE BUILDING PLAN ASSOCIATION, Architects, 106–108 Fulton Street, New York.

Residence, Design No. 1485

PERSPECTIVE.

DESCRIPTION.

GENERAL DIMENSIONS: Width over all, 67 ft. 6 ins.; depth, including verandas, 82 ft.

HEIGHTS OF STORIES: Basement 8 ft.; first story, 11 ft.; second story, 10 ft.; third story, 9 ft.

EXTERIOR MATERIALS: Foundation, brick; first story, second story, gables, dormers and roofs, shingles.

INTERIOR FINISH: Three coat plaster, hard white finish. Plaster cornices and centers in all principal rooms of first and second stories and in first story hall. First story floor double, with paper between. Top floors in kitchen, pantries and bath-room to be Georgia pine; elsewhere soft wood. Trim in main part of first and second stories, ash; in kitchen portion and third story, white pine; all to be grain-filled and finished with hard oil. Paneled backs under windows of hall and principal rooms first story. Picture moulding in main house, first and second stories. Chair-rail in servants' dining-room in basement. Main stairs, ash. Bath-room and kitchen wainscoted. Paneled wainscot in main hall.

COLORS: All shingling left natural to acquire weather stain. Trim, blinds and sashes, ivory white. Outside doors finished with hard oil. Balcony and veranda floors, dark drab. Balcony and veranda ceilings finished with hard oil.

ACCOMMODATIONS: The principal rooms and their sizes, closets, etc., are shown by the floor plans. Basement under the whole house with inside and outside entrances. Basement contains laundry with three set-tubs, servants' dining-room, servants' bath-room, store-room, wine cellar, furnace room, vegetable cellar and fuel-room. Four bedrooms and hall finished in third story. Spacious verandas and balconies. Open fireplaces in parlor, dining-room, library, sitting-room, and three bedrooms. Double sliding doors between hall and library and sitting and dining-rooms, and double folding doors connecting hall, parlor and dining-room. Two bath-rooms, with complete plumbing, in second story. The house is well arranged for a first-class summer boarding house.

COST: $9,000, † not including mantels, range and heater. The cost is based on ‡ New York prices for materials and labor. In many sections of the country the cost should be less.

Price of working plans (with full details drawn to large scale), specifications, and * license to build, ... $90.00

Price of †† bill of materials, ... 25.00

FEASIBLE MODIFICATIONS: General dimensions, materials and colors may be changed. Basement may be reduced in size. Servants' dining-room and bath-room may be omitted. The number of finished rooms in third story may be reduced, or the entire third story may be left unfinished. The veranda may be reduced in size. By reducing their number the second story rooms may be enlarged.

The price of working plans, specifications, etc., for a modified design, varies according to the alterations required and will be made known upon application to the Architects.

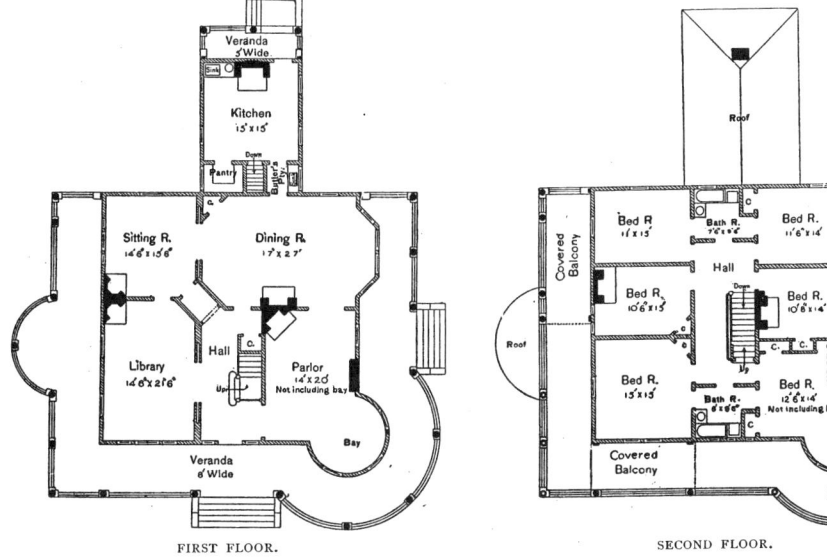

FIRST FLOOR. SECOND FLOOR. 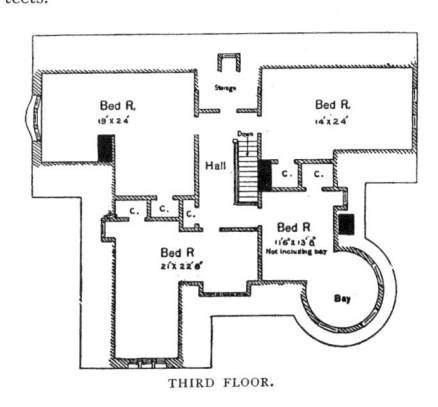 THIRD FLOOR.

103

Residence, Design No. 1486

PERSPECTIVE.

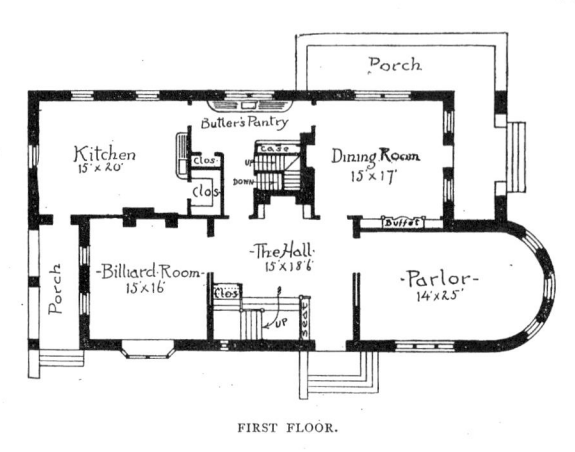

FIRST FLOOR.

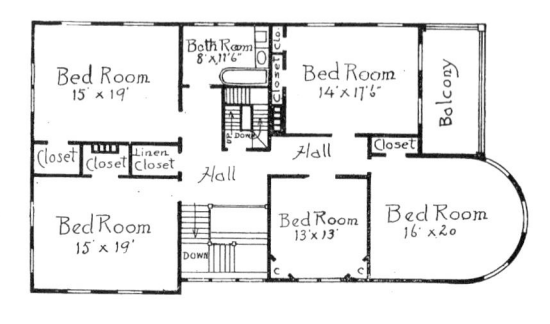

SECOND FLOOR.

DESCRIPTION.

GENERAL DIMENSIONS: Width, 71 ft. 10 ins.; depth, not including porch, 33 ft. 10 ins.

HEIGHTS OF STORIES: Cellar, 8 ft.; first story, 10 ft.; second story, 9 ft. 6 ins.

EXTERIOR MATERIALS: Foundation, stone; first story, porch piers, etc., field stone; second story, gables and roofs, shingles.

INTERIOR FINISH: Three coat plaster, hard white finish. Soft wood flooring and trim, except in hall, parlor, dining room and billiard-room, where oak is used. Main staircase, oak. Panel backs under windows in parlor, hall and dining-room. Picture moulding in principal rooms and hall, first story. Bath-room and kitchen, wainscoted. All interior wood-work finished natural in hard oil varnish.

COLORS: Trim, olive. Rear outside door, bronze green. Front door finished natural with hard oil varnish. Blinds, bronze green. Sashes and conductors, bright red. Shingles on side walls left natural. Roof shingles stained brown.

ACCOMMODATIONS: The principal rooms and their sizes, closets, etc., are shown by the floor plans. Cellar under the whole house with inside and outside entrances. Sliding doors connect hall, parlor and billiard-room. Attic floored and two rooms finished off. Bath-room, with complete plumbing, in second story. Sink, portable range and boiler in kitchen. Open fireplace in billiard room, hall, nook, and child's bedroom. Laundry in cellar. Attractive main staircase. Large butler's pantry and kitchen closet.

COST: $9,000, † not including mantels, range and heater.

The estimate is based on ‡ New York prices for materials and labor. In many sections of the country the cost should be less.

Price of working plans (with full details drawn to large scale), specifications and * license to build, . . $90.00
Price of †† bill of materials, ... 25.00

FEASIBLE MODIFICATIONS: General dimensions, materials and colors may be changed. Uncovered porch may be roofed over. Attic may be left unfinished.

The price of working plans, specifications, etc., for a modified design, varies according to the alterations required and will be made known upon application to the Architects.

Address, THE CO-OPERATIVE BUILDING PLAN ASSOCIATION, Architects, 106–108 Fulton Street, New York.

Residence, Design No. 1487

PERSPECTIVE.

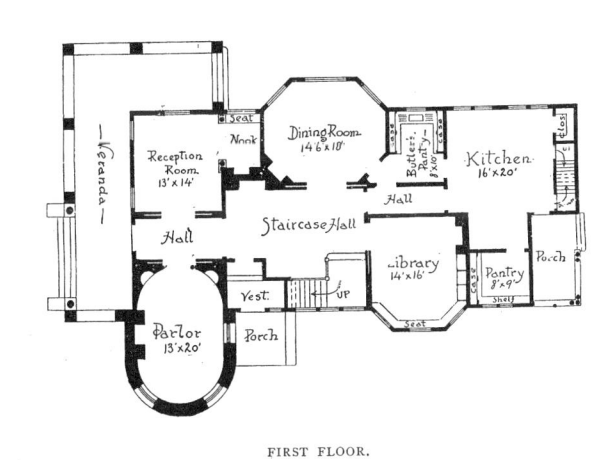

FIRST FLOOR.

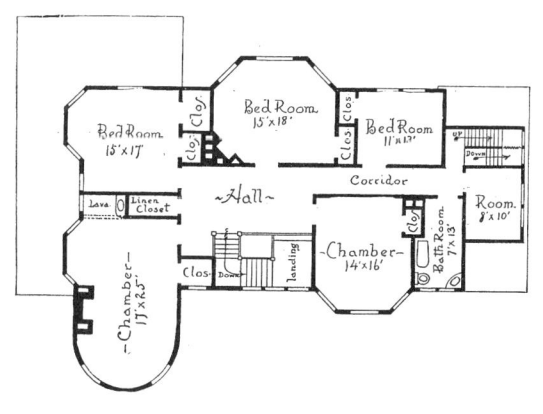

SECOND FLOOR.

DESCRIPTION.

General Dimensions: Width, including veranda, 54 ft.; depth, not including veranda, 68 ft. 6 ins.

Heights of Stories: Cellar, 7 ft.; first story, 10 ft.; second story, 9 ft. 6 ins.; attic, 9 ft.

Exterior Materials: Foundation, stone; veranda enclosure and posts and portion of first story, field stone; remainder first story, second story, gables and roof, shingles.

Interior Finish: Three coat plaster, hard white finish. Plaster centres in reception-room, parlor, library, dining-room and hall of first story. Flooring, North Carolina pine, except principal rooms in first story, where hard wood is used. Trim, white wood. Main staircase, ash. Bath-room and kitchen wainscoted. Chair-rail in dining-room. All interior wood-work, grain filled and finished with hard oil varnish.

Colors: Casings, cornices, bands, outside blinds, veranda posts, rail, etc., dark green. Shingling on side walls left natural. Shingle roofs dipped and brush coated brown stain. Sashes, white. Porch floor and ceiling and outside doors, grain filled and finished with hard oil.

Accommodations: The principal rooms and their sizes, closets, etc., are shown by the floor plans. Cellar under the whole house, with inside and outside entrances and concrete floor. Portable range, sink and boiler in kitchen. Sliding doors connect reception-room, dining-room, hall, library and parlor. Open fireplaces in the above named rooms and two bedrooms. Three set wash trays in cellar. Two rooms and hall in attic.

Cost: $9,860, † not including mantels, range or heater. The estimate is based on ‡ New York prices for materials and labor. In many sections of the country the cost should be less.

Price of working plans (with full details drawn to large scale), specifications and * license to build, ... $90.00

Price of †† bill of materials, ... 25.00

Feasible Modifications: General dimensions, materials and colors may be changed. Cellar may be reduced in size or wholly omitted. Any or all fireplaces and part or all of plumbing may be omitted. Sliding doors may be omitted. Veranda may be reduced in size or extended. Attic may be left unfinished.

The price of working plans, specifications, etc., for a modified design, varies according to the alterations required and will be made known upon application to the Architects.

Address, The Co-operative Building Plan Association, Architects, 106–108 Fulton Street, New York.

Residence, Design No. 1488

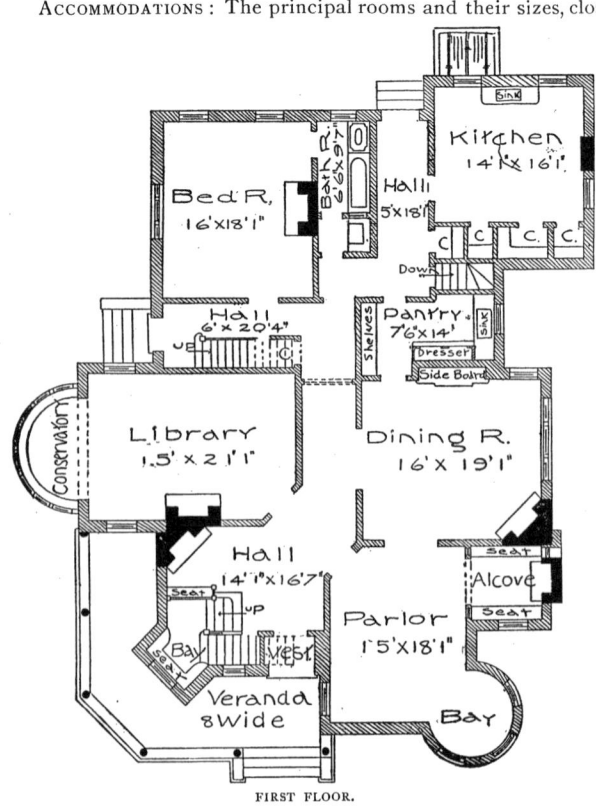

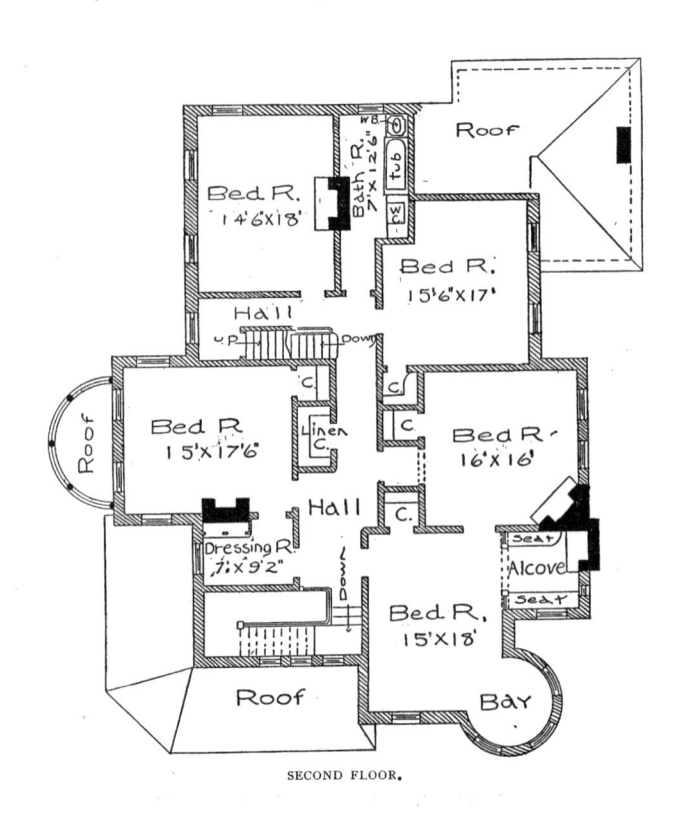

PERSPECTIVE.

DESCRIPTION.

GENERAL DIMENSIONS: Width, including conservatory and kitchen, 61 ft. 8 ins.; depth over all, 69 ft. 10 ins.

HEIGHTS OF STORIES: Cellar, 7 ft.; first story, 10 ft. 6 ins.; second story, 9 ft. 6 ins.; attic, 8 ft.

EXTERIOR MATERIALS: Foundation, stone; first and second stories, brick; gables, dormers and roofs, shingled. Outside blinds to all windows, except those of the conservatory, dining-room, first story bedroom, circular bay and cellar.

INTERIOR FINISH: Hard white plaster. Plaster cornices and centers in main hall, library, dining-room and parlor, and four principal bedrooms and alcoves. Yellow pine flooring in first and second stories; white pine flooring in attic. White wood trim throughout. Main stairs, oak. Kitchen, bath and toilet rooms, rear hall and pantry, wainscoted. Interior wood-work finished in hard oil.

COLORS: Brick-work cleaned down at completion. Trim, drab. Outside doors, stained cherry and varnished. Blinds, green. Sashes, dark red. Veranda floor, medium drab. Veranda ceiling, varnished. Wall shingles dipped and brush coated medium drab. Roof shingles dipped and brush coated dark red.

ACCOMMODATIONS: The principal rooms and their sizes, closets, etc., are shown by the floor plans. Cellar with concrete floor under whole house. Laundry under kitchen. Open fireplaces in all principal rooms of first story, and four bedrooms of second story. Bath-rooms in both first and second stories. Handsome staircase with bay on landing. Alcoves in parlor and bedroom over same. Four rooms and storage space in attic. Small conservatory off library.

COST: $10,000, † not including mantels, range and heater. The estimate is based on ‡ New York prices for materials and labor. In many sections of the country the cost should be less.

Price of working plans (with full details drawn to large scale), specifications and * license to build, . . . $100.00

Price of †† bill of materials, ... 25.00

FEASIBLE MODIFICATIONS: Heights of stories, sizes of rooms, materials and colors may be changed. Cellar may be omitted. Attic finish may be omitted. Sliding doors may be introduced. Fireplaces may be reduced in number, or all may be omitted. Part or all of the plumbing may be omitted. Laundry may be planned at rear of kitchen, instead of in basement. Conservatory may be omitted. Kitchen may be planned to take in the hall at side of it. Veranda may be extended in size or reduced.

Address, THE CO-OPERATIVE BUILDING PLAN ASSOCIATION, Architects, 106-108 Fulton Street, New York.

FIRST FLOOR.

SECOND FLOOR.

Residence, Design No. 1490

PERSPECTIVE.

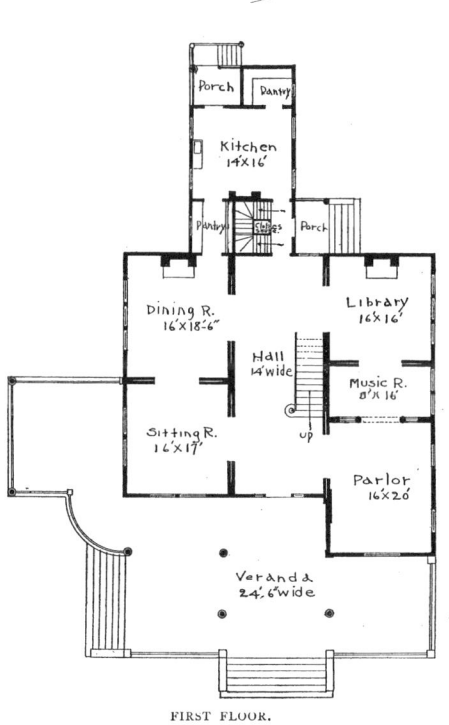

FIRST FLOOR.

SECOND FLOOR.

DESCRIPTION.

GENERAL DIMENSIONS: Width, 49 ft.; depth, not including veranda, 75 ft.

HEIGHTS OF STORIES: Cellar, 8 ft.; first story, 11 ft.; second story, 10 ft.; attic, 8 ft. 6 ins.

EXTERIOR MATERIALS: Foundation, brick; first and second stories, clapboards; dormers and roof, shingles.

INTERIOR FINISH: Hard white plaster, with cornices and centers in hall, parlor, sitting and dining-rooms, and library. Trim in hall and-dining room, oak; remainder of trim, soft woods. Flooring, oak in hall, vestibule and dining-room; yellow pine in laundry, kitchen and butler's pantry; all other floors, white pine. First story floors have rough under-flooring. Main stairway, oak. Main hall, vestibule, dining-room, bath-room and kitchen, wainscoted, Interior trim, etc., stained or painted to suit owner and finished in hard oil.

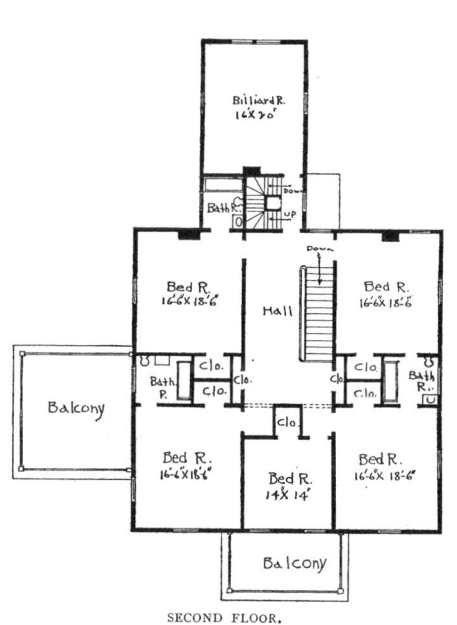

COLORS: All clapboards, blinds and rear outside doors, light terra cotta. Trim and rain conductors, light brown. Front door finished in hard oil. Sashes, bright red. Veranda ceiling, varnished. Veranda floor and all brick-work, oiled. Wall shingles dipped and brush coated reddish stain. Roof shingles dipped and brush-coated dark terra-cotta stain.

ACCOMMODATIONS: The principal rooms and and their sizes, closets, etc., are shown by the floor plans. Cellar under whole house. Bath rooms contain full plumbing. Three bedrooms and storage-room finished in attic. Music-room separated from parlor by columns and grille-work.

COST: $12,800, † not including mantels, range and heater. The estimate is based on ‡ New York prices for materials and labor. In many sections of the country the cost should be less.

Price of working plans (with full details drawn to large scale), specifications and * license to build, . . . $170.00

Price of †† bill of materials, ... $30.00

FEASIBLE MODIFICATIONS: General dimensions, materials and colors may be changed. Cellar may be reduced in size. Veranda may be extended around side.

Address, THE CO-OPERATIVE BUILDING PLAN ASSOCIATION, Architects, 106-108 Fulton Street, New York.

Residence, Design No. 1489

PERSPECTIVE.

DESCRIPTION.

GENERAL DIMENSIONS: Width through library and sitting-room, 48 ft. 2 ins.; depth, including veranda, 67 ft 6 ins.

HEIGHTS OF STORIES: Cellar, 8 ft.; first story, 12 ft.; second story, 10 ft.; attic, 8 ft.

EXTERIOR MATERIALS: Foundations, stone; first and second stories, brick; sides of dormers and all roofs, slate; ornamental work of dormers, copper.

INTERIOR FINISH: Hard white plaster; cellar ceiling plastered one heavy coat. Plaster cornices and centers in main hall, parlor, sitting-room, library, dining-room and large bedrooms of second story. Oak floor in hall and dining-room; white pine elsewhere in first and second stories. Double floor in first story, with paper between. Rough floor in attic. Oak trim in hall and dining-room; remainder of house soft wood. Main staircase, oak. Panels under windows of all principal rooms. Vestibule, main hall, dining-room, kitchen and bath-room, wainscoted. Front entrance doors, oak. All interior wood-work finished in hard oil, stained to suit owner.

COLORS: All brick, stone and slate work cleaned down at completion; brick-work, oiled. Outside cornices, mouldings and veranda rails, seal brown. Veranda posts, balusters and facia of all cornices, light brown. Copper work of dormers to be left clean and natural color of the metal. Veranda floors and ceiling, oiled.

ACCOMMODATIONS: The principal rooms and their sizes, closets, etc., are shown by the floor plans. Cellar under whole house, with concrete floor and inside and outside entrances. Ash-pits with chutes leading to fireplaces. Servant's bath-room and water-closet, and laundry, with stationary tubs, under kitchen. Billiard-room and one bedroom finished in attic. Open fireplaces in dining-room, library, hall, parlor, sitting-room and four bedrooms. Sliding doors connect principal rooms and hall of first story. Hat and coat closet under main staircase.

COST: $10,000,† not including mantels, range and heater. The estimate is based on ‡ New York prices for materials and labor. In many sections of the country the cost should be less.

Price of working plans (with full details drawn to large scale), specifications and * license to build, ... $100.00
Price of †‡ bill of materials, ... 25.00

FEASIBLE MODIFICATIONS: General dimensions, materials and colors may be changed. Attic may be re-planned for more rooms, or it may be left entirely unfinished. First and second stories may be frame or stone. Cellar may be reduced in size or omitted. Ash-pits, fireplaces and sliding doors may be omitted. Part of plumbing may be omitted. Front balcony may be replaced by a veranda roof. Tower balcony may be enclosed with sashes. Shingles or other materials may be used for dormers and roofs.

The price of working plans, specifications, etc., for a modified design, varies according to the alterations required and will be made known upon application to the Architects.

Address, THE CO-OPERATIVE BUILDING PLAN ASSOCIATION, Architects, 106-108 Fulton Street, New York.

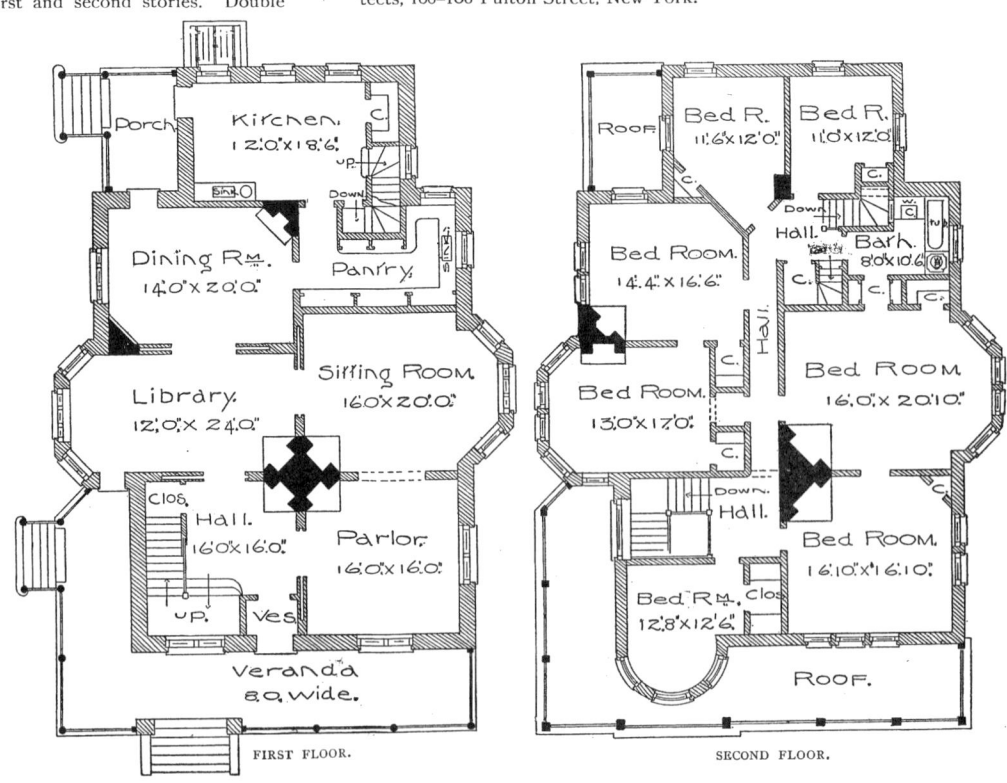

FIRST FLOOR.

SECOND FLOOR.

108

Residence, Design No. 1491

PERSPECTIVE.

DESCRIPTION.

GENERAL DIMENSIONS: Width, not including veranda and bays, 67 ft.; depth, not including bay and veranda, 79 ft. 4 ins.

HEIGHTS OF STORIES: Cellar, 8 ft.; first story, 11 ft.; second story, 10 ft.; attic, 9 ft.

EXTERIOR MATERIALS: Foundation, stone; first and second stories, stone, faced with broken range work; circular turret, shingles and panel work.

INTERIOR FINISH: Hard white plaster. Hard wood flooring and trim in principal rooms of first story and main halls of first and second stories. Hard wood main staircase. Soft wood flooring and trim in kitchen department, and in second and attic stories. All interior wood-work finished with hard oil and stained to suit owner.

COLORS: All stone work cleaned down at completion and repointed. All wall shingles of dormers dipped and brush coated terra cotta stain. Trim, cornices and other mouldings, dark brown. Sashes, dark green. Veranda floors and ceilings, oiled. Outside doors natural color, varnished. Roof shingles dipped and brush coated red stain.

ACCOMMODATIONS: The principal rooms and their sizes, closets, etc., are shown by the floor plans. Cellar under whole house. Stationary range in kitchen. Sinks in butlery and kitchen. Stationary tubs in laundry. Servants' water closet off laundry. Bath-room has full plumbing. Open fireplaces in hall, parlor, dining-room, billiard-room and library. Sliding doors connect parlor, hall, billiard-room, library and dining-room. Large main hall with handsome staircase and stained glass windows. Covered driveway with carriage mount and side entrance to library. One family bedroom and three servants' bedrooms, also billiard-room and hallway finished in attic; ample storage room in the attic. Large linen closet off second story hall. Wash basins in all principal bedrooms.

COST: $30,000, † not including mantels, range and heater. The estimate is based on ‡ New York prices for materials and labor. In many sections of the country the cost should be less.

Price of working plans (with full details drawn to large scale), specifications, and * license to build, ... $300.00

Price of †† bill of materials, ... 75.00

FEASIBLE MODIFICATIONS: General dimensions, materials and colors may be changed. Any or all sliding doors and open fireplaces, and a part of plumbing may be omitted. Hard wood flooring and trim may be used throughout.

The price of working plans, specifications, etc., for a modified design, varies according to the alterations required and will be made known upon application to the Architects.

Address, THE CO-OPERATIVE BUILDING PLAN ASSOCIATION, Architects, 106–108 Fulton Street, New York.

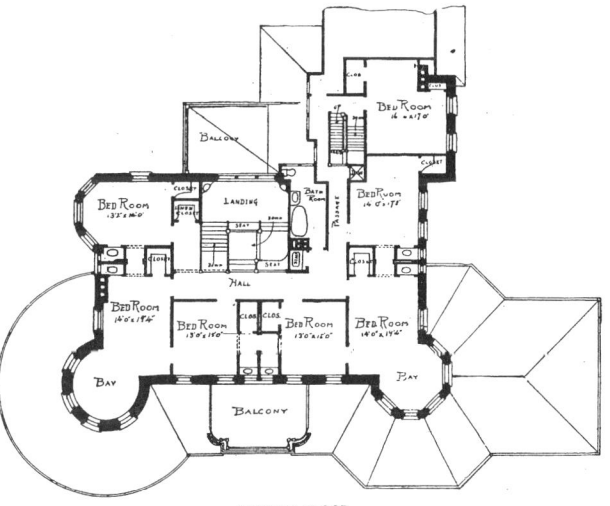

SECOND FLOOR.

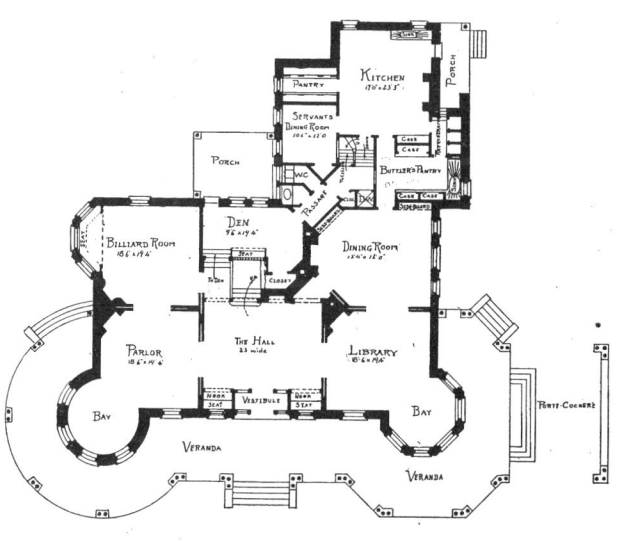

FIRST FLOOR.

Residence, Design No. 1497

PERSPECTIVE.

DESCRIPTION.

GENERAL DIMENSIONS: Width, 35 ft.; depth, including carriage wash and stoop, 64 ft.

HEIGHTS OF STORIES: Basement, 6 ft. 6 ins.; first story, 9 ft. 11 ins.; second story, 8 ft.

EXTERIOR MATERIALS: Foundations, stone; first story, clapboards; gables, dormers, ventilators and roofs, shingles.

INTERIOR FINISH: Second story bedrooms plastered for papering. Spruce flooring throughout. White pine trim in plastered rooms. The walls and ceilings of first story ceiled with yellow pine. Stairway, yellow pine treads and risers. All interior wood-work in first story, and in second story bedrooms, finished in hard oil.

COLORS: Stone and brick-work cleaned down at completion. Clapboards, Colonial yellow. Wall shingles dipped and brush coated Colonial yellow. Trim and cornices, white. Outside doors and sashes, dark green. Entrance porch ceiling finished in hard oil. Roof shingles dipped and brush coated silver stain.

ACCOMMODATIONS: The general arrangement of stalls, etc., is shown by the floor plans. Cellar or basement under carriage room for farm wagons, carts, tools, etc. Feed bins in second story, with chutes to first. Water and feed troughs and stablemen's water closet in stable. Work room or shop, with chimney, in first story. Wash stand at main entrance. Sliding doors to main entrance.

COST: $2,200, † not including stall fittings. The estimate is based on ‡ New York prices for materials and labor. In many sections of the country the cost should be less.

Price of working plans (with full details drawn to large scale), specifications and * license to build, ... $20.00
Price of †† bill of materials, . . . 10.00

FEASIBLE MODIFICATIONS: General dimensions, materials and colors may be changed. Building may be adapted to level grade and cellar or basement omitted. Any or all plumbing and chimney may be omitted. Four single or two box stalls may be placed where work room is now shown.

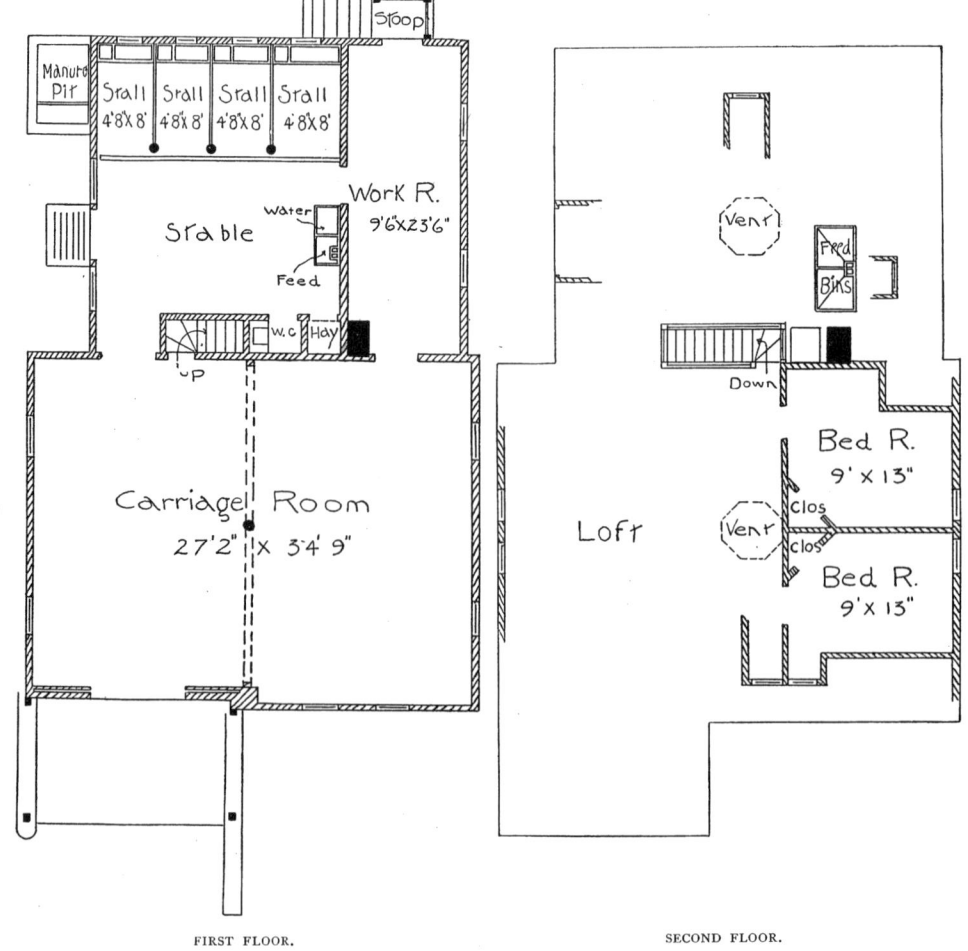

Address, THE CO-OPERATIVE BUILDING PLAN ASSOCIATION, Architects, 106-108 Fulton Street, New York.

FIRST FLOOR. SECOND FLOOR.